Applying Sociolinguistics

York St John College

Impact: Studies in language and society

IMPACT publishes monographs, collective volumes, and text books on topics in sociolinguistics. The scope of the series is broad, with special emphasis on areas such as language planning and language policies; language conflict and language death; language standards and language change; dialectology; diglossia; discourse studies; language and social identity (gender, ethnicity, class, ideology); and history and methods of sociolinguistics.

General editor

Annick De Houwer
University of Antwerp

Advisory board

Volume 15

Applying Sociolinguistics: Domains and face-to-face interaction
by Diana Boxer

Applying Sociolinguistics
Domains and face-to-face interaction

Diana Boxer

University of Florida, Gainesville

John Benjamins Publishing Company
Amsterdam/Philadelphia

™ The paper used in this publication meets the minimum requirements of American National Standard for Information Sciences – Permanence of Paper for Printed Library Materials, ANSI z39.48-1984.

Library of Congress Cataloging-in-Publication Data

Boxer, Diana, 1948-
    Applying sociolinguistics : domains and face-to-face interaction / Diana Boxer.
       p. cm. (Impact: Studies in language and society, ISSN 1385–7908 ; v. 15)
    Includes bibliographical references and index.
       1. Sociolinguistics. 2. Social interaction. I. Title. II. Impact, studies in language and
society ; 15.

P40.B678   2002
306.44--dc21   2002018540
ISBN 90 272 1850 1 (Eur.) / 1 58811 197 0 (US) (Hb; alk. paper)
ISBN 90 272 1851 X (Eur.) / 1 58811 198 9 (US) (Pb; alk. paper)

John Benjamins Publishing Co. · P.O. Box 36224 · 1020 ME Amsterdam · The Netherlands
John Benjamins North America · P.O. Box 27519 · Philadelphia PA 19118-0519 · USA

Contents

Permissions

Thank you to the following journals for granting permission to use modified versions of articles:

Chapter 2, part II:
Boxer, D. 2002. "Nagging: The familial conflict arena." *Journal of Pragmatics* 34: 49–61.

Chapter 3, part II:
Boxer, D. and F. Cortés-Conde. 1997. "From bonding to biting: Conversational joking and identity display." *Journal of Pragmatics* 27: 275–294.

Chapter 6, part II:
DeCapua, A. and D. Boxer. 1999. "Bragging, boasting and bravado: Male banter in a brokerage house." *Women and Language* 22(21): 5–11.

List of abbreviations

CA	Conversation Analysis
CDA	Critical Discourse Analysis
CCP	Cross Cultural Pragmatics
CJ	Conversational joking
DA	Discourse Analysis
DCT	Discourse Completion Task
ES	Ethnography of Speaking
ESL	English as a Second Language
FTA	Face Threatening Act
ID	Identity display
IP	Interlanguage Pragmatics
IS	Interactional Sociolinguistics
ITA	International Teaching Assistant
JT	Joke telling
L1	First Language
L2	Second Language
NS	Native Speaker
NNS	Non-Native Speaker
RID	Relational identity display/development
TOEFL	Test of English as a Foreign Language

CHAPTER 1

Introduction

1. Introduction

This book is about the real world of verbal interaction. Its aim is to demonstrate what can be learned from the study of face-to-face interaction. In doing this, it plays a dual role in informing readers about (1) recent research on talk in interaction; and (2) possibilities of applying knowledge gleaned from this research to optimizing interaction in everyday encounters. The following pages emphasize that face-to-face interaction is an important part of sociolinguistics: the study of language in society. Indeed, the analysis of face-to-face interaction is applied sociolinguistics par excellence. It is applied simply because when we take what we know about how we do oral discourse, we can apply it to everyday talk in order to learn how to be more happy and successful in all domains of life.

The fields of applied linguistics and sociolinguistics are viewed by some scholars as overlapping and by others as distinct. Indeed, there exist those who call themselves applied linguists who do not consider themselves sociolinguists; the reverse is also true: there are those who study sociolinguistic issues who do not consider themselves doing applied work. The primary question we must ask, given these facts, is what exactly does it mean to *apply* within the broad field of linguistics and the sub-field of sociolinguistics?

The moment we do "real life linguistics," that is to say, study what people actually do with the languages of their linguistic repertoire, we are applying linguistics. Any time we make a study of how language is *used* by its speakers or learners in interaction, we are doing applied sociolinguistics. Much of this endeavor of "applying" has to do with phenomena quite separate from the well-studied area of language learning. Indeed, a great deal of the confusion between the two areas, applied linguistics and sociolinguistics, derives from the view that applied linguistics deals only with language acquisition and pedagogy. When we consider "applying" what we know about what we do with language in face to face interaction, we easily see that the sociolinguistics of discourse is necessarily applied linguistics. In this volume we explore the vast array of phenomena of how language is used in the real world of verbal interaction.

This book, then, focuses on micro-sociolinguistic phenomena: the realm of sociolinguistics that is typically referred to as discourse analysis and pragmatics. Many definitions have been given of these two terms. For our purposes, discourse will simply refer to any study of language use at the level of utterance and beyond. In its larger definition, this subsumes both spoken discourse and written discourse, including stylistic studies in literature. Discourse analysis can focus on a variety of topics: "textual structure beyond the sentence, cohesion, speech acts, narrative organization of conversation, linguistic description of style, politeness and deference and the formalization of discourse structure (Sherzer 1983: 15).

The term *pragmatics* is used here simply to refer to what is meant by what is said or written. As such, it has to do with illocutionary force of utterances — the meaning underlying the surface. As Jacob Mey has so eloquently stated:

> Pragmatics is the science of language seen in relation to its users. That is to say, not the science of language in its own right, or the science of language as seen and studied by the linguists, or the science of language as the expression of our desire to play schoolmarm, but the science of language as it is used by real, live people for their own purposes and within their limitations and affordances (1993: 5).

The perspective of studying face-to-face interaction in various spheres of life is in essence the study of language as it is used by "real, live people" within these spheres or contexts. Therefore, the micro-sociolinguistic endeavor here is heavily involved in pragmatics as a sub-discipline of linguistics. This endeavor is based upon important theoretical/philosophical tenets underlying pragmatics, encompassing Gricean and speech act theoretical perspectives on language. The analysis of pragmatic phenomena in the research outlined in the pages to follow is largely based upon these roots in the philosophy of language. As analysts of face-to-face interaction, we build upon these philosophical roots to bridge theory with practice, or analysis.

1.1   Sociolinguistics: Micro and macro divisions

Applying sociolinguistics to the day to day life of individuals in societies spans macro-sociolinguistics as well as the micro-sociolinguistic phenomena discussed above. When we refer to macro issues, we include questions related to bilingual/multilingual communities. These issues include language contact and choice, language and nation, language status, language maintenance and shift, and all related phenomena (e.g. dialects and standards). Just where to draw the line between macro and micro is often difficult, leading us to the conclusion that there is no definitive demarcation; the distinction is indeed a fuzzy one. For example, the study of gender differences in language use spans both micro and macro-sociolinguistics. Sex/gender differences in lexical choice, speech act use, politeness and solidarity, for example, are micro phenomena. Nevertheless, the view that women and men are members of different speech communities by virtue of different rules of speaking, for example, (Maltz and Borker 1983), renders the study of sex and sexism in language a macro-sociolinguistic phenomenon. We will see in this book how macro issues such as these cannot be divorced from the application of sociolinguistics to everyday life.

There is a great deal of current interest in identity and identity development in the social sciences (e.g. Le Page & Tabouret-Keller 1985, Wiley 1994). Linguistic choices have to do with underlying and shifting identities. Our identity as speakers of a particular language, our identity as a member of any number of speech communities, our identity as an individual in a particular setting, our identity as it relates to others in our social group, our identity as it forms in the process of moment-to-moment group relationship display and development, are all relevant to applying sociolinguistics. In the following pages it should become clear that through our moment-to-moment language choices, our very identities are developed and displayed through language use. These phenomena are examples of applying sociolinguistics.

1.2   Domains

Sociolinguists and anthropological linguists have for several decades now advocated a concern with how talk relates to day-to-day action. For example, Hymes (1962) argued for an empirically viable sociolinguistics focusing on specific situations of speaking rather than on speech communities as analytical wholes. In the past several years, Bourdieu (1991) put forth a new notion of 'practice' that has now been widely adopted in discourse analysis, substantiating the role that communicative or discursive practice plays in sociolinguistic analysis. Thus, it seems clear that specific situations and discursive practices are best analyzed vis à vis the spheres of activity everyday action .

Following this line of reasoning, the manner in which this volume is organized follows Joshua Fishman's (1972) categorization of day-to-day language use into "domains." Specifically, I take those domains deemed worthy of investigation for multilingual communities, and apply them to the analysis of face-to-face interaction in mostly North American settings. In so doing, following Fishman, we borrow the five primary domains taken in Greenfield (1968): family, friendship, religion, education, and employment. In sociolinguistics, a domain refers to a sphere of life in which verbal and non-verbal interactions occur.

> Domains are defined, regardless of their number, in terms of *institutional contexts or socio-ecological co-occurrences*…Domains enable us to understand that language choice and topic, appropriate though they may be for analyses of individual behavior at the level of face-to-face verbal encounters, are… related to widespread socio-cultural norms and expectations. (Fishman 1972: 19)

By choosing to approach the analysis of face-to-face interaction within domains, we can clearly see the relationship between micro-sociolinguistics and macro sociolinguistics, between intra-group and inter-group verbal interactions.

Education is but one of the domains outlined by Greenfield and Fishman as a sphere of interaction. This domain has had primacy of focus in the recent history of applied linguistics. While second language acquisition and pedagogy have offered a burgeoning literature over the past thirty years, I caution researchers and students in the field of applied sociolinguistics to take a broad view of the educational domain. When applied sociolinguistics is the focus, we come to realize that other important areas of research endeavor in the educational domain merit careful examination. We must include areas of language use in education such as native speaker interactions in classrooms, face-to-face interaction in advising sessions, colloquia, and office hour encounters, as well as second language development. The chapter on the educational domain offers examples of these perspectives.

Family life, social life and work life are important domains for the study of real world linguistics. It is in these three domains that the elements of face-to-face interaction are salient. How we use language to interact with family members, friends, acquaintances, and colleagues informs how others perceive us. This perception affects how well we fit into groups, how harmonious or not are our relationships, and ultimately, how much we achieve a feeling of "belonging." This belonging is a part of a sense of membership — without it, we are left with isolation and alienation. Thus our interactional competence impacts greatly on our lives.

The family domain is fundamental to the building of identity through language socialization. It is in this domain that we are able to study the repercussions of face-to-face interaction with those most intimate to us on the social distance continuum. Social distance has been shown to be an important sociolinguistic variable in studies taking place in the social life domain. Yet family interactions have largely taken a back seat in the literature on discourse and pragmatics. For children, at least, day to day interactions with family members is the essence of formation of selfhood from the earliest understanding of parent-child language. The chapter on family talk explores consequences of patterns of verbal interaction in the family and about family matters. These interactions clearly vary with ethnic, regional, religious and racial communities. Differences in expectations for age and gender relationships, for example, are paramount in the building of value systems for groups and individuals alike. It is in the familial domain that couples communication can be microscopically analyzed with implications drawn for gender and language. Role expectations for children, women and men are revealed in the analysis of family discourse and interaction. Through such analysis, we are able to view the norms and values of families in societal perspective. How family members speak and are spoken to, expectations for participation, turn-taking, getting and holding the floor, relevant topics for discussion, are all important discourse phenomena in family interactions. We cannot explore these patterns without a discussion of how rules of speaking perpetuate and reflect cultural/societal values.

The chapter on social life explores in detail how we use language to make friends and successfully (or unsuccessfully) interact with other individuals and in groups. Here we clearly see the importance of applying sociolinguistics. This is the domain of face-to-face interaction with people we are getting to know, people we already know and with whom we have a friendship, and strangers thrown together into contexts of immediate interaction. How we build solidarity has consequences for consolidating our membership and ultimately our sense of well being.

The chapter explores such phenomena as phatic communication (Malinowski 1923) — in speech acts, events and activities — as well as ordinary day-to-day interaction such as greetings and partings. The sociolinguistic variables are an important reference point for describing what we know about social interaction; thus, several of these (e.g. gender, social distance) are taken as points of closer analysis. We also examine differences between various methodological approaches to social talk and the different types of findings yielded by these types of analyses.

What exactly is it that makes for smooth social interaction for some but awkward interaction for others? Why is it that some people are skilled at making friends while others are just unable to do so with ease? What are the factors that constrain successful social interaction? What does the term "successful" mean, anyway, when focusing on social life? These are all issues to be explored in the analysis of face-to-face interactions in the social domain. The literature in this sphere of activity is vast. Indeed, social interactions have been the primary focus of investigation in the sociolinguistics literature over the past decades.

The domain of work life has been the focus of some very interesting discourse research in recent years. As the US workplace has become more diverse, with more women, different ethnic groups and various racial groups having increased access to a wider range of jobs, the analysis of face-to-face interactions in the workplace has become ever more important in assessing access to career opportunities. Much of the recent research in the sub-field of language and gender has taken as its focus the workplace, studying the available opportunities and denied opportunities for women, as seen through the lens of linguistic interactions. Workplace discourse research is varied, with vast unexplored areas for the study of face-to-face interaction. For example, much has been made of the notion of "networking" in recent years. Networking is the knowledge of how to get to know people in the workplace who interact in groups of which we want to become a part. Little, if any research has taken the concept of networking as its focus. Likewise, face-to-face interaction in the culturally plural workplace of the present has been left largely unexplored. The chapter on the domain of work life reviews relevant extant research in sociolinguistics and offers many possible topics for further research.

This book takes another important sphere of life as a domain of interaction, that of institutional discourse. By institutional discourse I mean talk in face-to-face interactions with personnel in offices, medical and legal contexts, and bureaucratic interactions. Research on face-to-face institutional interaction is sparse. I take this as a separate area and attach a review of research in this domain to the chapter on work life. The literature on service encounters is included here, and illustrates interactions in status relationships as opposed to personal relationships, a distinction made in the field of sociology.

The remaining domain is that of religious life. Little sociolinguistic research has been carried out in this domain. Religion is becoming increasingly important to modern individuals and families; indeed, it is sometimes difficult to disambiguate social interactions from their religious counterparts. As the forces of modern society move people away from their families for career and educational opportunities, more and more individuals are turning to religious organizations for their sense of community. Thus, participation in religious life is a way to build a network of friends in addition to finding spiritual comfort.

The chapter on religious life reviews relevant research on face-to-face interaction in this domain.

1.3   Critical discourse analysis

An important thrust in the field of linguistics in recent years that is extremely relevant to any discussion of applying sociolinguistics is that which is known as Critical Discourse Analysis (CDA) or critical linguistics. These terms denote the analysis of spoken and written discourse to expose and study important societal problems stemming from manipulative and discriminatory language use by powerful groups. Critical discourse analysts approach language as a site for explicating the ongoing struggles of peoples of particular societies (e.g. racial, ethnic, gender and otherwise dominated groups). Through such analysis, aspects of contemporary societal problems can be better understood and perhaps reshaped to change society towards increased emancipation for the specific subjugated groups. Several British and European scholars have been closely associated with CDA, perhaps most notably Norman Fairclough (e.g. 1989, 1992, 1995), Teun Van Dijk (1983, 1989, 1993, 1996, 1998) and Ruth Wodak (e.g.1989, 1996, 1999), to mention but a few. This work is primarily concerned with demonstrating issues of prejudice, power and dominance in private and public discourse, including the media. CDA is the quintessential applied sociolinguistics, as its goal is to transform societal values through the exposing of harmful ways of speaking.

Fairclough (1995) asserts that it is of little use to study discourse as disconnected from social action. In comparing CDA with traditional approaches to discourse analysis, he claims that the latter suffers from serious inadequacies. He states, "...unless the analyst differentiates ideology from knowledge, i.e. unless s/he is aware of the ideological dimensions of discourse, the chances are that s/he will be unconsciously implicated in the reproduction of ideologies, much as the lay subject is" (45).

Many sociolinguists believe that solving societal problems is beyond the scope of the field, which is descriptive in nature. In other words, sociolinguistics describes language use but does not recommend action. Critical Discourse Analysis makes a direct effort to translate into action the societal problems exposed by the analysis. The study of face-to-face interaction in the domains of everyday life necessarily calls for reflection on the repercussions of what we do with words. Recommendations for subsequent action are therefore indirect. In a CDA approach, description comes first, then interpretation, followed by what Wodak (1989) terms "therapy." Linguistics is thus taken out of the realm of the academy and placed into a political action perspective. The descriptive orientation of sociolinguistics is taken to another level, that of explicating and working to solve the social struggles of people without power. Issues of ideology are paramount. The sought outcomes of CDA are described aptly by Van Dijk (1986) as cited in Wodak (1989):

> Beyond description or superficial application, critical science in each domain asks further questions, such as those of responsibility, interests and ideology. Instead of focussing on purely academic or theoretical problems, it starts from prevailing social problems, and thereby chooses the perspective of those who suffer most and critically analyzes those in power, those who are responsible, and those who have the means and the opportunity to solve such problems. As simple as that (Van Dijk 1986: 4).

Not all of the literature on face-to-face interaction overviewed in this volume takes a CDA approach. However, the aim of providing the overview and the specific examples in each chapter is to allow the reader an opportunity to reflect on issues of power. While the thrust of CDA is essentially the issue of language and power, the thrust of this book is somewhat different. I would characterize it as "power in language." What this means is that the intention here is not only to uncover harmful ways of speaking by powerful groups and organizations that result in the subjugation of people(s); the intention is also to provide examples of results of ordinary interactions that will help us achieve power in language. The sort of power here is *not* that of dominance; it is the power to present ourselves as we wish and thereby negotiate more successfully through the important domains of our lives. It is through talk-in-interaction that this negotiation takes place.

1.4   Organization of this volume

The chapters to follow take the domains separately for an analysis of recent research. Each chapter begins with a section describing the importance of studying face-to-face interaction in that specific domain. An overview of relevant research by sociolinguists, anthropologists, sociologists, communication researchers and others is offered to illustrate important thrusts in applying discourse analysis to real world phenomena. This overview is not meant to be exhaustive. Indeed, it would be impossible to review all relevant studies, as the literature in the fields has burgeoned over the past several decades. The research reviewed is mostly of the past twenty years. Where appropriate, none-theless, earlier seminal research is discussed or cited.

Following the overview of research that begins each chapter, an in-depth analysis of face-to-face interaction in that domain, carried out by myself either alone or with a collaborator, is outlined in detail. The chapter on family interaction contains an analysis that I undertook of "nagging" as a ubiquitous speech event in families; the chapter on social life contains a study on conversational joking and teasing that I undertook with colleague Florencia Cortes-Conde; the chapter on educational life contains an analysis of the use of sarcasm in the classroom discourse of higher education, researched collaboratively with Jodi Nelms; the chapter on religious interactions contains my own in-depth analysis of the face-to-face language of a Bat/Bar Mitzvah, the Jewish rite of passage of youth into adulthood at age thirteen; the chapter on workplace interaction contains an in-depth analysis of face-to-face interaction in a brokerage house, carried out in collaboration with colleague Andrea DeCapua.

An additional chapter is devoted to examples of cross-cultural face-to-face interaction in the domains. That chapter includes an analysis of gatekeeping encounters in higher education that I wrote with colleague Christina Overstreet. I have included this discussion because the literature on cross-cultural face-to-face interaction is indeed relevant to the present volume. Each of these chapters illustrates how we can study face-to-face interaction within a domain or cross-culturally, and what the findings imply for our happiness, success, and sense of belonging.

The literature reviewed demonstrates examples of the kind of work that has been carried out within the particular domain under discussion in various disciplines. Not all of the research derives from the field of sociolinguistics; however, it is all relevant to applications of sociolinguistics. For example, some very important recent research has emanated out of scholarship in the field of communications. Much of this work is based on the analysis of spontaneous data and is either analyzed ethnographically, microethnographically, or from a conversation analytic perspective (see the following section for an overview of these approaches). In each case, methodological approaches are discussed, and limitations of the analysis are drawn where relevant.

For the sake of limiting the scope to something reasonable for a volume of this size, for all of the chapters focusing on specific domains, the research reviewed and presented here by and large concentrates on interactions among native speakers of the English language in North American speech communities. The chapter on cross-cultural face-to-face interaction is clearly an exception to this narrow focus. As noted previously, the vast literatures on first and second language learning and bilingualism are not included in this book, for any attempt to adequately cover this literature in a volume of this nature would be nearly impossible. The domain of education, then, focuses on the literature in face-to-face interaction in higher education in the US. This focus, while admittedly narrow, offers one thread of research that is relevant to the educational domain.

Before concluding this introduction, a few words are in order concerning how to go about applying the findings of research in micro-sociolinguistic interaction. The first and foremost application is the potential of the research itself to make the reader conscious of the particular speech behavior under discussion. This is the ability of research to " … make the obvious obvious or the familiar strange " (Wolcott 1987: 41). We may or may not be aware of what goes on when we face others in talk. We may be oblivious to the fact that power is being wielded in subtle ways. We are brought to understand the existence of such phenomena by reading analyses of talk in interaction. The simple realization of the repercussions of what we do with words is often enough of a trigger for change. The challenge, then, is to take this knowledge base from the academy to the general public. This is what Wodak (1989) means by "therapy." Translating the knowledge to action is the charge of not only those who carry out the research but also those who gain knowledge from the dissemination of the work.

2.   Methodologies of research in face-to-face interaction

There are various methods that researchers have employed to study face-to-face discourse. In the preceding section I briefly discussed critical discourse analysis (CDA), and its relationship to more descriptive approaches to discourse analysis. An overview of the many methods used to analyze talk in interaction is clearly in order. It is my point of view that most good analyses of spoken discourse employ data that captures *spontaneous* speech among interlocutors, since elicitation instruments necessarily interfere with the naturalness of spontaneous discourse. Obviously, this perspective is not shared by all discourse analysts, especially those involved in studying interlanguage pragmatics. Indeed, great advances in elicitation instruments have been made in the past decade.

The majority of research reported in this book has employed naturally occurring talk as data. Having said this, there are various approaches to the analysis of spontaneous data among the studies cited herein. These approaches stem from developments in the disciplines of linguistics, sociology, anthropology, psychology and communications. Let us take a closer look at approaches to spoken discourse. For a complete and in-depth presentation, I refer you to Schiffrin (1994).

2.1 Discourse analysis

Recall my assertion above that discourse analysis is a term used to refer to any study of language beyond the utterance/sentence level. As such, I do not view discourse analysis (DA) as a *methodological* approach to research, though many scholars do. Within DA, we must distinguish between various methods employed in the analysis of the discourse data, whether oral or written.

Edelsky and Adams (1989) view the goal of DA as finding "abstract structures or universal rules governing the interpretations of sequences of units, such as Gricean maxims or Searle's framework for the well-formedness of speech acts" (25). They see DA as concerned with long sequences of talk, while conversation analysis (CA) "looks at small activities with big impacts (pauses, fillers, interruptions)" (ibid). It is clear that these researchers have a narrower description of discourse analysis than others. What they have attempted to do is compare and contrast discourse analysis and conversation analysis with the ethnography of communication or speaking. They assert that DA looks at participant attributes only as they pertain to the specific stretch of talk analyzed, while conversation analysis (CA) uses only what is in the transcription of the data. The ethnography of speaking (ES), in contrast, looks at non-linguistic variables such as setting, speech event, and participant attributes. These researchers clearly view two primary approaches to discourse analysis as CA and ES. Indeed, the two differ radically in their views of what constitutes relevant attributes of data, particularly, in their notions of context.

2.2 Conversation analysis

Conversation analysis developed during the latter part of the 1960's with the work of sociologists Harold Garfinkel, Harvey Sacks and Emmanuel Schegloff. Emanating out of 'ethnomethodology,' a branch of sociology, it is concerned with talk as important work in everyday life — a supreme accomplishment of synchrony. The interactionist perspectives of Erving Goffman's early work is closely related to ethnomethodology; however, where Goffman was concerned with all features of interaction, including gestures and clothing, conversational analysts limit their analysis to what can be gleaned from a transcript of conversation. Those involved in CA look for how talk is used to create and sustain reality. They are interested in "discovering the categories and systems that people use to make sense of the world" (Wardaugh 1986: 243). As such, CA has established, through careful analysis of turns and topic coherence, for example, that conversational interaction is highly organized. The CA approach views conversation as work performed with the end of "accomplishing the scenes of everyday life "(Ventola 1987: 17).

Much important and informative research has come from the CA perspective in recent years, as we will see in the pages to follow. In fact, CA is the quintessentially appropriate method for analysis of some kinds of talk, particularly when studying the manner in which talk in interaction unfolds. CA affords insights into speakers' knowledge of how the world works — uncovering the largely unconscious rules for the sequential nature of ordinary discourse.

2.3   Ethnography of communication

As distinct from CA, a widely employed approach to the analysis of face-to-face data is the ethnography of speaking or communication, ES, (Hymes, 1962). This methodology unites the classic anthropological approach to research, termed ethnography, with linguistic analysis. ES is an important way of studying language as it is used in a variety of contexts. Research carried out within this tradition is both holistic and emic, taking into account a variety of contexts as well as native viewpoints. Ethnographies of speaking have been carried out for some four decades now. Increasingly, the focus of ethnographic research has centered on communicative patterns, and the task of the ethnographer has become the study of language use in particular societies. The meaning of speech for particular speakers in specific social activities is a central concern for ES. The notion of context is primary, including spatio-temporal dimensions, participant attributes and goals of interactants. The fundamental anti-universalism that characterizes ES makes it an *emic* rather than an *etic* pursuit (Duranti 1983). Some of the sociocultural knowledge affecting speech behavior in particular contexts is below the level of consciousness of community members.

Some scholars engaged in ES research view its goal as the explication of diverse codes that fulfill functions within the community (Hornberger 1985; 1988). This perspective takes a macro-sociolinguistic perspective stance. In much the same fashion, however, ES can also look at the functions that particular speech behaviors have in a speech community and the way in which community members use various types of speech to fulfill these functions (a micro-sociolinguistic approach). ES is concerned with community members' perceptions and representations of their own culture; therefore, it must be able to describe everyday, ordinary uses of speech in addition to such phenomena as patterns of dialect and language use and ritualized speech events. Many of the studies overviewed in the following pages have employed ES techniques in the analysis of speech behavior, whether in the form of speech events, speech acts, or other speech activities.

ES and CA diverge specifically in their distinct notions of context. Where ES looks at speech acts and events giving relevance to the sociolinguistic variables (e.g. social status, gender, age), "for CA what is found in the transcript is the only legitimate source of knowledge for inferring participants' concern. For ES social identity and past history are equally important" (Duranti 1988: 223). Both CA and ES researchers are hesitant to claim universality for their findings. While the key ES concept of "speech event," and the constituent factors that characterize speech events are regarded as universal, cultural traditions differ in how they are defined and how they function. Likewise, for CA researchers the categories of adjacency, repair and turns, for example, are universal; however, the way in which these phenomena are realized varies from conversation to conversation, and thus constitutes an important focus of analysis. Hence, while CA and ES share some attributes, they also differ in important ways. As always, chosen methods of inquiry always depend on the questions being asked. What these two research traditions do share is an interest in analyzing stretches of talk (some long and some short) that are recorded and serve as retrievable data capable of close and careful analysis.

2.4 Interactional sociolinguistics

There are other traditions in the analysis of spoken discourse that are closely related to both the ethnography of speaking and conversational analysis. Interactional sociolinguistics (IS), sometimes known as microethnography, is a methodological approach to interactional analysis using video-taped data and taking into account non-verbal behavior such as facial gestures, postural shifts and proxemics. The focus here is on *interaction* rather than solely *discourse*, as the former includes non-verbal features in addition to talk and suprasegmentals. Work in IS derives from sociology, linguistics and anthropology. The specific focus of IS is the study of miscommunication between different ethnic groups. Thus IS research carefully examines the contextualization conventions (Gumperz 1982) of a particular interaction:

> To the extent that we can talk about conversations being governed and controlled by shared expectations, we must assume that these expectations are signalled and sharedness is negotiated as part of the interaction itself. We refer to those signalling cues that are seen to operate systematically within specific communicative traditions and to the communicative strategies to which they give rise as contextualization conventions. (Gumperz 1982: 17–18)

The particular purpose of IS is to study miscommunication in order to discover how it comes about and how it can be avoided. One of the purposes of IS, then, is to link problems in face-to-face interaction between different ethnolinguistic groups to larger macro-sociolinguistic issues.

Seen from the above perspectives, my view of discourse analysis is that it is an umbrella term for the study of any written or spoken discourse, whether it stems from linguistic, sociological, anthropological approaches or a combination of these. The sociological branch of analyzing spoken discourse is known as conversation analysis. The anthropological approach stems from ethnography, and when it specifically studies speech is called the ethnography of speaking or communication. ES typically refers to the collection of data from spontaneous speech by a researcher who becomes a participant observer. The data for ES is normally in the form of audio-taped interactions and/or field notes on these interactions, as well as in-depth interviews with consultants/ informants from the speech community. Interactional sociolinguistics is related to ES but usually employs video-taped data for studying both the verbal and non-verbal features of interaction. CA and IS are closely related in some studies; however, while CA studies the sequential organization of interaction, IS looks specifically at how miscommunication arises and the larger societal implications of such miscommunication.

2.5   Elicitation instruments

Elicited data is something quite apart from spontaneous face-to-face data. One of the most widely employed elicitation techniques for researching speech behavior, particularly speech act realization, has been the Discourse Completion Task (DCT) (see, for example, Kasper and Dahl 1991; Kasper and Rose 1999). The DCT is a specific type of questionnaire. It typically sets up a situation in which the speech act being studied (e.g. compliments, apologies, requests) or possible responses to them, are required by the subject. DCTs can be open-ended in that they set up a situation and then leave a blank for the speech act to be supplied; or they can be of a second type that provides a situation, gives a first turn, a blank space for a turn from the subject, and then a second turn for the fictional interlocutor. DCTs manipulate the socio-linguistic variables (e.g. status, age, distance, gender) in order to ascertain the subject's reaction to them. DCTs ordinarily take fewer than 20 to 30 minutes to complete. The reason for this time limitation is to ensure compliance with lack of fatigue. Unfortunately, limiting the time has the potential drawback of eliminating distractor items. However, without such distractors, subjects may begin to give rote, thoughtless replies to one specific speech act.

Much discussion has taken place over the years about other advantages and disadvantages of this type of instrument (see, for example, Beebe and Cummings 1996). One criticism of the DCT is that it is an instrument that makes a priori decisions about the sociolinguistic variables that are the most important in constraining speech acts. In fact, the DCT has been used mostly to study the patterning of speech act realization in different speech communities and within the field of interlanguage pragmatics, pre-selecting variables such as social status, gender and social distance, for example, in creating hypothetical situations to which the responder is supposed to indicate what she would say. There are several advantages to using such an instrument, as Beebe and Cummings (1996) outline in detail. One of the most obvious of these is the ability to collect vast quantities of data in a relatively short period of time, and in so doing find out about how different variables change the discourse, without having to capture those variables in action. In addition, as we will see in the chapter on cross-cultural interaction, when performance of certain speech acts in two or more languages is desired, the collection of data via an elicitation instrument such as the DCT is reasonable.

Let us take one speech act as an example of advantages of DCTs. In my own work on complaining and commiserating (Boxer 1993a), I collected 533 sequences of complaining behavior ethnographically. What resulted was information on certain gender combinations, most frequently women talking to women. I could have captured the different gender combinations more easily by employing a DCT instrument. As such, the situations could have been manipulated so that the responder would theoretically have been talking to either a person of the same or opposite sex. Had I used a DCT, I would not have needed to wait around in order to hope to overhear people engaging in naturally occurring complaint exchanges. I would only have had to manipulate the situations on a DCT to capture all the possible combinations. At first read this may sound like an ideal way to collect discourse data.

Upon further reflection, the drawbacks of using DCTs begin to appear. First, such an elicitation instrument asks people to tap into their intuitions about how they speak. When we compare what people say they would do with what they actually do, we find these intuitions to be notoriously unreliable (see e.g. Wolfson, Marmor and Jones 1986). Indeed, there are many problems inherent in using methodologies that rely strictly on intuitional data. People have a good idea of how they *should* interact, but reality often demonstrates that their linguistic behavior deviates greatly from this idealized notion.

Second, there is a real danger in pre-selecting the variables we think are important. In other words, we cannot possibly know what sociolinguistic variables are at work in specific speech exchanges without capturing naturally occurring exchanges and carefully analyzing them to see what variables *emerge* as important. Let us take a hypothetical example. How do we know whether age constrains how we give and receive compliments unless we capture people of various ages giving and receiving them? We may think age to be important and yet find, upon close analysis of spontaneous compliments, that age makes very little difference.

A third serious drawback of using elicitation instruments such as the DCT has to do with written versus spoken language. Asking people to write down what they would say renders the data invalid in my opinion. Written and spoken texts are indeed two very different genres. Having said all this, a disadvantage of naturally spoken data is that it may be disparate and not representative. Indeed, such data suffers from lack of generalizability. Recent advances in elicited data have made such data more useful than the original form of DCTs. Let us look at one such variation on elicited data, the role-play.

2.6   Role plays

To overcome at least the one drawback of DCTs, that they need to be oral rather than written tasks, many discourse researchers (particularly those studying cross-cultural discourse) have devised oral DCTs and role plays. These more closely approach natural spoken data. However, they still remain contrived insofar as participants are asked to indicate what they think they would say and do in a particular situation. In this method of data collection, two or more subjects are asked to play a specific role in a speech situation, acting out their roles while they are audiotaped or videotaped. Theoretically, the advantage of role-play date over DCT data ought to be that acting out what the subjects think they would say should come closer to producing natural language data. Some disadvantages of role-plays are that they are difficult to set up, conduct and transcribe, and, as some researchers claim, come no closer to spontaneous data than do DCTs. One other potential problem is that it may be difficult to find subjects who are willing to be videotaped. Furthermore, video-taped data is subject to the Observer's Paradox in a way that DCT data is not. Thus, it is my contention that, while role-plays are useful for intuitively reacting to strategic interactions (cf. DiPietro 1987), they are by no means representative of naturally occurring interaction.

One way that some researchers have refined role play tasks for data on spoken discourse is to get respondents to provide verbal report explanations after they have performed the role play. These verbal self reports allow immediate feedback from the participant about what s/he was thinking and feeling and what the discourse attempted to accomplish (for further information on this type of protocol, see Cohen 1996). At any rate, the important point regarding elicitation instruments is that they can be quite useful, particularly for piloting measures. Particularly when combined with ES, IS, or CA type of data, elicitation instruments can be quite useful indeed.

2.7 Sociolinguistic interviews

No overview of methods of capturing discourse data would be complete without a discussion of the sociolinguistic interview (cf. Labov 1966, 1972; Schiffrin 1988, 1994). The earliest pioneering sociolinguistic research by William Labov very cleverly employed the sociolinguistic interview to study phonological variation with attention to speech. The challenge in this research was how to capture the vernacular, that is, natural talk not constrained by the interview speech event. We all certainly recall the well-known technique devised by Labov to distract the subject from the interview by eliciting "danger of death" narratives. The underlying hope was that the subject would get so involved in narrating her story that she would forget about the norms of the interview situation and speak as she would in natural conversational narrative style. The by product of this distraction was the ostensible ability of the researcher to obtain spontaneous vernacular speech data. While most sociolinguists applaud Labov's pioneering work, some have been critical. Wolfson (1976) for example, asserted that there is no way we can be certain that the speaker is indeed producing anything akin to natural talk in such circumstances. Indeed, the speech events of naturally occurring conversation and sociolinguistic interviews are certain to produce different kinds of talk, regardless of our attempts at distraction. To get around this problem, Milroy (1980) captured spontaneous talk by leaving the tape recorder on when neighbors stopped by or when telephone calls interrupted the interviews. No doubt such talk is indeed more natural than the danger of death narratives, where the subject is talking to the researcher rather than a member of her own speech community or network. In any case, there is really no way that any researcher can be certain of overcoming the Observer's Paradox, even when recording "spontaneous" interaction. Any time a tape recorder is turned on and the speaker is aware of it, there is danger of talk that is somehow distinct from natural talk. This is especially true of videotaped data.

Deborah Schiffrin has employed sociolinguistic interviews in her research on narratives. However, Schiffrin makes no excuses for the naturalness of her data. She does not claim to be eliciting anything but narratives offered to the researcher. What she does do is interview individuals who are known to her and her family and about whose families and lives she has a good background. Thus, this sort of data offers something akin to spontaneous narrative, with the interviewer (Schiffrin herself) a participant in the conversations. In so doing, Schiffrin has been able to capture people talking about their talk and reflecting on their own identities and values. As such, the data, while elicited by the researcher, is of great value.

2.8   Radio and television talk

Many researchers of face-to-face interaction have employed data taken from radio and television talk shows and teledramas, genres that have become very popular over recent years. Talk show data may be similar to naturally occurring speech; however, the speech event is distinct. Given this fact, the norms and rules for interaction and discourse must differ from ordinary interaction. Teledrama talk offers a canonical approximation of spontaneous talk in interaction; however, we can never be sure how true to real talk these approximations are. Thus, we must be wary of studies that take radio and television talk as conversational data, claiming them to be 'conversations.' Media discourse is an important thrust in critical discourse analysis. The perpetuation of discrimination in the rhetoric of politicians, for example, and the wielding of power and persuasion in the language of advertising, as another example, are important loci of studying talk for applying sociolingusitics. They must, however, be taken for the types of talk that they are rather than representative of naturally occurring conversation.

2.9 Laboratory data

There is a large body of research in linguistics, sociology, psychology, and communications that studies talk in laboratory settings as data for analysis. Many researchers employ subjects who are asked to record their conversations about particular topics in a laboratory setting. Typically, these subjects are in some way compensated for their participation. They are asked to submit to either questionnaires and/or batteries of tests before or after recording. While much valuable information has been collected in this manner, the drawbacks of using such data for analysis of face-to-face interactions are evident. Laboratories are not natural conversational settings — they are neither family settings, social settings, religious settings, educational settings, nor workplace settings for the subjects involved. They may be adequate settings for subjects to talk *about* how they talk. As long as we keep this in mind, we will never be fooled into a belief that any laboratory study is capturing real world language.

2.10 Data approaches to research in this volume

Having offered you an overview of possible data collection techniques in approaches to discourse, it is appropriate at this juncture to indicate that much of the research discussed in the pages to follow employs recorded spontaneous speech in naturally occurring settings in the various domains. Where there are exceptions to this, descriptions of the methodologies employed are provided, with shortcomings and benefits discussed. By and large, then, talk in the domains reviewed here was captured by audiotaping, videotaping, or field notes in specific speech events reflecting domain-specific interaction. They are mostly analyzed from either ethnographic or conversational analytic perspectives, giving us a good view of domains and face-to-face interaction.

2.11 Conclusion

The manner in which research is carried out constrains research findings. This fact has long been known to researchers in the social sciences. Sociolinguistics is particularly vulnerable to differential interpretation of research results that have used different methods of data collection and analysis. How one studies a particular issue both determines and is determined by the research question(s). Thus, if we want to study the realization of a particular speech act in a particular speech community, we will choose to collect the data according to where, when, and to what degree that speech act appears in face-to-face interaction. If the speech behavior is rare, employing a method other than that which relies on naturally occurring speech may be in order. Having said this, one must understand the limitations of any approach and proceed with caution, hedging on claims that may be beyond the possibility of analysis when using any one particular method. A combination of approaches is always recommended, and triangulating data sheds new light on how and why people said what they did.

For example, as will be seen in the section on sarcasm in classroom discourse (Chapter four) the data was collected and analyzed using interactional sociolinguistic techniques (i.e. spontaneous interaction captured on videotape, including all gestures and non-verbal features). We made efforts to triangulate the data by playing back segments of the videotapes to selected participants in the event. In so doing, we were able to "get at" what was going on from more than just the perspective of the researchers, but also obtained feedback from the teachers and students involved in the classes.

How to approach discourse analysis is a question that can be answered only by the researcher and only according to what exactly is being studied. The following chapters ought to afford readers the ability to overview a wide variety of studies undertaken from multiple perspectives.

CHAPTER 2

Face-to-face in the family domain

1. Introduction

Face-to-face interaction in the family domain is of utmost importance in our daily lives. It is the locus of primary involvement with loved ones — spouses, partners, children, grandparents and extended family. How we talk to our family members often differs in striking ways from how we talk to those more distant to us in other domains of our lives. The crucial aspect of focusing on family talk lies in the fact that the stakes are high. Unfortunately, it is frequently in this very domain that we exert less effort in the interactional work that we do. As speakers we must come to terms with just how important it is to interact in constructive and fruitful ways with those nearest and dearest to us.

The assessment of the interactional work that we do with friends, acquaintances and even strangers as compared with close family members has been widely reported in the sociolinguistics literature. Wolfson (1988) put forth her "Bulge" theory of social distance and speech behavior, claiming that we do the most interactional work in the middle of the social distance continuum, that is to say, with friends, acquaintances, colleagues and potential friends. She analyzed several speech acts, including those she was most noted for researching, complimenting and inviting. She posited that, at least in her own North American speech community, people do less work of negotiation with intimates and strangers.

My own work (Boxer 1993b) on indirect complaints challenged this notion by plotting out solidarity-establishing speech behavior (e.g. commiseration responses to complaints) along the social distance continuum. Findings of that study indicated that we work almost as hard with strangers as we do with those in the middle of the social distance continuum. That is, we do a lot of politeness work with strangers in an attempt to establish a momentary solidarity, presenting our "face" in the best positive light. Wolfson's work and my own agree in one important aspect: that it is with close family members that we are most certain of the relationships and therefore do less of the "dance of negotiation."

While factors of politeness are an important consideration, factors of power and dominance are extremely relevant to the discussion of face-to-face interactions within families. For it is not merely that we tend to let down our politeness guard with those closest to us. It is even more an issue of exerting our power over family members lower in the pecking order (e.g. children; less powerful members of a couple; some elderly individuals). Linguistic choices reflect and perpetuate the social order. What we need to come to terms with is the following: *Linguistic choices have the power to transform the social order.* It is my hope that this chapter will cause us to reflect on just how to do this. Let us begin with an overview of some existing research on family interactions. We will then turn to an in-depth analysis of one speech behavior in the family setting, that of "nagging."

1.1   What do we know about family interaction?

From a discourse analytic point of view, we know very little about face-to-face interaction in the family domain. . The literature that does exist on family discourse has had two important foci: (1) discourse between parents and children; and (2) discourse between spouses/partners. While there is a substantial literature in the social sciences generally on family interaction, there is a relative paucity of published research specifically focusing on *language*. This situation is perhaps not so surprising regarding studies on parent-child and sibling interaction, since few sociolinguists have focused on family talk. However, given the burgeoning literature on gender and language over the past decades, it is striking how little is known about *couples* interacting in the family domain. Much of the research on gender differences in language use has been conducted in the domain of social life and, more recently, in workplace life. We begin our discussion with a look at family talk between parents and children and then proceed to couples talk. This general review of recent relevant research in the family domain will assess the potential impact of such research on interactions in families and among intimates.

1.2   Family talk

Child language socialization is the principal focus of sociolinguistic research in families, and much of this body of work takes the speech event of the family dinner as its setting. The reason for the preponderance of studies on dinnertime talk seems obvious: It is around a meal table that we are literally face to face and (ideally) not focused on any goings-on other than the task of sharing a meal and conversing with each other. The sharing of a meal around a table may indeed be the only time during the busy day of the modern family that parents truly engage in with children. It is largely via such conversation and the non-verbal behavior that accompanies it that the values and beliefs of a family unit are inculcated. Family face-to-face interaction shapes who we are and who we become as we progress from childhood to our adult selves. How much of our identities are shaped by early socialization is, of course, still an open question in the nature/nurture debate. Nonetheless, no human speaker of any language nor member of any speech community can deny that we are largely shaped by how we are spoken to as children and how we are taught to speak. These patterns persist or are consciously shaken off by those who reject their own rules or norms of community and of family. Whatever the conscious or unconscious choice may be, few would deny the primacy of language socialization.

The manner in which children are linguistically socialized appears to be undergoing a transformation that reflects life style changes over the years. While much of the research on dinnertime talk has been published over the past decade, we realize that the very event of family dinner has undergone changes in recent years. Indeed, the family dinner speech event seems to be rarer and rarer as both parents and children have become increasingly involved in their busy lives and less often sit down together to share a meal. If dinner table talk has been the primary locus of child socialization, and if it is disappearing from the modern family, we are led to wonder what kind of language socialization setting will take the place of family dinner talk? For the moment, however, let us take a closer look at research on this speech event.

Research by Jean Berko-Gleason and her colleagues is an example of studies that offer important sociolinguistic insights into child language. Her work over the years has focused on how parents talk to children, particularly on gender differences in language socialization (e.g. Berko-Gleason 1987; Berko-Gleason and Grief 1983; Grief and Berko-Gleason 1980). A recent study (Ely, Berko-Gleason, Narasimhan and McCabe 1995) analyzed spontaneous audiotaped dinner table conversation to study the incidences of reported speech in adults vs. children during dinner talk. The goals of the study were to describe who uses reported speech, what types of reported speech are used, how such talk is modeled by parents for their children, and the repercussions of reported speech usage. The study's importance lies in its findings of how parental speech behavior influences the linguistic socialization of children through modeling and mimicking. The didactic element of this type of talk lies in the indirect lessons on what is valued enough to be reported. The selection of topics to report reflects what family members deem worthy of discussion.

It is important to note that there are three types of reported speech: direct, indirect and narratized, all of which reconstruct prior discourse. The study's findings indicate that children as young as two years of age report past speech events in dinnertime conversation with adults; however, children by and large use direct reported speech, frequently quoting other children. Much of the research on child language socialization, by Berko-Gleason and others (e.g. Johnstone 1993), has found vast gender differences in reported speech use by both children and adults: girls use reported speech twice as much as boys; mothers used all kinds of reported speech far more than fathers and children.

Indeed, one of the most important findings, corroborating previous re-search on gender socialization, was that mothers, much more than fathers, influence their children's narratives, in terms of both form and content, and that mothers also encourage and engage in communication more with their young, especially daughters. The authors offer an example that explains the importance of such parental talk to children:

> "by attending to [her] mother's quotation of her own past speech, the child learns which of the many utterances she had made are deemed remarkable. In this way, reported speech provides listeners an opportunity to reinterpret past speech, and speakers, in recalling and reflecting on past speech, both redefine and reaffirm the discourse practices of their community." (Ely et al. 1995: 214).

This greater attention to language use by women and girls has been reported widely in the literature on differential socialization of the genders. Women use and view language as a means to engage and negotiate relationships much more than men, who view such negotiation in a more competitive perspective, with actions speaking louder than words. Thus dinnertime talk is an important locus of gendered linguistic socialization. It is not only how we talk to our daughters and sons, but also how we as spouses talk to each other that serve as models for our children's conversational competence. The importance of din-ner table conversation for child socialization goes largely unnoticed by family members, its worth often taken for granted. The linguistic roles we take on, as parents, older siblings and younger siblings, are important in setting the stage for the child's linguistic development. We model and encourage or discourage certain types of speech behaviors and participation structures, and assign or deny rights and obligations in conversational interaction.

Along the same lines of research endeavor, a very informative body of research on family dinner table conversation, emanating from a large study funded by the National Institute of Child Health Development, has been conducted by linguistic anthropologist Elinor Ochs and her students and colleagues. In a series of published articles resulting from that grant, (Ochs and Taylor 1992; Ochs and Taylor 1995; Taylor 1995; Ochs, Smith and Taylor 1996) the authors report on just how influential family dinner table talk is on family conversational role development.

The corpus for these studies consists of 100 family dinner table narratives that were videotaped in homes with two-parent families with at least two children. The researchers divide narrative roles into: introducer, protagonist, primary recipient, problematizer of protagonists or other co-narrators, and problematizee. Detailing these roles here is important for demonstrating the fact that they reflect who gets to be the subject of a problem and thus whose problems get to be explored. Ochs and Taylor (1992) showed how family narrative activity reflects and perpetuates values as well as familial hierarchical relationships. Role distribution, the authors say, is "not random among family members but rather (re)instantiates a political structuring of family roles and privileges" (202). This role distribution is coordinated among family members, and one of the primary functions is to socialize children into the type of problem-solving inherent in the speech event, instilling social and moral values and creating a unique family bonding. If in fact the family is the locus of values-instilling behavior, we can see the importance of family interaction and understand the need to keep families talking with open channels of communication. Analyzing family talk gives us the opportunity to reflect on the unconscious choices we make that perpetuate roles and values.

These studies found that family members orient themselves to particular roles of wife/mother, husband/father, and child in dinnertime narratives, defining their particular identities within the family structure. Indeed, they found that children were typically the protagonists in the stories told around the table. Despite this fact, children were rarely the introducers; moreover, they were "nobody's preferred primary recipients" (Ochs and Taylor 1992: 323). In other words, the children were the subjects of narratives but neither the initiators nor the individuals specifically addressed. This seemingly simple fact may have important repercussions for identity development of children, empowering them less than other members of the family and ignoring a ratification of their importance as participants. Clearly, relationships of power are evidenced in these stories and reports, with children's activities placed under scrutiny. This role relegation provides opportunities for the adults to evaluate, including both criticism and praise.

Just as children's lives were open to scrutiny by parents through such problematizing narratives, so were mother's lives. However, this was not true for fathers, who never were the subjects of such exposure and regulation. Problematizing was done primarily by fathers, who tended to be the most critical. Family co-narration tends to place women and children in the subject role of narration but not in the role of agents themselves. How exactly does this happen?

Ochs and Taylor (1995) examined how gender roles are perpetuated in these narratives in their piece entitled "The 'father knows best' dynamic in dinnertime narratives." They found a typical pattern: the father is set up as the judge and critic of other family members through the co-narration of events by others. For example, fathers/husbands tended to problematize their wives much more often than the reverse. While men's problematizing tended to be critical of their wives, women's problematizing was characteristic of resistance to being problematized. Women unwittingly exposed themselves to problematizing in their prevalent role of introducer, accomplishing what the authors indicate as "shooting themselves in the foot" (113). Furthermore, when women did problematize men, they acted as problem solvers; husbands tended to dismiss the possible solutions. Thus, women open themselves up to male scrutiny and criticism.

Both parent/child interaction as well as couples interaction are relevant in this research. More than twenty-five years of sociolinguistic research focusing on language and gender has found women to do what Pamela Fishman (1983) termed "conversational shitwork." Because women are socialized to be nurturers, even in talk, we open ourselves up to scrutiny and loss of power. A by-product of this phenomenon is what it models for children around the dinner table as in other family speech events. Both boys and girls absorb the linguistic roles their parents play, and take on these roles as gender- appropriate ones as they grow. Males learn to problematize and criticize, and that their criticism is to be valued.

Ochs, Smith and Taylor (1996) focus on dinnertime narratives as "detective stories" by allowing family members to solve others' problems jointly. This, in turn, "gives structure to family roles, relationships, values and world views" (39). In fourteen families that were the subject of this study, some families ate together around a table, while others members ate when they wanted and not together, minimizing the opportunities for family socialization through dinnertime talk. Those that ate together had increased opportunities for a wide range of problem-solving activity, which is typically accomplished through co-narration. They also provided opportunities for adults to wield power over children. The ability to co-narrate brings about gradual relaying of relevant information, and sharing of storytelling rights in such a way empowers participants to socialize each other.

Detective story co-narration, with its concomitant probing for more details into a story, needs to involve intimacy, or it oversteps boundaries. This type of conversational activity is thus only appropriate in family or similar social contexts. It is the prerogative of families to participate in this sort of probing and co-narration. To participate in such activity outside of the family domain would likely be inappropriate speech behavior. Clearly, factors of status and power are relevant to doing this kind of conversational work. In families it is typical of parents to wield the power.

Notwithstanding this typical state of affairs, Taylor (1995) found that at times it is the children of the family who "know best." She focuses on one family's interaction one evening, during which a parental "fight" ensued on videotape. The children's reactions to the fight are explicated through their attempts at what Taylor terms "spin control" (303). The children of this family were very aware that a parental fight was in fact videotaped, and they were clearly more embarrassed by it than their parents. Because of this realization, they put forth a valiant attempt to preserve the family's face for the researcher. In so doing, they demonstrated that they recognized talking "mean." Their spin control, in their conversations with the researcher, tried to minimize the chaos inherent in the scene and thereby maximize what they perceived as a much-needed re-affirmation of order.

This corpus of research has many important implications for family dynamics. It is easy to see how children's and women's roles are reflected and constrained by how they are spoken to; how much access to the floor they get; how they are placed into positions of scrutiny through speech acts (e.g. criticism and its opposite, praise); and how they either fight for new roles or accept what is expected.

A recent study by Kendall (2000) took family dinnertime conversations as a context for analyzing how parents create and sustain gendered identities at dinnertime. It is a case study of one family with two working parents who carry out differential roles during the dinner speech event. These roles and their enactment are shown to reflect and perpetuate gendered identities. Despite the fact that both parents were involved in demanding full time careers, Kendall's frame analysis yielded a vast distinction in the roles each played. While the mother evidenced agility in carrying out multiple roles simultaneously, the father played far fewer roles vis à vis the family dinner dynamic, and these roles were not overlapping:

> "…a framing analysis reveals that the mother accomplishes multiple tasks simulta-
> neously by maintaining multiple frames throughout dinner, stepping in and out
> of frames as the situation requires. In this way, she performs a dexterous balancing
> act at home, providing evidence that the greater demands on women at home
> extend to, and are partly constituted by, linguistic interaction." (Kendall 2000: 9).

In other words, not only did the mother perform most of the duties of providing food, but she also wore many other hats. Kendall identified a total of eleven
possible frames falling into three categories. The dinner category consisted of
the frames of 'head chef,' 'hostess,' 'miss manners,' 'caretaker,' and 'teacher.'
The conversational category subsumed the frames of 'co-participant,' 'facilita-
tor,' 'journalist,' and 'playmate.' The managerial category consisted of two
frames, 'time and motion manager' and 'social secretary.' Kendall's finding
was that the mother in this family created and sustained all but one of these
frames, the 'playmate,' which (in addition to 'co-participant') was the only
frame created and sustained by the father, who did so in a "one-frame-at-a-
time" manner. This is all to say that despite the ostensible move toward
egalitarian sharing of domestic duties in dual income families, this case study
revealed a persistence of traditional gendered roles at dinnertime that modeled
traditional gendered identities for their ten year old daughter.

These roles are clearly different in different speech communities. Expectations not only vary from family to family, but also clearly differ from society to
society. What counts as appropriate dinnertime talk certainly varies with different ethnic, regional and racial groups. Because of this variation, a look at an
example of research into language socialization cross-culturally is worth noting
here. Israeli researcher Shoshana Blum-Kulka (1990) has studied dinnertime
narrative activity with a focus on politeness, comparing US Jewish families with
Israeli families. The researcher coded videotaped dinner talk in these two
groups for evidence of social control via directives. While directives are certainly part of parent -child talk in many if not all known societies, Blum-Kulka
characterized Israeli "straight talk" as even more direct than most. This corroborates earlier research by Blum-Kulka and others (e.g. Katriel 1986) on
directness differences between different groups in Israeli society.

An important aspect of this study by Blum-Kulka is its exploration of the
child's need for independence versus involvement in American vs. Israeli

families. While she found independence to be more important for Americans, involvement was more important for Israelis. Blum-Kulka terms family discourse as a "domain-specific politeness system" (269). Indirectness has a different meaning in the familial domain than in others. In other words, within the family domain, indirectness and politeness do not carry the same meaning as in the social domain. Indeed, directness is more expected within families as opposed to other domains, since it may indicate higher involvement and thus more caring. Blum-Kulka shows how directness for Israelis can function as polite deference, indicating not only power but also intimacy. Thus, she sees parental discourse, albeit replete with directives, as essentially polite.

Americans and Israelis mark their directives for politeness in different ways. Israelis prefer solidarity politeness, employing mitigation such as nick-naming, while Americans prefer conventional politeness, using indirectness and explicitly socializing children in politeness expectations of the speech community. For example, many of us who are members of North American speech communities will recognize that families take turn-taking rules very seriously in family dinnertime talk. Turns are explicitly negotiated, and the floor is typically allocated by parents. In Israeli families, this is accomplished much more implicitly.

This example of cross-cultural variation in familial talk is illustrative of how we must be suspect of positing universals in norms of face-to-face interaction. While it is likely that many societies have some kind of talk at meals, the expectations for the participation of children and other family members differ widely. In some, for example, children are to be "seen and not heard." In others, children are expected to speak up. Rules of discourse and pragmatics vary greatly. Family and societal value systems are always reflected in the analysis of face-to-face interaction in talk at home.

Narratives by mothers rather than children are the focus of Deborah Schiffrin's 1996 study on the sociolinguistic construction of identity. Her data comes from sociolinguistic interviews in which she asks questions of her interviewees that elicit narratives. From a methodological perspective, the data captured is indeed "face-to-face," but is elicited through questions by the researcher (for a complete overview of the sociolinguistic interview, see Schiffrin 1994). Schiffrin (1996) demonstrates how narratives produced by two women of a specific ethnic group (Jewish), display their familial values.

Each of the women tells a story about a family member who did something that conflicted with family expectations, thus threatening family solidarity.

The two problems are: (1) a grown offspring who was dating someone inappropriate; and (2) a daughter-in- law who refused to use terms of address appropriate to the family (e.g. addressing her mother-in-law without a title, such as "mom"). Both stories are on the theme of integrating outsiders into the family domain, a sweetheart on the one hand, and a new family member on the other. The narratives center around the desire for family solidarity in this Jewish-American subculture. The mother's narrating of her daughter's dating a gentile demonstrates her negative evaluation of her daughter's actions. In the second narrative, not being addressed by a specific name by a daughter-in-law is perceived as marking an uncertain relationship, something to be avoided when integrating outsiders into a family. These narrative accounts are told to the researcher rather than serve as direct confrontation with the perceived "offender." Thus, they resort to constructed dialogue and reported speech rather than spontaneous face-to-face familial interaction. They do demonstrate, however, the belief that talk can solve problems. The parallel conflict is indirect here rather than direct. Even by relating the conflict to an outsider, the problem can be thought through. The data is reflective of problems in face-to-face interaction in the family domain. The family "provides our first set of social relationships …; it also remains a traditional nexus of social life and cultural meaning for many women." (Schiffrin 1996: 170).

Family talk is the basis for indexing appropriate social and linguistic roles and for challenging these roles. The manner in which parents and children talk to each other and talk about each is clearly reflective of family beliefs and values.

1.3   Couples talk

I would like to reiterate here that the past quarter of a decade has spawned a veritable wealth of research on gender differences in conversation; however, surprisingly little of this research has been carried out in the family domain. I referred above to Pamela Fishman's (1983) research that analyzed the work women do in couples talk to sustain conversation with their partners. Although her data was limited to recorded conversations of three couples, she found that women do a majority of the work to keep conversations going with their partners and spouses, despite a seeming lack of interest of the male partners.

A more recent study by De Francisco (1991) takes off on this research, extending Fishman's methodology by adding interviews with seven couples. Gender role behaviors are explored here, with all seven couples exhibiting what she termed quite typical gender role behavior. She studied talk time, question-asking, topic initiations, topic success/failure, and turn-taking. In general, men's behavior served to silence the women, first by non-responses to women's talk, and second by interruptions. As in Fishman's research, while women encouraged talk, the men demonstrated a preponderance of put-down type of speech, or as she terms it, "patronizing" and "teachy" behaviors (418). Some examples offered by the author were sermonizing and using slower speech with more careful articulation as if the talk were addressed to a child. In order to avoid conflict, the men preferred light talk or no talk at all.

An important unpublished research endeavor on couples interaction in families is well worth noting here. In a dissertation and beyond, D'Amico-Reisner (1985; 1993), analyzed adult scolding within the family domain. She found that such scolding is extremely rare among interlocutors who are not intimate; thus, the majority of this speech behavior is found in private talk among spouses and partners. This type of disapproval exchange serves to establish what the author calls "behavioral expectations" and "boundaries of interaction." Studying disapproval exchanges diachronically, D'Amico-Reisner (1993) called these exchanges, "songs and dances." These are defined as the reoccurring themes of disapproval in the lives of intimates. Demonstrating definable themes that are motivated by unmet expectations, occurrences of direct disapproval were found in this research to evolve, dissolve, or change shape over the course of time; moreover, they gave melody to other speech activities. A number of interactional effects were documented that included ganging up, undressing, stacking, blending, and extending the amount of talk. Evidence from the data indicated semantic patterns that connected "songs and dances" with one another through time.

Her continuing research on the theme of disapproval reflected a delicate struggle to balance power with solidarity in the most intimate of social relationships. She identified several interactional patterns of "songs and dances": *leashing*, the appropriate complementary behavior to an initiating "dressed" (mitigated) utterance of disapproval (acceptance through justification, remediation, and/or apology); *spiraling*, where an opposing "undressed" (unmitigated) occurrence leads an exchange to spiral out of control; and, *downturning*, where interlocutors who begin to spiral jointly negotiate down to resolution. This work demonstrates that differences in conversational style alone are insufficient to explain individual instances of disapproval when an intimate social relationship is diachronically examined.

Adult scolding is but one example of a type of language and behavior used in conflict situations between intimates in the family domain. How conflict is managed among couples is the focus of a study by Alberts (1990) which takes a conversational analysis perspective combined with quantitative measures to study the use of humor in managing couples' conflict talk. Realizing that humor is a potentially positive conflict management strategy, she wanted to ascertain how exactly it functions, both positively and negatively. Humor in this context can indeed be a double-edged sword (Boxer and Cortes-Conde 1997). While it has the ability to diffuse a situation, it also can express malice.

Alberts employed an instrument to elicit talk about conflict among 40 couples. They were given a battery of tests and then selected for being adjusted but in conflict about a particular issue. Each couple was instructed to discuss items from a battery on which they had indicated disagreement, and their conversations were audiotaped for up to one hour of talk. Humor strategies employed in these discussions were subsequently analyzed. Alberts found only 38% of the couples to use humor at all, and those that did employed various sorts of humor (e.g. sarcasm, jokes about self, jokes about the partner). These instances of humor were coded as either hostile or benign. An important finding was that how the humor is met seemed to indicate the potential to arrest or continue the conflict cycle. There was a correlation between the use of negative humor and the extent of maladjustment of the relationship: "...it appears that the nature of the couples' relationship influences the type of humor used, that in turn influences how effectively the conflict is managed." (116). The opposite was also found to be true. Better adjusted couples used humor as a means to bring the conflict to a close.

While conversational humor has been amply studied in the social domain, Albert's study is one of the few to study humor in the familial conflict arena. The analysis of such verbal strategies as humor for resolving conflict has the potential for fruitful applications. The study of aggressive humor and how it differs from humor that diffuses conflict can teach us how to more effectively manage our most intimate relationships.

There is widespread general interest in effective communication. A perusal of many lay magazines yields advertisements for self-help literature and audio-tapes to help people become better communicators and networkers. Few of these focus on our most important relationships, that of the family. Let us take a close look at one specific speech behavior that occurs in the familial domain, that of nagging.

2.   An in-depth example of family speech behavior: Nagging

"Nagging is the repetition of unpalatable truths."
Baroness Edith Summerskill

The speech behavior having the semantic label of 'nagging' is one that occurs principally within the familial arena and is relevant to both parent-child communication and couples communication. Because it is widely agreed that nagging is unpalatable, as the above quote indicates, the question that arises is: why is nagging so ubiquitous in the domestic context?

Nagging occurs among family members in an attempt to accomplish the everyday necessary tasks of family life. Nagging as a speech event is typically an attempt by one family member to get other members of the unit to carry out household tasks. Why is it that one family member, usually an individual with given power inherent in a role, will nag, while another with the same given power will issue a request without having to resort to nagging? This section focuses on such issues, analyzing nagging with regard to the sociolinguistic variables of gender, social distance, social status, and power. Topics or themes of nagging are also discussed, as these reflect aspects of relative importance of tasks to participants in the event.

Nagging is both a speech event and a speech act that is part of the larger event. Neither event nor act has been systematically studied in any speech community in which English is spoken as a native language (nor does it appear to have been described elsewhere). Analyses of closely related speech behaviors have appeared in the sociolinguistics literature, and these include griping (Boxer 1993a), complaining (DeCapua 1989; Olshtain and Weinbach 1993), and adult scolding or disapproval exchanges (D'Amico-Reisner 1985). Nagging shares qualities with these speech behaviors; however, it is distinct in several ways. Complaining occurs over a wide range of interlocutor relationships and in many of the domains of interaction. Indirect complaining or griping has been found to occur in all domains and across the social distance continuum, and small gripes are often heard between total strangers in an effort to establish a momentary solidarity based on a shared negative evaluation (Boxer 1993a). Direct complaining rarely occurs among interlocutors of great social distance, since it is, in Brown and Levinson's (1987) terms, a Face Threatening Act. When a person complains in order to remedy an offense, it is the antithesis of rapport-inspiring (DeCapua 1989). Disapproval exchanges do indeed occur most often where the relationship has already been established and where the disapproval has less chance of hindering the relationship. Recall that D'Amico-Reisner (1985) found that adult scolding, or disapproval, occurred most frequently between intimates who were fairly equal regarding social status; speakers who were status equals but neither intimates nor strangers seldom participated. Clearly, such disapproval exchanges prevail among interlocutors with a power relationship giving one individual the right to disapprove (e.g. parent to child in the socialization process). Nevertheless they are distinct from nagging in that they are often the result of non-compliance with a previous request issued among intimates.

Aside from disapproval and griping, another related speech act is criticizing. Perhaps the most closely synonymous to nagging is the speech behavior commonly termed "pestering." Clearly, a componential analysis of folk terms would yield related terms to nagging that could be teased apart and analyzed to ascertain the nuanced distinctions in these speech behaviors.

As we have seen in the previous section of this chapter, the body of research on family face-to-face interaction has by and large studied discourse of the family dinner speech event. These studies analyzed such phenomena as narratized speech, gender socialization, role distribution in families, instilling social and moral values, judging and criticizing. Nagging has been left virtually unexplored. Likewise, the literature on couples' intimate speech behavior has, surprisingly, omitted nagging. This study is a first attempt at analyzing nagging in one US speech community.

2.1   Methodology

Data for the study consist of seventy sequences of spontaneous speech collected in family settings. Graduate and undergraduate students in my own classes in Linguistics gathered data. Students were enlisted to voluntarily write down nagging sequences as they occurred in domestic contexts. These situations varied from interactions with roommates and parents (for undergraduates) to interactions with spouses, partners and children (for graduate students). Thus, a variety of contexts and interlocutor relationships are represented, with a considerable age span of participants, from late teens to early middle age. All spontaneous data are in the form of field notes taken immediately following the nagging speech event.

In addition, I conducted five quasi-ethnographic interviews, with three women and two men, in order to delve more deeply into folk perceptions of nagging in this academic community. Interviews took place over the course of several months of data collection. Since from the spontaneous data it began to appear that occurrences and perceptions of nagging differed for women and men, the insights of individuals of both sexes were obtained. Also, the consultants' ages spanned some thirty years, from mid thirties to mid sixties, in order to uncover any generational differences in perceptions of nagging.

I refer to these interviews as "quasi-ethnographic" because they took place only once with each consultant. Typically, in interviews that are truly ethnographic, interviews take place several times with each consultant, tapping into native speaker implicit knowledge about the language under investigation (Spradley 1979). With speech act studies carried out by researchers who themselves are members of a speech community, I have found such interviews to be most fruitful when done once for approximately an hour with each consultant (for further details on ethnographic interviewing for speech act analysis, see Boxer 1996).

2.2   Nagging as a speech event

Data for this study indicate that nagging as a speech event incorporates several sequential acts: the first move is a request. When the request is repeated it becomes a reminder. When a reminder is repeated it become nagging. Thus, nagging requires a prior request and reminder.

Clear syntactic and semantic patterns emerged. The initiating speech act of the event, the request, is typically in the form of a command or a hedged request: With intimates, it is often "bald on record" (Brown and Levinson 1987), as in "make sure you take the clothes out of the dryer as soon as it buzzes" (from wife to husband). With those who are less intimate (or more careful of politeness) it may be couched in the form of an interrogative having the illocutionary force of a directive: "why don't you change your shirt?" (from a girlfriend to her boyfriend in a relatively new relationship).

The second move by the initiator follows (sometimes after a lapse of time) an addressee's non-compliance with the request. It typically takes the form of a question that is indeed an interrogative, not a request or suggestion. Examples would be: Did you hear me? or Did you do as I asked you to do? This second move is the reminder. It takes the interrogative form in order to ascertain compliance or non-compliance.

The third or subsequent move by the nagger is often an exclamation of some sort that expresses exasperation:

> Look at this. It's all wrinkled!
> I give up, I'm not asking you any more!
> Never mind, I'll do it myself!

A final, culminating speech act in the nagging event can either be a scolding or a threat, depending on the relationship between interlocutors (e.g parent/child).

2.3   Topics/themes of nagging

Nagging focuses on a variety of topics that revolve around domestic issues. The focus of nagging is typically something important to the nagger but not important to the person being nagged. Themes of nagging run the gamut of asking a family member to do a chore (e.g. take the clothes out of the dryer; clean the garage; take out the trash; start dinner) to asking a family member to *stop* doing something. Chores/errands accounted for approximately 43% of the data. Asking someone *not* to do something or to stop doing something accounted for approximately 26% of the data. Most of the remainder of the sequences involved attempts by the nagger to get another person to call someone, either to find out information or to call them to stay in touch. Miscellaneous exchanges focused on such nagging as telling a grandchild to eat more; telling a class to get their first drafts in; and sermonizing to grown children about the need to teach the young children more about religion.

One of the female consultants, a middle-aged professional with a husband and two grown sons, talked about topics of nagging with a retrospective insight into how it occurred with her own family:

> In my experience nagging has to do with matters of control and order in the environment or with schedules — matters that in the total scheme of things are relatively minor, but the person doing the nagging wants control of the environment or of schedules, that is, someone who's chronically late or whatever ….In other words, the wet towels lying around… are a threat to how I want my environment to be.

> I think I also take it more personally — all those little annoyances drive me crazy, while in the grand scheme of things they are very unimportant. Of all the kinds of things I've nagged about, if something were to happen to the person who I love but nag to death, I would say I'd give anything to have them back, they could leave all the wet towels they want.

These reflections provide insight into the relative importance or unimportance of the themes of nagging in domestic life. While the focus of nagging seems at the time to be important to the nagger, it may be understandable why it is unimportant to the recipient of the nagging.

Nagging of children was typically on themes that would do the child some good, even though the child may not have realized its importance. These exchanges focused on such topics as taking medicine or doing homework. The following is an insight from one of the female consultants on nagging about homework:

> As for homework, you want them to be successful in their own right. You have the perspective that they lack, that these grades and learning matter for the future, and as a reflection of you, I think it's a really pretty rare parent that is so detached from their children that they don't see them in some sense as a reflection.

Parents do not wish to see the natural consequences of having their children ignore such important requests. To not take medicine, for example, might result in continued symptoms. Parents try to control such aspects of life for children, and often resort to nagging do so. Natural consequences for the child necessarily mean natural consequences for the parents. Parents understand these consequences better than their children.

2.4 Status and power

Nagging is an act that is irritating and frustrating to both naggers and recipients. It is not surprising that topics of nagging tended to focus predominately on getting household chores done. Inevitably, one family member ends up being the "cleaning boss," and the individual in this role has inherent rights and obligations to assign chores. The question that arises is, does this role of "boss" really have power? Most of us know that this kind of "boss" must deal with frequent reneging on duties within the family unit. Perhaps children can get away with this in families, where unconditional parental love reigns. With couples, however, the case is somewhat different. The sort of power possessed by the nagger is distinct from true power typically found in social and professional relationships.

People with this latter type of inherent power seem never to need to issue the request more than once. Let us consider the following two sequences, issued first by a mother to her teenage son (1) and by the same mother to her teenage daughter (2):

(1) A: Mother, to B: Son, just before a party when trying to clean up:
     A: What are you doing now?

B: Cleaning my aquarium

A: I need for you to help clean up, not make new messes. Please do the carport!

B: Okay

One half hour later:

A: Son, I need the carport cleaned

B: Okay

A: Have you started it yet?

B: No, not yet.

A: Fine. I give up. I'm not nagging you any more. I'm really angry now.

(2) A: Mother; B: daughter, age 19, at home from college on vacation

A: B, Would you please empty the dishwasher?

B: Okay, in a minute.

Twenty minutes later:

A: B, I need the dishwasher done right now.

B: Yeah, I heard you.

One hour passes (A is angry now)

A: B get down here right now and do what I've asked you to do!

B: Chill, mom. I said I'd do it.

Contrast these above sequences with the following (3) in which the father issues a directive to son in sequence (1) above:

(3) Father, A, to teenage son, B:

A: B, would you come downstairs please and put away those tools.

B: Okay. (Immediately obeys).

The father in sequence (3) had no need to nag. Indeed, as the individual who gathered this data indicated, his children immediately comply with his requests.

Exchanges (1) and (2) above stand in sharp contrast to (3). Sequence (3), where the father issued one directive and only one, is reminiscent of requests/directives in workplace interactions where jobs need to get done. Nagging is rare in the workplace precisely because the rights and obligations of roles are strictly circumscribed. Indeed, the consequences of not carrying out one's assigned tasks are clear-cut. Notwithstanding systems of tenure, the majority of jobs have assigned duties. If a worker does not carry these out, the natural consequence is likely to be loss of one's job. Thus, bosses ought never to have to nag employees, for if a request becomes a reminder and the task is not accomplished, the result is firing.

In the interview data, only one consultant talked of a co-worker, a status inferior, who nags. She describes her secretary's nagging:

> I have a secretary that nags. She nags about formalities in the office. The office deals with clients, and there has to be a little spontaneity because not everyone is on time. Sometimes everybody comes at once. So you just have to get them in without the paper work. So she nags, and she nags until … even though you say you understand, she still nags. She gets so mad. She has to keep things in order. If we take the patients before the paperwork is done, it has to be put in order later, and it's confusing for her. I see it as nagging and I think she has to lighten up a bit.
>
> *She won't get fired if she keeps nagging?*
>
> No because she keeps our office together.
>
> *So she has some sort of power. More than most secretaries do.*
>
> Oh yeah, she does. Nobody is organized enough. I guess we allow her to do it because we need it, we have to have it.

The issue of power/status/authority here is analogous to the familial situation. While the secretary is indeed a status inferior in some respects, she takes on a very important role in this workplace. Without her efforts the office would fall apart. In some manner, then, this worker is responsible for running things smoothly, just as is the "cleaning boss" in a household. Given that the place could not function properly without her efforts, she has the right to nag and, indeed, on some level this nagging is, while not exactly appreciated, considered justifiable by the counselors. She does not have to worry about losing her job. They need her. In contrast, she does not have the power of being a status superior to the counselors; therefore, she must resort to nagging at times. If indeed she had such power, she would need only to issue a request.

In contrast, we do not typically fire our family members (though we do more with partners and spouses than with children). Nagging, or causing someone to nag, thus has dire consequences in families. While it has been known to lead to divorce, it rarely leads to disowning children. This may explain why nagging is a persistent speech behavior in the domestic arena between parents and offspring. Just why some parents nag while others need not do so must lie in family members' perceptions of power of the person issuing the request. Certainly, awareness of the consequences of our speech behavior can lead to more harmonious familial interactions.

2.5   Gender and nagging

There are instances in the data where the nagging is repeated many times. Issues of power (or lack of power) are clearly demonstrated in such examples. A person whose role in a family (e.g. parent; spouse) gives her/him the right to request something from a family member, is able to have the request carried out quickly if there is perceived power. This appears to be the key to why it is that women are so frequently the naggers. If indeed gender is a "master status" as West (1984) asserted, this comes as no surprise. Tannen (1990) had the following to say about the gender stereotype of women as naggers:

> That women have been labeled "nags" may result from the interplay of men's and women's styles, whereby many women are inclined to do what is asked of them and many men are inclined to resist even the slightest hint that anyone, especially a woman, is telling them what to do. A woman will be inclined to repeat a request that doesn't get a response because she is convinced that she *really* wants him to do it. But a man who wants to avoid feeling that he is following orders may instinctively wait before doing what she asked, in order to imagine that he is doing it of his own free will. Nagging is the result, because each time she repeats the request, he again puts off fulfilling it (Tannen 1990: 31).

Tannen hints of power play in this tug of war between the sexes when it comes to such speech behavior as nagging. Power emanates from style differences, in her view. We must wonder which comes first — the style or the power? One male consultant reflected on this issue, in talking about his former partner's nagging:

> She nagged me because she was weak. The person who's nagged starts to grow until there's an eventual satisfaction. ... You [the nagger] start out with power and you get half way through it and you're probably at your weakest point.

One female consultant, a sixty-five year old secretary with six grown children, put a positive spin on female nagging. She said that mothers tend to nag while fathers don't because we expect things to be the way we want them. Men don't place as much importance on domestic organization as women:

> It's a part of the nurturing thing to be after the family to do the things we're supposed to do.

Semantic perspectives on the lexical term "nag" may point to inherent semantic derogation indicative of terms typically associated with women. Such terms, while once having been neutral, have, over a period of time, taken on negative semantic loads. The noun "nag", as defined by Webster's Dictionary, is "a small light horse." This over time became derogated to mean an inferior or aged or unsound horse. This source even gives one old definition as "prostitute." Indeed, the examples offered there all have female subjects as naggers: "She's a good wife but she does nag so;" "She nagged her husband at every opportunity." It seems clear that the speech act has come to be known as female activity, despite the fact that the original definition made no specific reference to "female" horse.

One distinction between female and male terms of reference is the apparent perception by one of the male consultants that we tend to refer to male nagging as "hounding." Pursuing the semantic load of the two terms, we immediately sense a difference. To the native English speaker, nagging is a negatively tinged behavior, and, indeed, so is hounding. Going back to the nouns from which the two terms are derived, however, we are able to notice glaring distinctions. While a nag is an inferior or unsound horse, a hound is a useful hunting dog.

Only six of the seventy sequences involved men nagging women: four in which a husband nagged his wife and two with a boyfriend nagging the girlfriend. In one, the husband asks his wife, every time she is about to get into the car, not to slam the door. This falls into the nagging speech event because it has been requested repeatedly for several years, every time the couple gets into the car. It follows a single incident early in the relationship in which she slammed the car door so hard that it hurt the husband's ears.

In another sequence, the boyfriend and girlfriend are living together, and he deems it time to begin dinner preparations:

(4) A: Female graduate student in linguistics, age 25 B: Male graduate student in MBA program, age 29. Relationship: intimates
       Situation: Both studying. They talked about preparing dinner. B asked A to cook rice.
     B: Did you cook rice?
     A: No, not yet. Isn't it too early?
     B: Could you cook it right now?
     A: Okay
     B: No! We just have to warm up curry! It will take 5 minutes and rice takes 30 minutes.
     A: Yeah, but that means we have to eat dinner at 5:30
     B: Okay, but don't be too late.
     (Both studying again after thirty minutes), in a minute.
     (after a minute)
     B: Can you... Never mind!
     A: okay, okay.
     (A walked in the kitchen and cooked rice).

He wanted her to cook it but gave up trying. Perhaps in this particular relationship such activity was perceived as her role, and either he would not do it, or she knew how to make it better. He was obviously hungry and she was not.

In contrast, in two thirds of the data women were the naggers. There were twice as many mothers nagging sons as wives nagging husbands, contrary to what one might expect. This could be an artifact of the data collection. Recall that students in linguistics classes, many of whom were undergraduates, collected some of the data during Thanksgiving weekend. While the female undergraduates collected data on their mothers nagging their brothers, the male students collected data on their mothers nagging them. An example follows:

(5)   B has many points on his driver's license and is in danger of losing his car insurance. He has gotten a ticket for expired registration in the past and it is now time to renew his registration. On the phone with his mother, A.
A: Have you renewed your registration yet?
B: No, not yet.
A: You know you won't have insurance if you got any more points on your license. You got a ticket for that last year.
At the end of the conversation:
A: You're going to send your registration in this week?
B: No, but I got the form and I'll send it when I finish my exams

(6)   A typical example of wife nagging husband. A (young mother, age 25) wants to take a shower after giving the kids a bath. Their daughter, C (age 4) wanted to draw and A asks B (husband, late 20's) to play with their daughter:
A: B, Mary wants to draw and color. I have to shower.
        Can you play with her? All the crayons and papers are on the table already.
B: Ok.
While A is coming out of the bathroom she hears Mary complain to her father:
C: But dad, you too have to paint!
A: I asked you to play with her.
B: (who was reading the newspaper) Ah! I have to draw too?
As A gets dresses she hears C again asking her father to draw with her.
A: B, you can't read the paper now! We have two kids.
        One plays with one and the other one plays with the other.
B: No response. He goes to play with their young son.

One of the female consultants had the following insight into gender and nagging:

> If most nagging is domestic and women are responsible for the domestic part of life, then these issues are going to resonate more with them than with the men. Even women in their twenties who are married or partnered are more responsible for that sphere of life even if they're working.

One of the male consultants gave his insight:

> Well, don't take offense, but it's only been since the beginning of this century that women have begun to have authority. When women are coming from the other end, they feel that they're not as authoritative as men, so they have to keep asking and keep asking. honey, take the garbage out. And the man says to himself …"I'll take it out when I get around to it."

This consultant corroborated exactly Tannen's perspective on nagging and gender styles. The issue is a difficult one to disambiguate. Clearly, power and authority enter into conditioning for all speech behavior. We speak in a certain way due to our socialization. If girls are socialized into cooperative styles emphasizing symmetry and boys into hierarchical styles emphasizing status (Maltz and Borker 1983), it is no wonder that women nag the boys and men in their lives. In a world of cooperation women may expect compliance with reasonable requests; nevertheless, when confronted with the hierarchical style of boys and men, it just does not work. Requests need to become repeated reminders that turn into nagging. If our styles constrain how we request and the responses to requests, then by nagging we lose power. Without power we are forced into nagging. The cycle is vicious.

2.6 Social distance

Nagging is scarce with interlocutors who are not intimate. As with much speech behavior, the social distance variable is a strong determinant of the speech event (c.f. Wolfson 1988; Boxer 1993b; Spencer-Oatey 1995). Thus, nagging is a speech event that is not typically encountered except at this extreme end of the social distance continuum. One rarely hears of nagging among friends and acquaintances, for it is within this arena that interlocutors find themselves in the process of negotiating relationships. As is indicated in the "Bulge" theory of social distance, in the middle of the continuum occurs most of the delicate dance of negotiation.
Female consultant:

Nagging is repetitive action, asking someone to do something repetitively. It's mostly in the family. I don't nag my friends.

Why not?

Because I want them to stay my friends. So, I guess I take for granted the family.

When friends and acquaintances develop a closer relationship, they may begin to develop speech behavior that approaches that of the domestic scene. Of course, this is particularly the case with roommates, since domesticity is inherent in this context. Several undergraduates and graduate students offered spontaneous nagging sequences among roommates. The following insight was offered by a middle aged female graduate student:

I nag my roommate to take out the trash. He agreed to be responsible for trash when he moved in, but he has to be reminded every time. I have seen him put trash into the container when the lid won't close. Even then, he will turn around and walk away. We go through this little routine twice a week.

With close friends who are not roommates, nagging about a non-domestic theme can cause the person nagged to perceive the nagger as irritating and eventually lead to the demise of a friendship:

(7)   College girlfriends. Almost every weekend the same thing happens. A calls B on the phone on Friday night: The phone rings,
       A: Hi Jill, this is Kim. What are you doing tonight?
       B: Hi Kim. Well, I think X is having a party that we're going to and then we'll probably end up at the Salty Dog.
       A: Hmmm, ok, well who all is going?
       B: (names the various people)
       A: Well, I can't decide what I want to do, so why don't you just take my beeper number and call me.
       B: Ok, give it to me again.
       A: Don't forget to beep me. You didn't call last week.
       B: Yeah. I swear. Sorry about that.

B commented on A's nagging:

I have such a hard time contacting someone via beeper, because I think it's ridiculous for a student to have one (anyone other than professionals). With this mindset, I go to parties with her number in my pocket even though it is inconvenient to use the phone at some loud party or at a bar. I also have the tendency to get involved with conversations and forget the time. In any case, she always calls me and I always forget.

2.7 Conclusion

This analysis of the speech event we commonly term "nagging" indicates that it prevails in the family arena, and, indeed, is the source of a good deal of conflict within this domestic domain. While it is somewhat beyond the scope of sociolinguistics to provide solutions to speech behaviors that are problematic in face-to-face interaction, the mere description of the act or event provides a heightened consciousness about the variables conditioning the speech behavior. Certainly, nagging is a face-threatening act. The reasons why we participate in such an event with only certain interlocutors is worth a good deal of reflection.

Several of the consultants interviewed for this study indicated that they have a new awareness of nagging and that probing of their tacit and explicit knowledge of such talk has opened their eyes to what they are actually doing when they nag or are the recipients of nagging. Certainly, with the emergence of the variables of gender, power/status and social distance as strong determinants of nagging, we are able to examine more closely what exactly transpires in such a speech event. Implications of the study are clearly indirect. Nagging is yet another example of the undeniable fact that what we do with words affects our most important relationships.

3. Conclusion: Face-to-face in the family domain

Certainly, how we talk with members of our families affects the most important people in our lives. What can we learn from the analysis of face-to-face interactions in families? This question is timely and important. While the applications are indirect, the heightened awareness such study brings about is a first step toward family harmony with offspring, partners, and elders. I would venture to characterize the application of this kind of analysis of face-to-face interaction as having great potential to solve real world problems. The understanding of how our linguistic usage affects child socialization and relationships between couples and other family members is a critical first step in the creation of a more egalitarian society. The transmission of societal norms and values begins in interaction with family members from early on in childhood. The creation of a more democratic interactional schemata must begin in the family domain. When otherwise subjugated family members are given a voice, traditional power relationships are challenged. It is true that parents have the important job of teaching children the norms of appropriate speech behavior.

Rules of politeness take years to be fully inculcated. However, more than just appropriateness and politeness are taught in family interaction, as we have seen in the preceding pages. Such rules as who gets to "know best" are also implicitly taught. The seeds of transforming traditional power and dominance relationships are sown at home.

Note

1. A brief overview of Brown and Levinson's Politeness theory can be found in Appendix B

CHAPTER 3

Face-to-face in the social domain

1. Introduction

Social life is the domain in which most of the existing research on the discourse of face-to-face interaction has concentrated. It is easy to see why the analysis of 'ordinary' social interaction has been the focus of so much attention by scholars in linguistics, sociology, psychology, communications and other inter-disciplinary fields. Despite the fact the ordinary or mundane is typically not something of interest to research, for analysts of conversational interaction in the social domain the study of the work that so-called 'ordinary' interaction entails is fascinating. The reason is that in discourse analysis, that which is mundane, and thus seemingly effortless, is indeed a work of incredible synchrony. How people make sense of each other's contributions in conversation, how we know what people mean by what they say, how we are able to respond to interlocutors appropriately and accurately by accessing a vast schema of information that is not in the actual conversation, is the focus of this fascination.

That everyday conversation is by and large interactional rather than transactional (Brown and Yule 1983) is what makes the analysis even more interesting. In other words, in social conversation our aim is typically to establish rapport with others, not necessarily to convey information. The fact that we do so much of this kind of talk indicates that social conversation forms the very backbone of relationships. The subtleties of just how this is accomplished have been the focus of much recent research in sociolinguistics. We deal here with the analysis of social conversation from various methodological perspectives, ranging from ethnographic and conversational analytic, sociolinguistics' roots in anthropology and sociology, to more quantitative research studies.

Any attempt to do justice to a review of literature on conversational interaction in social life can be daunting. Clearly, the overview that follows is intended to be exemplary rather than exhaustive. Various perspectives are taken here as the focus of analysis: speech act and speech event studies both from ethnographic and CA perspectives; studies that focus on gender and language in social life; studies that take one of the other sociolinguistic variables as the point of analysis. These are some ways of looking at social interaction. In other words, various perspectives are offered here. Methodological issues are important in the present discussion, for how we approach a particular type of data influences the issues addressed and thus the findings yielded by the questions that are asked.

For example, a recent thrust in applied linguistics specifically and in the social sciences generally has been the study of the issue of identity. Sociolinguists are interested in how identity is displayed and developed because as conversationalists we have at our disposal a vast repertoire of identities that may or may not be relevant to a particular interactional context. This development or display (performance) is instantiated in the moment-to-moment unfolding of interaction. We choose to present ourselves in a certain way, featuring some of our identity characteristics, depending on our interlocutor's identity, role, and/or power in society. Our social identities are multiple. We may at the same time be a woman, have a certain job or career, be of a particular ethnic/religious/racial group, participate in various smaller communities (e.g. sports teams, choirs, community organizations); be a member of a certain political party, and on and on. Every time we participate in social interaction we display some of these individual and social identities. Likewise, identity is co-constructed through interaction. That is to say, it is neither fixed nor stable, but fluid, and depends to a large degree on where, when, and with whom we are interacting. Research that takes into account the relevant sociolinguistic variables is able to reflect on just how identity constrains and is developed by and through conversational interaction. This is particularly significant in the social domain, where the aim of conversation is to create, affirm and reaffirm social relationships.

Let us now turn to an examination of recent research in the domain of social interaction to take a closer look at how we use language to tell our interlocutors something about ourselves. In so doing we display who we are to establish a rapport or solidarity with others, forming a relationship or becoming a member of a group or community. This chapter culminates in an in-depth study of identity development and display through conversational joking and teasing that I carried out in collaboration with colleague Florencia Cortés-Conde.

1.1   What do we know about social interaction?

It seems fitting to begin an overview of recent work in the language of social interaction with a discussion of phatic communication (Malinowski 1923), for this sort of communication is quintessentially social. It has no transactional benefit. Phatic communication, sometimes called "small talk" (J. Coupland 2000), is that which on the surface appears to be unimportant in that it offers very little to an interlocutor in terms of information exchange. Nonetheless, phatic communication conveys important information about interlocutors' needs and wishes. For example, certain speech acts and their responses (e.g. complimenting/responses to compliments) tell an addressee that s/he is approved of. This kind of information is conveyed indirectly through the speech act. Saying something such as "I like your shirt" is therefore often more than just a compliment — it is frequently a solidarity marker. Phatic communication, or small talk, is an important social lubricant. In the words of Erving Goffman: "The gestures which we sometimes call empty are perhaps in fact the fullest things of all" (1967: 91).

1.2   Phatic communication, speech acts, events, and activities

Perhaps one of the most widely used examples of phatic communication is the greeting "how are you." Most native speakers of North American English have as part of their communicative competence the knowledge that this expression is indeed a greeting and not a question inquiring about health. Other societies have similar phatic greetings, such as the question "have you eaten?" in Chinese. Communicatively competent members of speech communities recognize these formulae as greetings (i.e. interactional) rather than requests for detailed information (i.e. transactional). The extent to which the question "how are you" is phatic is reflected in our propensity, as native speakers, to answer with a phatic "fine," even in contexts outside the social domain (e.g. doctor's office visits). The greeting and its typical reply is so deeply ingrained as part of our communicative competence that our tendency is to offer the phatic response regardless of the context. Only after realizing that the question is seeking information do we go on to offer information about how we are.

This phenomenon was studied by Coupland, Coupland and Robinson (1992). They analyzed responses by elderly individuals to the greeting *how are you?* as an opening to interviews in which they were asked about their health. The authors' intent was to demonstrate the differences between the use of phatic communication and the conveying of real information. Analysis of elderly people's responses was a logical choice here, since the *how are you?* question ostensibly asks about health and the fact that elderly people's talk is very often focused on health-related issues.

Given this intersection of contextual variables, the authors were able to pinpoint exactly when the *how are you?* question elicited either a phatic response or an informational one. The focus of the piece was how the respondents proceeded to health related disclosure after an initial phatic response to *how are you?* There were, indeed, some clearly phatic responses, and these often came hand in hand with thanking formulae. Unqualified negative responses (non-phatic), were also found in the data, but were deemed anomalous, given their abnormal propensity of disclosing intimate details to strangers on first meeting. These two extremes were rare in the data. The majority of responses were somewhat intermediate between phatic and non-phatic. Many of these adopted what the authors called "good news, bad news" formats. (Coupland et al. 222). While initial responses tended to be phatic, this was mostly at the opening and used as a means of holding off the face threat of telling bad medical news.

This study has important implications for social interaction and beyond. Where elderly interlocutors are participants in interaction, the typically phatic *how are you?* may only be initially responded to in a phatic manner. It appears to depend entirely on who is asking the *how are you?* question. It is certainly amusing to hear a phatic response to *how are you?* when the asker is not asking for social reasons. Our immediate visceral inclination to respond to this question phatically, even in non-social contexts, gives credence to the strength of the spillover from social to institutional talk. Given this, we must ask if the *how are you?* question is at all relevant to anything other than ordinary social talk.

The phatic nature of greetings is reflected in the fact that many speech acts may be used to realize greetings. Other studies on greetings in North American English have found that the phatic "*how are you,*" merely scratches the surface of formulaic greeting rituals. Eisenstein, Bodman and Carpenter (1988) offer a good example of research that clearly demonstrates the multi-functionality of speech acts used in greetings. The native-speaking portion of this study employed natural observation techniques to uncover nine categories of greetings. These ranged from "greetings on the run" to what they termed "greetings for special purposes." The researchers found eight purposes for greeting, showing how greetings overlap with other speech acts such as complaining and apologizing. Data collected on buses in New York City, for example, showed many complaints as greetings (e.g. "this bus is really crowded"). The nine greeting topics ranged from the phatic *how are you?* to discussion of problems. In other words, greetings can be phatic or, time permitting, lead into conversations conveying information (after the initial reply "fine"). Thus, greetings can be quick and formulaic or lead into rapport-inspiring social conversation. Clearly, "greetings on the run" most often reaffirm a momentary solidarity. Those greetings that lead to further elaboration in social talk have the potential to lead to the exchange of personal disclosures that may result in social bonding.

Despite the fact that the greeting *how are you?* is not intended as a request for information, as a greeting it has the potential to lead into other kinds of social talk that can build bonds between interlocutors. Clearly, when we participate in greeting rituals we give and receive signals about the availability of our interlocutor for further talk. These signals are both non-verbal and verbal. A greeting on the run, for example, will have non-verbal cues (e.g. continuing movement away from us) that make it obvious that a conversation will not ensue. However, when the greeting co-occurs with a lingering to talk, we must know the appropriate next step. A more specific question than "how are you," focusing on some aspect of an addressee's life, is more likely to open an extended conversation. Talk about health-related issues is not always what the greeter, in asking the *how are you?* question, really wants to talk about. The formulaic answer "fine" may be a signal to engage in talk about another topic. Clearly, among the elderly, ensuing talk about health is more common as a next topic proceeding from the greeting. Here the sociolinguistic variable of age is paramount. Finding a next topic of mutual interest is key in proceeding from greetings to other conversation.

Whether or not greetings lead to a conversation that establishes bonds between interlocutors, anything beyond a greeting on the run, (that is, even a short exchange) necessitates an appropriate parting ritual. Consider the following, in which two female students passed each other on the way to class on campus:

A: Hey, how are you doing?
B: Fine, how about you? Going to class?
A: Calculus, I hate it! (keeps moving)
B: Ugh! Well, catch you later.
A: Yeah, see you at the meeting.

While partings have been found to be formulaic at times, the precise initiation point and moving to closure is a fine-tuned "dance." Findings from research on social conversation indicate that partings, like greetings, can function to bring interlocutors closer to each other, when carried out with finesse. In the sequence above the interlocutors had a brief complaint/commiseration exchange in which a momentary solidarity was established regarding dislike of calculus. The greeting, while on the run, led into a brief exchange where the participants engaged and parted with a promise to participate in a later meeting at which they both are expected to be present. The parting affirms their relationship as part of a group that is scheduled to meet. Thus the sequence, despite being on the run, does important interactional work for these interlocutors.

Telephone partings were described early on in a CA analysis by Schegloff and Sacks (1973). In that seminal study they noted closings of phone conversations to proceed in steps that frequently incorporate one or more pre-closing sequences. A less well-known early study on telephone partings (Clark and French 1981) found goodbye exchanges to be virtually absent from most face-to-face conversations in which routine information was requested. Only when some personal information was exchanged between interlocutors was some kind of *goodbye* heard. The researchers found that people employed leave-taking formulae if they felt they had become more than superficially involved with their addressee (i.e. if some minimum amount of rapport had been established).

The fact that greetings often operate as leading to the development of relationships is not surprising; the indication that partings may also fall into this category is somewhat less obvious. Indeed, there are speech acts that do not upon superficial reflection appear to be rapport-inspiring in the social domain, but which, upon close reflection, can function positively. One such behavior is that which is commonly known as the "refusal." Beebe, Takahashi and Uliss-Weltz (1985) conducted a cross-cultural study on US/Japanese differences in refusal strategies that merits attention here. The researchers studied refusals in response to requests, invitations, offers and suggestions and found that it is among status equals who are potential friends that refusals are most elaborated. Elaborated refusals frequently led to long conversational exchanges that were intended to build rapport while at the same time saying "no." While we tend not to think of refusals as solidarity-establishing speech behavior, we see from sociolinguistic research how refusals can serve to affirm or reaffirm a relationship. Thus, even speech acts that have a negative semantic label, such as refusing, can be manipulated by competent speakers to serve them positively in social conversation.

Refusals are of course responses to other speech acts, such as the four mentioned above. Among these, requests have been most widely studied, but primarily from the perspective of cross-cultural differences (cf. Blum-Kulka 1982; Blum-Kulka, Danet and Gherson 1985; Blum-Kulka, House-Edmonson and Kasper 1989; Fraser, Rintell and Walters 1980). Ervin-Tripp (1976) was among the earliest studies to look at requests/directives among speakers of American English. Her findings yielded six types of requests ranging from embedded imperatives to hints. Ervin-Tripp's study was one of the first to note that, in social conversation at least, this speech act tended to be realized less directly under conditions of decreased solidarity or familiarity between interlocutors. Later speech act research, as we will see below, has confirmed this patterning and led to some theoretical work on indirectness in social interaction.

One subset of the speech act of requesting, favor asking (Goldschmidt 1993), has found that mitigating for indirectness increases the likelihood of compliance, given that asking a favor constitutes asking for something that is outside the boundaries of normal obligation. Because of this, people generally ask favors of others whom they believe are willing and able to carry out the task in question. Goldschmidt found that more modification and politeness are employed if the task is perceived as too great or if social distance is perceived to be great. In other words, the weight of the imposition and distance, two variables in Brown and Levinson's (1987) politeness scheme, are most important in how favors are realized. Goldschmidt found that 85% of responses of favor-asking in her data received positive responses, and she posits that this success derives from the fact that we tend not to ask favors of those who are either unwilling or unable to comply. The study gives insight into an aspect of a particular North American value system as it is reflected in the types of favors that are appropriate to ask and the kinds of responses and negotiations which follow a request for help and/or service. The importance of knowing what is appropriate or not in asking favors lies in the inherent fact that the speech act involves asking for something outside of the addressee's daily routine. Because doing a favor usually requires some time and/or effort (on the part of the addressee) and entails no role-related obligation on the part of an addressee to fulfill the task, how to ask a favor is an important part of social communicative competence.

Offers are also speech acts that precede refusals (or acceptances). An in-depth study on this speech behavior (Rabinowitz 1993) outlined how native speakers of American English give and receive offers. Clearly, offers are rapport-inspiring, since they extend support, help, or some kind of potential benefit to the addressee. In this way, offers can be seen to be the flip side of favors. That is to say, they extend a potential benefit without it being requested. The offerer commits herself/himself to convincing the addressee to accept, but by doing so runs the risk of imposing on the recipient's negative face. Rabinowitz explained that this is the reason for the existence of a large proportion of IF-clauses in offering — to mitigate imposition and thereby give the addressee a face-saving way to refuse. Regardless, a response of either refusal or acceptance is always expected in American English. Misperceptions often occur in offering due to the potential mismatch between an offerer's view of what is of potential benefit to the receiver and the addressee's perception of the potential benefit. Understanding this point can be important in avoiding conflict and misunderstandings when offers are involved.

Within English-speaking communities, scholarly studies on a range of other speech acts have been published over the past twenty years. The early work of Nessa Wolfson cannot go unmentioned here, due to its pioneering methodological approach to data collection and analysis. Wolfson was greatly influenced by the theoretical work of Dell Hymes, with whom she studied. This is clearly seen in her writings, specifically in Wolfson (1989), where she strongly advocates an ethnography of speaking approach to the analysis of naturally occurring speech data.

Wolfson is most remembered now for her extensive study of compliments in North American speech communities. Her work on invitations (Wolfson 1979; Wolfson, D'Amico-Reisner and Huber 1983) is less known but very important for the study of social interaction. She became interested in studying how Americans use invitations after hearing foreign students repeatedly complain about how speakers of American English are insincere when they extend ambiguous invitations that are rarely followed through. By using in-depth ethnographic observation and field notes, these researchers discovered that such gambits as "let's get together some time" or "we should really have lunch" are not only *sincere* but also show something important about the way in which North Americans interact. They found that self-protection against the risk of rejection was at work in the use of what appeared to the learners to be insincere invitations. The average speaker of US English is so anxious to avoid rejection that s/he offers a "lead" in order to ascertain an addressee's interest in getting together. Hence, it is not lack of desire to get to know an addressee better, but quite the opposite: by offering a lead which is non-specific with regard to time and place, a speaker is attempting to assure that both interlocutors are able to save face. What is important is the concept of negotiation inherent in offering an ambiguous invitation as a lead. It is the mutual cooperation of the speaker and addressee that results in a successfully negotiated invitation.

Invitations share the attribute of being rapport-inspiring speech behavior with other types of speech acts, perhaps the most extensively studied being that of complimenting (Pomerantz 1978; Wolfson 1981, 1988; Wolfson and Manes 1980; Manes and Wolfson 1981; Knapp, Hopper and Bell 1984; Herbert 1990;

Holmes 1988). The result of this research is a wealth of information on how this speech act and its responses are realized across English-speaking communities. Wolfson's work on compliments established the most common syntactic and semantic patterns used in complimenting behavior in American English. Moreover, this research, along with the other studies above, has contributed greatly to our knowledge of how complimenting behavior reflects underlying cultural values.

The knowledge of how to give compliments and respond to them is an important part of native speakers' communicative competence in social life. While Wolfson's work concentrated primarily on the initiating compliment, other studies have looked at responses as well. Pomerantz' (1978) study stands as a first in its CA approach to the study of compliment responses. Her research focused on the notion that Americans are torn between not wanting to appear immodest and not wanting to insult the complimenter by denying the truth of a compliment. Pomerantz found that we tend to avoid these dangers by downgrading compliments. We do this through minimizing or denying the value of the attribute being complimented. Thus, to accept a compliment by saying something along the lines of "I like it too" would appear to be lacking in humility. For this reason, we tend not to hear this type of response in American English. On the other hand, we need to temper our downgrading so as not to invalidate the complimenter's positive sentiment. This fine line is something most of us negotiate successfully without realizing it. In other words, a reply such as "this horrible thing, it's so ugly" would probably be going too far in invalidating the compliment. Pomerantz showed how we temper our responses to strike an appropriate balance between self-praise avoidance and validation of the compliment.

A CA approach to the analysis of compliment data, such as that used by Pomerantz, allows for an investigation of the ways in which interlocutors use their real world knowledge and practical reasoning to compliment others. A good example of a more recent study on complimenting behavior using CA techniques is Boyle (2000), who asserts that CA allows for an analysis of complimenting from a phatic communication point of view that ethnographic analysis misses. Boyle claims that through CA, implicit complimenting can be studied by investigating the unfolding of the speech act. Implicit compliments are implicated through supposition, as, for example, 'I wish I were as adept as you are at...' (fill in the blank). Boyle argues that the ethnographic approach of data collecting through field notes renders the researcher unable "to reveal the complex, local, interactive constitution of a compliment"(29). Boyle maintains

that the field notes typically employed by ethnographic approaches to compliment studies do not allow the researcher to study compliments from this
perspective; therefore, they are limited in their ability to adequately analyze the
speech behavior.

The problem with recording was explained by Wolfson's assertion (1981)
that compliments are rather rare in ordinary social conversation. To overcome
this difficulty, Boyle used transcripts of radio talk programs, in which implicit
compliments could be readily analyzed. He found that such data yielded
implicit compliments that, contrary to the explicit compliments studied by
Wolfson and others, were not formulaic. Using CA techniques to analyze this
recorded talk, Boyle claims, allows for the analysis of indexical knowledge (i.e.
knowledge of the nature of the objects and occurrences in the real world).
Through a CA approach, one is able to distance oneself from a speech act
analysis per se and look at the entire sequence of talk surrounding the act.

Boyle contends that CA's approach to analyzing implicit compliments
allows for using only a few samples of data to draw examples of how such
compliments are instantiated in moment-by-moment interaction. An example
offered in Boyle's study was a transcription of a radio interview of a discussion
about a musician's difficulty in getting his work released because of his open
homosexuality. On the topic of the interviewee's difficulties becoming known
as a musician, the interviewer (BB) clearly showed his commiseration with the
musician (MC), aligning himself with MC by using various techniques that are
demonstrated through CA analysis. One such technique is his use of implicit
complimenting, which Boyle shows to assume a shared schema of indexical
knowledge of the audience, when BB says to MC: "you've worked with
Elizabeth Taylor." This counts as an implicit compliment by indexing the
interviewee's success as an actor, even though he has had troubles as a musician.

> Thus, for many the name of Elizabeth Taylor would index fame, wealth, glamour,
> success, excitement, talent and beauty, among other things, and the information
> that the actor has worked with Elizabeth Taylor would lead many listeners to infer
> that MC must surely possess some exceptional qualities. Rather than specifying
> those qualities, however, BB refers to the achievement of having worked with
> Elizabeth Taylor and allows the audience to infer the compliment that is implicit
> in the utterance. (Boyle 2000: 37).

Boyle explains that implicit complimenting such as this enables the individual
being complimented to respond without the difficulty of deciding whether to
reject or accept the compliment (cf. Pomerantz 1978, who claimed that accep-

tance of compliments is dispreferred). An implicit compliment allows for acceptance without suggesting vanity. Boyle goes on to show how this implicitness not only allows MC to agree, but also makes it easier for BB to establish greater rapport between himself and MC through displaying a "reciprocity of perspectives" (38) that abounds in phatic communication of this nature.

Avoidance of self-praise, as found by Pomerantz and Boyle to be important in the uptake of compliments, is an important aspect of social bonding. One of the drawbacks of a CA approach to speech act data is that it analyzes only what is in the transcript. Sociolinguistic variables rarely if ever enter the analysis. Ethnographic approaches, on the other hand, look at gender, age, status, social distance, and social class, to name but a few of these variables, and analyze how the speech act covaries with differences in these variables. Thus, each approach has advantages and disadvantages. While it is true that CA can aid in an analysis of the act as it is unfolding, it too has its limitations.

An ethnographic study that found this self-praise avoidance to be an important reflection of the American value of equality can be found in Herbert (1986). That study looked at American cultural values reflected in complimenting behavior in a comparison with South Africans. The study found that Americans, when compared with South Africans, tend to minimize or reject the compliments they receive, thus further working toward the building of solidarity by stressing equality with their interlocutors. Herbert concluded that since South Africans function in a society in which social stratification is more obvious, they automatically assume solidarity with status equals and thus are likely to accept compliments more freely. This contrast gives an insight into social values in US society when compared with others in which the social context differs greatly. The point is that in much of the American middle class, the push toward the establishment of solidarity in social talk is paramount, and the fact that we tend to downgrade compliments in our responses gives evidence to support this.

Wolfson's "Bulge theory" (1988) is based on precisely this concept and derives from her extensive study of invitations and compliments. Based on the study of these two speech acts, Wolfson theorized that most speech acts would plot out in a similar way. That is, Wolfson claimed that what strangers and intimates have in common is the relative certainty of their relationships. Given this, neither group works very hard at the give-and-take of negotiation so characteristic of interlocutors in the middle of the social distance continuum, friends and acquaintances, who do conversational laor to establish bonds. This is very true of compliments, which are used as social strategies with the goal of opening conversations, establishing points of commonality, affirming or re-affirming solidarity, and thus deepening friendships.

My own in-depth work on troubles-talk, or complaining behavior (Boxer 1993a) took this theory to task (see Chapter 2 on family interaction). In this analysis of complaints and their responses I found that indirect complaining, or griping (complaining that is not directed at a person responsible for an offense or capable of remedying an offense), is more often than not done in an attempt to establish common bonds. In other words, in ordinary social talk we gripe to others about a range of troubles, many of them not serious (e.g. the weather, being overworked, the bus being crowded, the line at the bank being too long). My findings indicated that the preferred response was one of commiseration. That is, this sort of phatic troubles-telling is frequently undertaken by inter-locutors to open and sustain conversations and relationships. This was particu-larly true of women. Along the social distance continuum, I found that even total strangers engaged in this type of conversational exchange, and agreement or commiseration abounded as responses among strangers. It was among intimates that responses differed, with higher instances of contradictions and advice given. These findings run counter to Wolfson's "Bulge" in that it found strangers to be willing to establish a momentary solidarity, while intimates needed not do so. Wolfson claimed that at neither the intimate nor stranger end of the social distance continuum do interlocutors work to establish rapport. The complaining data showed that they do at the maximum end of social distance (strangers). Thus, the bulge was skewed, at least for griping responses.

Claims have also been made for how apologizing behavior follows a similar pattern to the Bulge (cf. Holmes 1989, 1990); nonetheless, the actual data on which these claims were based were never plotted out, just as Wolfson's compliment and invitation data was not.[1] The speech act of apology has been extensively studied since the late seventies, and has important implications for social communication. Similar to extant research on requests, much of the research on apologies has been carried out within the traditions of cross-cultural pragmatics and/or interlanguage pragmatics (e.g. Cohen and Olshtain 1981; Olshtain 1983; Olshtain and Cohen 1983; 1987; Kim, 2001) or has taken as its focus English-speaking countries other than the US (e.g. Holmes 1989, 1990 in New Zealand; Owen 1980 in England). The interest in apologies as remedial exchanges stems from Goffman's early volume *Relations in Public* (1971), where he noted that remedial exchanges "change the meaning that might otherwise be given to an act, transforming what could be seen as offensive into what can be seen as acceptable" (109). Here Goffman provided a fruitful theoretical foundation for more systematic empirical research on apologies.

One rather early apology study that focused on North American English speakers (Fraser 1981) focused on strategies of apologizing. Fraser found that apology formulas are often followed by acknowledgements of responsibility, promises of forbearance, or offers of redress, depending on the severity of the violation. With specific reference to the building of rapport, Fraser notes that "the more formal the situation, the longer and more elaborate the apology" and that "as the degree of familiarity increases between the interactants, the need…to provide elaborate apologies decreases"(268–69). Thus, Fraser's data, much like my own data on complaining and commiserating, indicates that, contrary to the "Bulge," we are more likely to offer a more elaborate apology with strangers or acquaintances. Among intimates apologies are either less likely to occur or are simpler and shorter in form.

Not all speech acts are less elaborated among interlocutors of close social distance. One good example is advice-giving. One of the problems in ascertaining how advice covaries with social distance is that this speech behavior has been studied more by using talk show data than social interaction data (e.g DeCapua and Dunham, 1993). The reason for this seems clear: the researcher is able to collect a large amount of data in a short amount of time. Capturing spontaneous advice ethnographically is a challenge; nonetheless, using talk show data yields findings on a speech event that is different from ordinary social conversation.

My work on complaining and commiserating yielded a good deal of spontaneous data on advice as a response to troubles talk. Perhaps not surprisingly, it was a rather large category of responses by males to complaints, particularly female complaints. This response occurred most often in family/intimate interactions. In the social domain, among friends and acquaintances, males were more likely to give advice than commiserative responses, but not as much as with their partners in family setting. The offering of advice in a "social" troubles talk encounter has great potential to be face-threatening. Indeed, complainers do not always seek advice when telling of troubles. That study found that much griping was carried out for the sole purpose of venting, and when this was the case the complainer just wanted the addressee to be there as a supportive listener. Support was typically offered via outright expressions of commiseration. Most complainers did not want to solve the particular problem under discussion, and when the interlocutor offered advice it frequently caused friction. Tannen (1990) corroborates this notion in her discussion of differences in troubles talk approaches between women and men.

When advice is offered it needs to be tempered with sensitivity to the context so that the advice is not presented as imposing authority. A very informative study on just this issue was published recently by Goldsmith (1999) focusing on what she termed "content-based resources." In order to study these resources, the researcher employed both qualitative and quantitative techniques. Elicitation instruments enabled her to collect large amounts of data on varying contents.

One can give advice that highlights the hearer's distress, underscore the hearer's weakness, or suggest that the problem is under the hearer's control. Goldsmith found that it is this latter type of advice that is preferred by tellers of troubles. She demonstrated how advice giving could take advantage of content-based resources:

> More skilled speakers have face-related thoughts as part of their representation of a situation and have a better understanding of how to select face-relevant content and express content in face-sensitive ways. This perspective does not deny that politeness forms (i.e. indirectness and redress) are relevant to face, but it shifts our focus: Rather than presuming given content (e.g. an idea about an action the other could take to solve the problem) and asking "How do messages vary in the form or style used to express that content?," this alternative perspective leads us to ask "How do the contents (and forms) speakers express vary and how does this variability represent different identities and activities?" (Goldsmith 1999: 308).

To ascertain how advice giving can take into account identities and activities, Goldsmith undertook two studies to show that content has implications for a hearer's face. The first sought to find out the common topics in troubles talk. Her methodology was to have individuals respond to hypothetical situations. She terms this method a "naturalistic experiment," following Tracy (1989). After finding the common ways that advice-givers respond to another's problems, Goldsmith carried out a second study to ascertain how these topics are related in regard to a hearer's face. The questions asked touched on some of the following issues: Is a hearer free to reject the advice? Does the advice criticize the hearer? Is the advice considered `butting in' by the hearer? Does the advice take into account the hearer's identity? In her detailed analysis, Goldsmith shows how what we may perceive as face threatening, from Brown and Levinson's point of view, can in reality be face-sensitive when content-based resources are taken into account. For example, "Combining advice with statements that the problem is serious might honor positive face by simultaneously accepting that the other has good reason to be concerned and portraying the other as capable of effecting change" (Goldsmith 1999: 322). Thus what we might think as an inappropriate response, validating the seriousness of a complaint, may indeed be content-sensitive and therefore appropriate in certain contexts. Goldsmith's findings are indeed interesting:

> As predicted, content that asserted that the other's problem is not severe, that his or her emotional reaction is inappropriate, and that the problem is uncontrollable were negatively associated with regard for positive face. The contents that were positively associated with regard for positive race were unexpected. Although saying not to have the emotion or that the emotion is temporary might be face threatening alone, these contents may be heard as reassuring when they accompany a solution to the problem (Goldsmith 1999: 326–327)

Goldsmith's study adds to our knowledge of how to give advice with sensitivity, augmenting Brown and Levinson's (1987) theory of politeness. It is informative for ordinary social conversation, as troubles-telling is a prevalent speech event, and advice-giving can either work to build rapport or alienate interlocutors from each other. This research gives detailed analyses of how to go about being a sensitive interlocutor to friends. Goldsmith shows how contents work in combination and that "different combinations of the same contents could project different identities" (1999: 328). Socially supportive advice shows sensitivity to a complainer's negative stance, and does not diminish its importance by statements that minimize the trouble. Such statements are very problematic when they co-occur with advice. On the other hand, advice accompanied by a statement like "don't worry" can be face honoring.

Methodological considerations are important here. Whether to analyze a speech act through ethnographic methods, to employ quantitative techniques, or to examine the unfolding of a speech event through CA techniques, should be determined by what questions are being asked. Studies such as Goldsmith's validate the combination of approaches to data analysis to get at the heart of a particular issue. Research on the language of social interaction carried out through varied methodological approaches gives us a clearer view of different perspectives on speech behavior. Ethnography of speaking approaches that utilize spontaneous speech data enable us to analyze how members of specific speech communities actually realize speech acts and participate in speech events. Quantitative techniques, as we have seen above, afford the opportunity to collect larger amounts of data that can then be corroborated with data that is based on actual conversations, either audio-recorded or from field notes.

Recorded data allows for analysis of the unfolding of an event or activity, but is limited in generalizability. Combining techniques is sometimes useful for ascertaining what we really do in social interaction.

1.3   CA and speech activities

We have seen in the research overviewed above on speech acts that many of these studies have taken an ethnographic approach to data collection and analysis. This methodology lends itself nicely to speech act research, since it analyzes the act and its responses as a reflection of the sociolinguistic variables. Fewer speech act studies have taken a CA approach (e.g. Pomerantz 1978; Boyle 2000) but in so doing have demonstrated some of the advantages of analyzing talk in interaction through these techniques. CA is ideal for studying such phenomena as topic development and topic shifts, overlapping speech, intonational and prosodic effects on interaction, and adjacency in utterances.

The journal *Research on Language and Social Interaction* has over the past several years advocated utilizing CA techniques for insights into speech activities (speech acts and beyond) in the social domain. An example of advocacy of CA is an article in that journal by Malone (1995) on "altercasting." This concept is defined as follows by Weinstein and Deutschberger (1963: 454): "altercasting is projecting an identity, to be assumed by other(s) with whom one is in interaction, which is congruent with one's own goals. It is posited as a basic technique of interpersonal control" (in Malone, 1995: 149). Malone's article purports to analyze social conversation from what he terms a "perspective display sequence (ibid). What this means precisely is taking on the perspective of the addressee in an attempt to cast her or him in a supportive role of what the speaker has to say, before the speaker has even said what she or he proposes to say. This is all done with the goal of obtaining support for what is about to be said. Strategies of altercasting include preempting disagreement through such conversational devices as prefaces and disclaimers. This is accomplished through manipulative moves such as opening a multiunit turn through prefacing (e.g. let me ask you something), which allows a speaker to hold the floor without appearing to violate norms of appropriateness for multiunit turns. Malone terms these "conversational traffic signals" (152) that present the addressee with an implicit understanding that later talk will make everything clear. They thus establish footings (mutually agreed upon orientations to an issue) or alignments that will be acted upon in subsequent talk.

Malone illustrates altercasting with an excerpt from a conversation between five graduate students having a friendly conversation about their discipline, Sociology. A male speaker does the altercasting by using a multiunit turn
that establishes a shared identity (alignment) between the interlocutors. His
purpose in doing so is to tie his own sociological interests (qualitative and
theoretical) with the more quantitative approach of his present interlocutors.
His altercasting is done in a highly mitigated manner. He attempts what
Malone sees as co-implicating one of the female interlocutors in order to
subvert any disagreement on her part about what he is about to say on the
matter. In so doing, he tries to get her on his side of the intellectual argument.
"Altercasting gets done turn by turn as each interactant anticipates what is
likely to happen and how to respond to what has just happened in order to get
to where he or she wants to go" (Malone 1995: 154). In such a manner the
recipent (addressee) is cast in the role of assisting the speaker. By co-implicating the support of the most quantitative person in the group, who happened to
be a woman, the speaker made it more likely that his claim about sociology
would go unchallenged.

The issue at hand here is the methodological one: how it is that CA can be
used as a tool for understanding how altercasting (and other speech activities)
is accomplished. Malone claims that a turn-by-turn analysis of unfolding
interaction is the analytical key to unlocking such moves. While this may
indeed be true, I would suggest here that referring to the existing sociolinguistic variables in a conversation gives further insights into interaction. In the
example that Malone gives, there is no analysis at all of the fact that the
addressee (who is altercasted) is female and the speaker (the altercaster) happens to be male. To *not* analyze natural speech data with reference to variables
such as gender (and social status, age, etc.) is to miss an opportunity to
understand the important role played by individual and social identity.

Let us take another CA study as further example. Maynard (1998) is a CA
analysis of praising versus blaming the messenger in the speech activity of
delivery of news. The author asserts that messengers seek to avoid blame in the
delivery of bad news and work to claim credit in the delivery of good news.
Maynard shows that when good news is received, recipients tend to offer
congratulations and gratitude almost immediately; conversely, when bad news
is received, recipients covertly assign responsibility to the messenger, but do so
in a delayed fashion. Indeed, deliverers are seen to often work to avoid being
blamed, since, of course, bad news is discrediting. Through CA techniques,

Maynard shows just how the turning from blame to casting the deliverer as victim is interactionally achieved. Techniques such as reciting evidence and being logical are used to deflect a deliverer's responsibility in bad news conversations. Such work is difficult. On the other hand, deliverers of good news frequently "prospect for compliments…in a partially disguised manner" (365). There is a tension between this prospecting for compliments and a more humble outlook of not wanting to be perceived as seeking self praise. "Regularly, deliverers who have good news for recipients may interject their own agency in a way that, as argued earlier, prospects for the recipients' displays of appreciation" (382).

CA lends itself nicely to an analysis of a speech activity such as delivery of news. It allows for a moment-by-moment analysis of the instantiation of talk in interaction. What it does not offer is information on how conversational moves reflect who is talking with whom. For example, we can envision how a status difference between interlocutors can have a strong effect on the uptake of bad news. Social status as a sociolinguistic variable constrains the rights and obligations that are inherent in who may say what to whom. In social conversation among equals we might indeed see posturing by the news deliverer to receive appreciation or deflect blame. Here the *domain* of interaction determines the role relationship and thus the rights to participate in certain speech activities. In the workplace domain, for example, a situation in which a boss delivers bad news to an employee would probably not contain the same types of moves on the part of the recipient as in ordinary social conversation. Hence, since sociolinguistic variables are constrained by the domain of interaction, and the variables affect how people talk to each other, CA analyses such as that of Maynard might be enriched by ethnographic information that adds to the information gleaned from the research.

1.4   Interlocutor variables and ethnographic approaches

Sociolinguistic context and the sociolinguistic variables that affect and constrain social interaction need to be accorded a primary locus in the study of face-to-face interaction. Clearly, as we have begun to see, the domain of interaction is in itself an important primary consideration. Contextual variables such as speech situation and topic always have an important effect on the manner in which verbal interaction ensues. Interlocutor variables — social status and power, social distance, age, social class, race, ethnicity and gender —

are of great import in face-to-face discourse, since who we are talking to determines what we way and how we say it.

Many of the speech act studies reported above based their findings on interlocutor variables that emerged in the analyses. An excellent example of a study of speech behavior larger than the speech "act" is Beers-Fagersten (2000), which analyzed swearing among college students. The study was a large-scale ethnographic investigation of the use of swear words among students of various racial, ethnic and gender groupings. Beers-Fagersten's analysis was based on a wide spectrum of spontaneous swearing collected in the form of field notes around campus settings. These data were then corroborated by distributing questionnaires to 60 of the students she had recorded, then taking a small subset of these students with whom she conducted in-depth ethnographic interviews. Beers-Fagersten's findings indicated that ethnicity, gender, and particularly race figured strongly into the realization of particular forms of swearing, reflecting an in-group solidarity and serving to keep outsiders at arms length. Males generally, and African-American males in particular, viewed swearing behavior as proscribed for certain groups.

Clearly, interlocutor variables such as race and ethnicity figure importantly into any analysis of speech behavior. These are perhaps most clearly seen in the domain of social interaction. Let us turn to examine one of the most widely studied of these interlocutor variables, that of gender/sex.

1.5   Gender and social interaction

A large body of recent research on language in social life has been conducted with gender/sex as the focus of analysis. Early essays on the inferiority of women's language and thinking (e.g. Jesperson 1922) appeared in the linguistics literature and seemed to be uncritically received, despite the fact that they offered no empirical evidence to substantiate their claims. More systematic gender and language research dates back to Robin Lakoff's 1973 work positing that the language that women use (e.g. tag questions, empty adjectives) both reflects and perpetuates women's powerlessness and inferior status in all spheres of interaction. While Lakoff's assertions about women's language were also not empirically systematic but rather based on intuition and observation, her work did serve to spark a great deal of more rigorous research seeking to debunk her claims.

The introductory article of the 1983 collection entitled *Language, Gender and Society*, by Barrie Thorne, Cheris Kramarae and Nancy Henley is an excellent overview of a decade of research following Lakoff. The book is seminal in describing gender and language research ranging from the use of the generic masculine he/man (Martyna, that volume) to male inexpressiveness (Sattel, that volume). The book has been followed by dozens of other books and journal articles on the topic of language and gender, offering multiple perspectives on issues in social interaction as well as the other domains. Several annual and biannual conferences on the theme now regularly take place, most notably the Berkeley Women and Language Conference, which publishes all of the presented papers, and the meetings for the Organization for the Study of Communication, Language, and Gender, a conference connected to the journal *Women and Language*. These fora offer opportunities for becoming acquainted with cutting edge research in the field. While early gender and language research focused primarily on the social domain, more recent studies have investigated issues relevant to all of the other domains. Indeed, a brief glance at current publications indicates the great diversity of present-day research in gender and language.

An important debate in the field at present is the issue of whether women's language is devalued because it is *deficient* (e.g. Lakoff 1973), because of men's *dominance* over women in our society (e.g. Fishman 1978), or merely because it is *different* (e.g. Tannen 1990). Cameron (1996) offers an excellent overview of these perspectives and the traditions from which they stem. According to her, the *difference* approach has been popularized precisely because it is so marketable for self-help literature. Books that talk about celebrating differences are not only politically correct but make it easy to rationalize an attitude of "I'm okay and you're okay." These take the stance that if only we could learn to understand each other's ways of speaking, we would be able to live together more harmoniously. What they fail to take into account is the power dynamic in modern society, in which women's ways of talking, doing, and indeed, being are devalued because they are the ways of the powerless. As long as that which is male is taken as norm, women's language will be derogated. Cameron (1996) states:

> If we accept that differences in speech style cannot be understood in isolation from differences in speakers' social positioning — the activities they are expected to undertake, the personal characteristics they are encouraged to develop, the sources of satisfaction available to them — the question becomes whether those who typically use a particular style of discourse are thereby being excluded from (or conversely, are monopolizing) not only certain verbal practices but, more significantly, a range of social practices. (Cameron 1996: 43).

The *dominance* position can be clearly understood by the view that differences in linguistic practice stem from differences in access to social power. Cameron claims that feminist linguists seek not merely to describe this dominance situation, but to *deconstruct* it. Other feminist linguists go even further, seeking to elevate women's language use as not just "different but equal," but superior (cf. Tromel-Ploetz 1994).

In order to limit the scope of the following overview, the examples included here focus only on *adult* female social interaction, and serve to illustrate the importance of studying gender/sex as a sociolinguistic variable in the domain of face-to-face interaction in social life.

1.6 What do we know about gender in face-to-face social interaction?

Language and gender research has employed various qualitative and quantitative techniques to ascertain characteristics of women's talk as well as women's language as compared with men's language. A piece by Candace West (1995) is an overview of how a CA viewpoint serves as an ideal method for demonstrating women's conversational competence. West esteems CA's approach to analyzing talk in interaction vis à vis gender and language because, from her perspective, it privileges the study of the "temporal and sequential organization" of conversation. Because of this, it is quintessentially concerned with competence in conversation: opening and entering into conversations, turn-taking, repairs, and closings, for example. West's view is that by taking a CA approach to analysis of a piece of data, we are able to see how gender differences are enacted in unfolding talk.

West takes up the term "competence" to take to task traditional views of women's roles in interaction, the *difference* approach, and the preeminence of positively evaluating all that the powerful of society do as superior or as "norm." She draws from her own previous work as well as that of others to explicate her stance. For example, she takes issue with Lakoff's assertion that tag questions are examples of women's powerlessness in talk by using Pamela Fishman's (1983) data on couples' interaction at home. Recall that Lakoff's claim that tag questions indicate lack of self-assurance in talk did not rely on systematic evidence as data. West argues that in order to make this kind of claim about women's language use, we need to carefully study context, including intonation. Relying on spontaneous recorded data, such as that of Fishman and others, a wave of research found that women's tag questions serve a facilitative function that shows women to be supportive and confident.

Fishman's data on tags and backchannels are shown to be displays of active listening through "turn by turn demonstrations of interest and support" (West 1995: 115). Mens' backchannels were delayed responses showing their lack of interest in the ongoing talk.

West likewise takes to task Tannen's work (e.g 1990; 1994) on gender and language. The problem, she says, with Tannen's *difference* point of view, in which women and men are viewed as members of two different speech subcultures, is that "…within the United States, women have been required to reinterpret men's behaviors to make sense of them — but not the other way around" (West 1995: 111). Citing some of her own research to demonstrate women's superior communicative competence, she discusses West and Garcia's (1988) finding that women shift topics more collaboratively than men, thus showing conversational competence. Women were also more adept at generating new topics, but not unilaterally, as did men (unilateral shifts created disjunctures).

Taking up Goffman's (1967) notion of "polite accord" as a requirement for conversational competence, West cites her own study of physician's directives (West 1990), in which she found that male doctors more often used 'impolite' forms, while women doctors used proposals that "minimized status differences between themselves and their patients" resulting in 67% compliance as opposed to 50% for male doctors. All of these points demonstrate women's abilities to guide and organize the flow of messages between speakers to achieve smooth transitions between conversational topics, to maintain polite accord in conversation, and to elicit compliance with their directives" (West 1995: 124). By studying unfolding interaction as these studies did, West claims we are able to clearly see women's competence in conversational interaction.

Candace West is one gender and language researcher who has successfully employed CA techniques to illuminate the *dominance* issue. Ethnographic and quantitative approaches have been used by other researchers to demonstrate a wide range of gender and language findings. A rather early study that is greatly relevant for social interaction from a social psychological perspective was carried out by Aries and Johnson (1983), who focused on conversation between close friends of the same sex. Using a questionnaire format followed by statistical analyses of the responses, the researchers found that female friends conversed more frequently and in more depth than did males about personal issues. Female friendships focused more on sharing of deep feelings, while male friendships focused more on activities. The topic of sports was the only one on which men focused more frequently than women. Women were found to be more disclosing on intimate topics. The authors conclude that "...males may see a close friend as someone to confide in about personal matters, but sex-role pressures restrict the frequency and depth with which they can express themselves to other men" (Aries and Johnson 1983: 1193).

Examples of more recent research on gender and language in the social domain using laboratory data is Freed and Greenwood (1996) and Greenwood and Freed (1992), who studied the functions of questions in conversations between pairs of women friends. Data were taken from eight recorded conversations in which the dyads were asked to talk about how friendship differs for women and men. The study's findings call into question some previous findings in gender and language research. Studying specifically the amount of questions asked, the researchers noted that in half of the pairs, one member of the dyad consistently asked more questions than the other. Greenwood and Freed (1992) assert:

> "Since sex differences cannot be held responsible for this imbalance, we doubt that sex differences alone are responsible for the imbalance in the number of questions used in cross-sex conversations, as claimed by Fishman (1978,1980) " (199).

Fishman's (1983) study of cross sex conversation among intimate partners noted that the female partners asked many more questions than the men, and Fishman attributed this quantitative (and qualitative) difference to women's conversational "work" in keeping the conversation flowing. We see from evidence from same sex social interaction that there may indeed be a tendency for one member of a conversational pair to predominate in question-asking, and this may not be a result of gender differences at all. Greenwood and Freed's findings on same sex interaction thus call into question Fishman's conclusion about question-asking.

Greenwood and Freed (1992) found sixteen types of questions grouped into four general categories. While younger women in the study tended to use more relational questions than older women, even this group did not use this type of question more than 29% of the time. The conclusion to be derived from this data calls into question another generally held belief about women in interaction which was popularized by Tannen (1990). In that publication, Tannen characterized female interaction as dominated by "rapport" talk, as opposed to the "report" talk so typical of men. This assertion is not borne out by Greenwood's and Freed's study of questions. The authors claim, "notions about `rapport' talk as described by Tannen are overgeneralized and misleading (Greenwood and Freed 1992: 205).

When research is carried out to test assertions about women's language, we can clearly see the need for empirically systematic data. Freed and Greenwood (1996) were able to study female-female social talk through elicitation in a laboratory setting. This approach enabled them to collect a larger amount of data than would be possible through the capturing of spontaneous talk. One of the problems with previous studies in the field, as we have seen, is that conclusions have been based on small samples of talk in interaction, such as Fishman (1983), who studied only a few couples' talk and then generalized the findings to male-female conversation on a wider scale. When female-female talk is systematically analyzed and compared with female-male data, we see that such speech behavior as question-asking may be somewhat idiosyncratic rather than a by- product of gender of the interloctutor. Likewise, when female-female talk is analyzed, we are able to see the vast array of topics discussed. While CA methods enable careful analysis of talk in interaction, they are limited in generalizability due to small data samples. Thus, we need to be careful with the conclusions drawn and the generalizations made.

Other qualitative approaches, such as ethnographic analyses of gender differences in language use, afford certain advantages in their data analysis. A case in point is the genre of gossip, a speech event that has been so generally attributed to female interaction to be denigrated. Indeed, this derogation is typical of women's language. J. Coupland asserts:

> Since it has often been women rather than men who have been stereotypically associated with generating small talk and 'gossip,' the deprecation of small talk and the deprecation of women have been mutually reinforcing social processes (2000: 7).

While there have been several studies on female gossip, a recent ethnographic investigation by D'Amico-Reisner (1999) showed how gossip could be used as a positive speech activity in the talk of close female friends. This research explored how indirect conflict talk facilitates an avoidance of direct conflict talk: a) by providing a stage for detailed, privileged information-sharing that enables interlocutors to guide their relationships with one another; and b) by providing an alternative stage for direct conflict with an absent other, allowing for the venting of frustrations, the provision of emotional support, an the co-construction of sense-making. It suggests that while co-constructed indirect conflict narratives enhance solidarity and intimacy in close female friendships, they also contribute to communal intimacy and solidarity in friendship circles.

These findings on woman talk are highlighted in a recent volume by Coates (1996). This was an in-depth ethnographic study of adult female verbal interaction. While the speech community studied was British, the research is well worth mentioning here due to its focus on how everyday talk among women is eminently supportive. Talk among the women studied revolved around topics having to do with people and the women's own lived experiences. The exchange of stories, replete with mutual self-disclosures, was shown to create and sustain for these women an intense level of sharing through collaborative talk. Coates states: "the mutual self-disclosure that is typical of women friends' talk allows us to talk about difficult subjects, to check our perceptions against those of our friends, and to seek support" (52). Indeed, all participants shared in the construction of talk through collaborative floors (cf. Edelsky 1981) and overlapping speech. Questions were used to draw others into the conversation and "promote connection" (201).

Ethnographic methods allow for a thorough analysis of certain aspects of conversation. As we have seen in the two studies described above, these include topic (e.g. talk about experiences; talk about others) speech behaviors (e.g personal disclosures; questions), and conversational organization (e.g. overlapping talk; collaborative floors). While this latter category of the sequential organization has been largely studied through CA techniques, it also lends itself to ethnographic analysis. Questions that can begin to be addressed ethnographically are sometimes nicely fleshed out through structured interviews designed to elicit instances of certain speech behaviors. These interviews differ from ethnographic interviews in that they are intended to elicit specific speech data rather than emic perceptions of linguistic behavior.

A study of Black women's language use in social interaction by Karla Scott (2000) illustrates just how this can be done. The piece is a view of language as it covaries not only with gender, but also with race and class. These latter two variables have been somewhat neglected in face-to-face discourse studies. Scott's study focuses on the analysis of two discourse markers, 'girl,' and 'look' that are ubiquitous in the social talk of a group of young African-American women studied. While her data derives from recorded spontaneous speech, it is supplemented with data on these discourse markers emanating from interviews with a subset of the population spontaneously recorded. The study takes the perspective that these discourse markers are employed when these women switch styles between the out-group code and the in-group code, displaying their ability to navigate multiple identities. In the in-group code, 'girl' is used as a solidarity marker; however, 'look' marks a difference in identity with those who do not share the in-group norms. Thus, both of these discourse markers are shown to have importance in marking social distance. The study is important in highlighting the contextualization cues that signal identity. The different identities naturally develop and are displayed when these women cross boundaries between Standard American English and African American Vernacular English (AAVE), with accompanying differences in prosody:

> In their responses and reported speech the use of the word 'look' illustrates the women's need to assert identity in a world where it is not shared or understood: 'look' says I am different from you, you don't understand.' As a marker of social distance it functions in the same way as 'girl,' which says 'I am like you and understand' (246).

Through ethnographic data supplemented with elicitation through structured interviews, Scott was able to draw on a rather large sample of the two discourse markers to study how identity is signaled through their use. By exploiting more than one methodology for getting at a particular speech phenomenon in a particular speech community, the analysis is able to offer a comprehensive picture of one group's way of negotiating gender, race and class identities.

The negotiation of identity is a topic of widespread discussion in current studies on face-to-face interaction. In social talk this phenomenon is particularly salient, as we choose to present selected aspects of who we are in negotiating social relationships. One interesting speech behavior prevalent in social conversation is conversational humor. Humor tells our interlocutors that we are individuals who are enjoyable company. The study of conversational humor offers a great deal of information about identity display and identity development. Let us take a look at an in-depth study of humor in social conversation that I carried out with colleague Florencia Cortés-Conde.

2.   An in-depth analysis of social talk:
Conversational joking and identity display

In much of Western civilization, humor is an essential ingredient of everyday interaction and of socialization. Conversational joking has been studied by various linguists over the past two decades (e.g. Phillips 1973; Davies 1986; Straehle 1993; Norrick 1994) and across cultures and ethnic groups (e.g. Schieffelin 1986; Miller 1986; Eisenberg 1986). Nevertheless, there has been little attempt to sort out the factors that contribute to the functions of joking and teasing in social interaction.

First, we draw a distinction between conversational joking (CJ), or situational humor, and joke telling (JT). We then attempt to disambiguate that which is ordinarily referred to as "joking" from "teasing." Where does word play fit in? What are the functions and outcomes of verbal interactions that involve joking, teasing and word play? Which of these activities leads to stronger social bonds between participants and which serve as negatively-tinged behaviors that function to alienate interlocutors from each other? In this study we focus on situational humor as a means for analyzing the way identity is displayed and how relationships are affirmed and reaffirmed through such display. We assert that an even more important part of CJ can be not only the display but also the development of a *relational* identity among participants which leads to a sense of membership in a group. In so doing, we take into account various approaches to the concept of identity display and development, including "performed social identity" (Erickson and Schultz, 1983), and positioning (Hamilton, 1995). We show that conversational joking, when it involves teasing, functions on a continuum that ranges from bonding to nipping to biting. We focus on CJ in its various forms and discuss in detail the myriad types of activity it engenders, the sociolinguistic variables that condition its use in ordinary social conversation, and the varied outcomes of the speech genre.

This study takes an ethnography of speaking approach to the data collection and analysis. The data consists largely of transcribed sequences of audiotaped conversations among interlocutors of varying relationships. A small portion of the data was derived from field notes.[2] The data was collected through participant-observation; it was not originally collected with the intention to study joking as a speech behavior but merely as samples of spontaneous speech in social interaction. Conversational joking as a salient speech activity emerged from the analysis. As members of the speech community studied, we used our in-group knowledge in locating occurrences of situational humor.[3] Twenty-two sequences were selected as representing the types of CJ present in everyday talk.

Conversational settings include homes, restaurants and bars, stores, and gyms. Interlocutor relationships vary from friends and acquaintances to strangers, with most being status equals. Ages vary from thirty to mid forties. Both genders are represented; however, there are fewer male-to-male transcriptions than other gender combinations. This is no doubt due to the gender of the researchers. Notwithstanding, part of the ethnography of speaking approach taken here stems from field notes taken on observations of varying gender combinations in face-to-face interactions.

2.1   Conversational joking and "joke-telling"

Conversational joking is clearly a different speech activity from joke telling. Joke telling is a highly conventionalized and socially bound speech behavior; CJ or situational humor is a play frame created by the participants, with a backdrop of in-group knowledge, encompassing not only verbal features but also suprasegmentals and non-verbal communication. In situational humor 'being there' becomes a very important part of 'getting it.' In joke telling the cues are highly formalized and socially marked. The cue is often an introductory statement such as "listen to this funny one," or, "I've got a good one, let me see if I can remember it." In CJ, however, creating the play frame is fundamental, since the humor not only emerges in the situation itself but from the appropriate cues that make it a laughing matter. There are no set formulae to clearly indicate the play frame. We can see this in the following example.

> (1)   Two academic colleagues, both assistant professors, Alice is female and in her forties; Bill is male and in his thirties. The setting is at Happy Hour, Friday evening in a bar.
> Alice: I'm thinking of getting this hair cut short, wash and wear, so that I can swim more easily.
> Bill: Oh, but how can you improve upon perfection?
> Alice: Don't give me any of that silver tongued devil crap!
> Bill: But I'm perfectly sincere.
> Alice: Yeah, right!

While they are both equal in status in the academic setting, A is a few years B's senior, both in age and in length of time in the department. Given this, A feels free to joke with B by challenging his possible attempt to flatter her. At the end of the segment B seems to interpret the exchange as a possible conflict when he says that he was being sincere, indicating he wasn't trying to flatter. The intonation pattern of this utterance signals his interpretation of her utterance as seriously annoyed rather than joking . The question is whether A is really annoyed at B's attempt at flattery, or just joking. In other words, this might not be a joking matter.

   As this example shows, the need for a clear play frame is as necessary in CJ as in joke telling, but intentional or unintentional ambiguity due to a lack of highly conventionalized means for signaling the 'play' frame can be problematic. In joke telling one might not get the joke, but there is no doubt as to the intent of the speech genre; in CJ, not getting it might result in a possible conflict. Misunderstandings and/or misfires are, thus, more likely and imply increased risk beyond the level of loss of face.[4]

2.2 Types of conversational joking

We consider *joking* and *teasing* as two very distinct activities, despite the fact that the distinction between them in the existing literature remains murky. Joking is often viewed as a superordinate genre encompassing teasing, word play, and such verbal devices as sarcasm and mockery. Such is Norrick's (1993) view of CJ. We assert that joking differs from teasing in important ways that have the potential to lead to differing outcomes in a conversational exchange.

Much of the existing research on the subject has focused on *teasing* as a means of socialization (particularly of children) and has concentrated on its inherent ambiguity as a means of social control (e.g. Eisenberg 1986; Miller 1986; Schieffelin 1986). In her study of Kaluli society, Schieffelin discusses teasing and shaming as related speech genres that function as a means to socialize children in the art of manipulating others in order to obtain what one needs and wants. Eisenberg states that teasing works as a means of social control precisely because of the inherent ambiguity that either allows someone to play along by teasing back or to feel shamed by a lack of understanding of the play frame. Miller also captures this ambiguity in her consideration of teasing as "the ability to stand up for oneself, to speak up in anger, and to fight if necessary" (1986: 200). Since it is not the intention of these studies to delineate the differences between teasing and other types of humorous interactions, they analyze teasing as a speech genre in its own right.

In our study, teasing emerges as one of three humorous speech genres, the other two being joking about an absent other and self-denigrating joking. In distinguishing these three types of CJ we take into account the recipient and object of the joke as important parameters. Given our definition, only teasing can bite or nip, since this activity must be directed at a participant. On the other hand, joking and self-denigration can bond without intentional biting. In this bonding relationality is developed.

2.3 Teasing

Teasing requires that the conversational joking be directed at someone present. This person is either the addressee or a hearer and becomes the center of an interaction in which a humorous frame has been set up. Teasing runs along a continuum of bonding to nipping to biting. Because this is a continuum, these constructs are not mutually exclusive and the boundaries are not always clear. As with all talk, much depends on the identification of context, and indeed the exact message cannot be interpreted without encoding/decoding the meta-message. This metamessage can be "made apparent, either by a disclaimer... or by the use of contextualization cues, such as exaggerated intonation, laughs, or winks (Eisenberg 1986: 184). Thus, "the playful nip denotes the bite, but it does not denote what would be denoted by the bite" (Bateson 1987: 180). On the other hand, if the tease is not accompanied by appropriate cues, it can actually bite.[5] There are clear cases of teasing that bonds without a nip or bite; clear cases of teasing that bites and that therefore does not bond; and less clear cases where a bite can actually serve to bond (e.g. among intimates). Each of these cases depends heavily on shared schema. "Teasing creates tension, as one is never completely sure which way an interaction might swing, owing to the unstable nature of many of the teasing frames" (Schieffelin 1986: 167). An example illustrates the possible nip:

> (2)   Family setting: Bob: male who is ill; Molly: female friend; Denise: wife of Bob.
>
> Bob: I walk at the edge of the envelope, every day. I wake up, "I am still here." And then I continue on, I push myself out of bed. I thank God. You become religious.
>
> Molly: Well, I'll tell you, you've gotta change your perspective on things a little bit.
>
> Bob: Of course you do. I was telling [my wife] my perspective is deeply changed. Now I have to help others who have the disease.
>
> Denise: **You don't have enough energy to help anybody right now.**

The couple in the above sequence uses teasing in the place of quarreling as a regular part of their verbal interaction. In this specific case, Bob has had a long illness and has not been able to do much in terms of household activities. The fact that there is an audience, Molly, takes the interaction out of the family domain and places it squarely into social talk. This contributes to the play frame for diffusing a potentially conflictive situation. The nip is inherent in the statement that Bob cannot help others if he does not have any energy to help his wife. Possibly because this is social talk, the tease is a nip rather than a bite. "Teasing and shaming [can be attempts] to inhibit or change a person's actions as well as convey a particular affective message about the relationship of those individuals involved and an audience or potential audience of family, peers and community" (Schieffelin, 1986: 166). In teasing, speakers often wish to reconcile attempts to change behavior with maintaining existing bonds with their interlocutors, particularly with intimates. Suprasegmentals and non-verbal features of the interaction are important cues that distinguish whether the tease is one that bonds, nips or bites. Given different contextualization cues (e.g. lack of audience, intonational contours, stress), the nip could be a bite. Clearly, a shared schema is essential in the uptake.

2.4 Joking about absent others

(3) Chatting at home: Two close female friends.
  Bonnie: Back problems are the scourge of modern man [sic].
  Cheryl: The spine is just ill designed
  Bonnie: Exactly. We're not supposed to...
  Cheryl: *I. M. Pei* [noted architect] *must have designed it.*

The above example is illustrative of joking about an absent or imaginary third party. We consider *joking* any type of verbal activity that creates a play frame, but does not make any of the participants in the conversation the center of the playing. Indeed in aiming the humor at an absent other party or parties, the interlocutors, joker and hearers, unite in a clear bond. Thus joking is safer than teasing. There is less ambiguity and the bond is clearer. We tend to do this kind of joking with friends, for it is rapport-inspiring.

We consider word play as a sub-category of this type of joking. The topic, or the form that the word play takes, can constitute a type of bonding against another represented in the words chosen with which to play. Hill (1993) considers the use of junk Spanish — terms such as 'No problemo' and 'Hasta la vista, Baby' — as a form of word play used against a threatening other (in this case the Chicano community). This form of word play can also be used to diffuse a conflictive and threatening situation such as that of migration. Moyna (1994), studied word play among a small, expatriate Uruguayan community in Gainesville, Florida, finding such examples as:

(4) "Vengo de la Infiernary" (I'm coming from the infirmary).

The play on words is from "infierno" meaning "hell." The equation of the university infirmary with hell is a comment on the US health care system. Another play on words in Moyna's data was:

(5) "Gailesbiano," (Gay/lesbian)

This was intended to refer to a resident of Gainesville, instead of using the more appropriate translation "Gainesvileano."

The absent other(s) are those who are not members of this expatriate community. As such, the word play functions to create a special in-group terminology that bonds the participants and unites them against the "others." While other speakers of Spanish within the larger community would have an understanding of the terminology, the special meaning created by the in-group could only be appreciated by those who created it. From this perspective then, we view word play as subsumed by joking.

2.5   Self-denigrating humor, or self-teasing

Another category in our taxonomy is self-denigrating humor. It consists of any play-activity that makes the speaker the center of the verbal playing. The speaker and referent are one and the same and the put-down must be initiated by the speaker. Self-denigrating humor can fall under the rubric of griping, as shown in the following example (Boxer, 1993a):

(6)   Two female strangers in swimming pool:
      Ann: What is this supposed to work on, your legs, stomach?
      Barb: Your legs mostly. I don't think it does much for the stomach.
      Ann: Oh, I'm not interested in the thighs. They're beyond hope.
      Barb: I've gained five pounds since I started swimming five years ago

By complaining about one's own physical, emotional or intellectual shortcomings, speakers show themselves self-effacing, allowing the addressee to perceive them as approachable.

Norrick (1993) explored the use of self-denigrating jokes to present positive self-images:

> Funny personal anecdotes end up presenting a positive self-image rather than a negative one. ... they convey a so-called sense of humor, which counts as a virtue in our society. They present a self with an ability to laugh at problems and overcome them — again an admirable character trait. So apparently self-effacing personal anecdotes redound to conversational rapport and positive face for the teller in several ways at once. (47)

Thus, self-denigrating humor is one of the three categories of conversational joking. These involve, respectively, (1) a verbal play that is directed towards an absent third person (or group), (2) a present participant, or (3) is self-directed. Joking and self-denigrating humor are safer forms of humor than teasing, since the brunt of the joking is not present.

We examine next the factors that might influence verbal play as well as the outcome of this play in terms of participants' interaction.

2.6 Outcome and function of verbal play

Having defined the play frames as three distinct types, we must next examine what occurs inside the frame. Tannen (1993) suggests that in most everyday conversation, realignment between participants is continually being negotiated. Hall (1993), in her study of *chismeando* (gossip) among Dominican women, characterizes this particular oral practice as one that creates and articulates the social position and relationship of the participants. Erickson and Schultz (1982) highlight how "performed social identity" is achieved through social interaction in interviews. Others speak of "positioning" in family interactions (Hamilton 1995) and "footing" (Goffman 1983) as indicating changes in the frame. All of these imply a connection between participants that is taking place and/or changing. Their principal aim is to explore the *structure* of the interaction. Our intention is to build on their analysis and explore the general processes that have *functional* consequences regarding the creation of identities. Realignment negotiation can have two possible outcomes: (1) the display of individual identity; and/or (2) the negotiation of a relational identity with others and *through* others.

Identity display (ID) and relational identity display/development (RID) can be the most important functions of joking, teasing and self-denigrating humor. The participants not only display identity but create new ones based on their past, present and future relationship. While identity display has been presupposed in the literature on everyday conversation, the fact that participants develop a *relational identity* through such speech events as conversational joking has been largely ignored. We believe that it is in situational humor that one can observe with most clarity the RID, because in joking and teasing we can display our identities as friends and members of an in-group. For transitory encounters RID can imply a low risk activity, where the relational identity is also transitory. For friends this is a high risk game where the relational identity displayed is based on past encounters, and where the encounter taking place might re-affirm or weaken the existing relationship. If this is a high risk game we are led to ask why people play it. The fact is that if the negotiation of RID is successful through the joking and teasing, the outcome will be the much sought-after result of bonding between participants.

2.7   Joking that bonds

Joking that bonds is a widely used strategy in uniting interlocutors against the foibles of an absent other. Bonding against others who are perceived as different allows us to become a unit without having to define what we are for each other. What makes us part of an in-group is having in common an "out group." Relational identity is not necessary in this uniting; what is the commonality is the word play and/or poking fun at others. In this there is identity display through reducing the "others" to some laughable characterization that makes them different from us.

We have found numerous instances of joking that bonds. The following sequence is part of a longer conversation in which two women are discussing a clothing store:

(7)   Close female friends.
       Bonnie: I found even a funnier store than Harry's. It's called Larry's. She
       [the saleswoman] said, she starts in with me that I should have been there a
       few weeks ago cause "there was gorgeous" [merchandise]
       Cheryl: That's a typical line.
       Bonnie: Typical.
       Cheryl: They had gorgeous. [laughs]
       Bonnie: "We had gorgeous. We had gorgeous." She sits down and crosses
       her legs and I'm getting undressed. Well, I'm not an extremely modest
       person among my friends, this strange lady is sitting there, so I tell myself,
       "Bonnie, don't be silly," she sees ladies in various stages of undress.

This is a case of joking against an absent other using constructed dialogue. It exemplifies female storytelling with identity display through exaggeration and voicing. The fact that the participants are close friends allows for much freedom in the exaggeration, causing humor. This is merely identity display, but *relational* identity display in that part of the humorous effect is the common knowledge of the "typical" line "we had gorgeous." Here both RID and ID have a bonding effect. The RID has a regional aspect to it, for it is inherent in the common identity of the interlocutors as New Yorkers. This is evident in their use, not only of constructed dialogue, but of dialect variants within it. This constitutes uniting against the other despite the fact that the participants also belong to the same wider community as the "other." The uniting is against the lower social class evident in dialectal differences that encompass phonological and lexical distinctions.

2.8 Self-denigration as a case of ID

It would seem that self-denigration, unlike joking or teasing, will always in-volve identity display. Self-denigration does not typically constitute a case of RID. The following is an example of the function of such joking among women in a service encounter. A customer has requested that an employee (whom she perceives as a sales clerk) allow her to enter the fitting room. The employee tries to open the fitting room with a key and has trouble.

  (8)   Salesclerk: **The manager is always the worst!**

Paralinguistic and extralinguistic cues such as intonational contour and eye gaze allow the customer to perceive the statement as a joke, that is, that the sales clerk is really the manager. This is a clear example of identity display in that only through the self-denigrating humor is the employee able to identify herself as a person of higher status in the commercial establishment. At the same time, by presenting herself as human and therefore not altogether com-petent, she creates a positive image for herself in minimizing the power inher-ent in her position.

Women seem to do this type of joking more than men. As Tannen notes, women tend to "downplay their authority while exercising it" (1994: 177). Indeed, there appear to be striking differences in self-denigrating joking be-tween females and males. We explore these differences further below in the discussion of gender.

2.9 Teasing that bonds: RID and ID

The maximum form of bonding we have found in our data is among women talking about men. In our definitions, teasing can imply a nip or bite, that is, a playful bite within the teasing frame. Recall that the nip can denote the bite without actually biting (Bateson 1986). Nevertheless, as we have seen in se-quence 1, the play frame is not always easy to interpret. A misfire can occur and the playful nip can indeed become the bite. In fact, because the nip can become a bite it is a very useful tool for social control. We have found numer-ous cases among family members in which the teasing disguises the bite, or makes it tolerable.

The fact that teasing can hide aggression is not new, as we have seen above (cf. Miller 1986). What is new is that there is a certain type of teasing with no pos-sible bite in it, and thus can only have the function of intimate bonding and RID.

(9)   Two close female friends on weekend ski retreat
      Carol: Ooh, my feet got cold, I don't know why my feet got cold all of a
      sudden.
      Jane: You need a hot drink. You're drinking cold soda.
      Carol: I know. I can't drink hot drinks.
      Jane: You don't drink hot drinks, it's not part of your religion.
      Carol: Right [laughs].

These are close female friends in which the addressee teases the other about not drinking hot drinks. It bonds them by showing that she knows this about the other, displaying a past history. This is relational identity display that demonstrates insider knowledge, despite the fact that they had not seen each other in some two years. In this sequence RID occurs between women who have not seen each other in some time, but who were close friends. We find that the teasing reaffirms closeness as one of the major goals of the conversation.

In sum, teasing always implies RID, since the teased and the teaser are present and participate actively in the play. The RID in teasing can have an outcome that ranges from bonding to biting. The bond developed in a teasing frame can become more intense, but the risks are high with certain interlocutors. Quite distinct from teasing, which is for the most part a RID activity, joking can function as either ID or as RID. Self-denigrating joking typically implies ID. We can postulate a continuum of RID to ID, with teasing showing the maximum RID to self-denigration showing the minimum RID and maximum ID. As always, it is a question of degrees.

2.10 Factors affecting the type of verbal playing

Two sociolinguistic factors have emerged as having the strongest effect in joking and teasing: social distance and gender.

2.10.1 *Joking and social distance*
High risk teasing typically takes place among interlocutors who are intimates. Recall that according to Wolfson's Bulge theory (1989), what strangers and intimates have in common is the relative certainty of their relationships. Thus, one would expect high risk teasing to take place among these two groups of extreme social distance. Recall that Boxer (1993b) showed this not to hold true for at least one type of speech behavior, complaining and commiserating. In teasing, interlocutors take the risk of biting only with intimates, not with strangers or acquaintances. This is so far borne out in the data for the present study.

Relational bonding is frequent among interlocutors of medial social distance, that is friends and acquaintances, as well as among strangers. Among friends, the type of teasing that bonds derives from a need for affirming or reaffirming friendship. With strangers, however, the bonding is through joking and word play, not through teasing. Strangers establish a momentary bond through conversational joking and especially word play that functions as displays of the individual identity of the speaker. An example illustrates:

(10)   Two female strangers in line at a pharmacy. (Referring to Dr. Scholl's corn pads)
A: They used to make these smaller, but now this is all I can find.
B: Maybe corns are coming in different shapes these days.
A: This is the third place I've looked and this is all I can find. And there are only a few in here, where there used to be about twenty.
B: Inflation. They don't want to charge more, so they just give you less.
A: Maybe they're thicker or something.
B: Technology of foot pads is improving.

Identity display is evident here. Strangers can present themselves in a certain way by joking to show their highly developed sense of irony. It tells the hearer that the speaker has a sense of wit and thus has the potential of functioning to create a momentary bond. Despite the fact the above interlocutors are strangers and know that this interaction is a limited and temporary one, the attempt at humor serves to make light of a situation and to establish a momentary good will. The bond cannot be termed "relational," as it is clear that no relationship will be formed. It is with intimates that we see the bite, not with interlocutors on the other extreme of social distance. The following is an example of family members joking/teasing with a nip:

(11)   Gail, Rose: female sisters-in-law. Dave: husband of Gail
Gail: I have a fungus infection in my ear.
Rose: What kind?
Gail: It's from an infection I had many years ago and it never left my ears.
Rose: You can't do anything about it?
Gail: No. Once you have it you can't get rid of it. *It's like athlete's foot in my ears.*
Gail and Rose: [both laugh]
Dave: *She crawls through the locker room.* [all laugh hysterically].
Gail: I get crusty, and when I get up in the morning I can't hear because there's fluid in my ears.

Dave: *In her sleep sometimes, the whole bed shakes cause she's got her fingers in her ears…it wakes me up when I'm sound asleep!*

First, the joke is a self put-down that displays identity, using a humorous analogy. Second, Dave teases Gail by carrying the analogy further, displaying his own humor. He continues with the identity display through the joking/teasing. The teasing nips.

Thus, where joking with strangers/friendly strangers establishes a momentary bond through performed social identity, it is with intimates that we tend to see the teasing that nips or even bites. With intimates we have a past history of RID that allows us to play with the frame. With strangers, on the other hand, where no past history has been created, we need to display our identity, to show them we are 'good' people, not dangerous, 'witty', safe to be around.

2.10.2 *Gender*

Gender strongly conditions the type of verbal play that occurs in everyday talk. We have seen intimations of this in a few of the above sequences, in which teasing bonds through RID. Women and men appear to employ different strategies of injecting humor into a conversation. We note clear differences in the data between the male propensity to use verbal challenges and put-downs and female attempts to establish symmetry. For example, the topic of bodies/figures/physique takes on a different form for women and men. Women frequently employ verbal self-denigration through irony about their own physical shortcomings. The goal might be to establish some common bond by telling the addressee that we are not full of conceit. Males appear to feel freer to tease *others* about bodies. This is seen in the following:

(12)   Adult men playing basketball at a gym
        A: *Man you've got a big butt. How can you lumber down the court?*
        B: (No response)

This could be interpreted as a real bite, but if the interlocutors are close enough it is merely a nip. This type of nip was interpreted by the male participants as typical speech behavior of male bonding during athletic competition. When consulted about their teasing, the interlocutors indicated that in such activity as basketball playing (in North American speech communities) men will pick out the physical weakness of the opponent and use it as a tease. This teasing serves to establish and/or reinforce hierarchy. For women, on the other hand, to tease about bodies is to touch something that we have been trained to take seriously. After all, if we don't care about our bodies we are not doing our job. If women's work is to look good, teasing about this is to touch a place of real insecurity (M. J. Hardman, personal communication). Thus it will only happen in self-denigration.

Verbal self-denigration about appearance seems to be more a female activity than male. Quite distinct from the type of teasing that men typically engage in, we have found striking instances of teasing that bonds among women. We have seen how with teasing a nip can become a bite, especially among family members. The clearer cases of teasing that bonds, however, are found among female friends that are bonding as women in resistance to some wider held norm.

(13)   Two female friends
        Ellen: I was thinking of a lemon cake for dessert but it's $15.00. Who wants
        to spend $15.00 for a cake?
        Fran: Oh, you mean you're not going to bake it yourself?

This is a fairly typical case of female bonding through teasing. The fact is that they know neither one likes to bake. This background knowledge and the tease that plays upon it creates a bond of solidarity through relational identity display as well as reaffirmation of shared identity (e.g. we don't bake). Thus, while diffusing the complaint, the response serves another, important function, that of RID — a RID in which the tease has neither nip nor bite but that bonds.

According to Van Dijk (1988), discourse creates and transmits social representations and social norms. He also adds that resistance to that power can also be discursive. In the cases of teasing that bonds that we have seen, the participants seem to be involved in resistance to the social representation of women. The RID they are displaying is not one that accommodates to what is or was considered to be the model for women.

2.11 Conclusion: Conversational joking and identity display

We have attempted here to sort out the fine distinctions in joking/teasing behavior, the variables that condition their use, and the possible outcomes of such exchanges in the context of face-to-face interaction. It is part of our communicative competence as native speakers of any language to understand the functions of such activity, but these functions and their limits are certainly below the level of consciousness. First, it is important to understand how far one can reasonably go with joking or teasing on certain topics and with certain interlocutors. An insight into what bonds and what bites can contribute to more felicitous interactions. Some of us overstep the boundaries, particularly with conflictive topics, interlocutors of certain social distance relationships and of the other gender. We have seen, for example, that conversational joking can function to display identity among strangers; we have seen that self-teasing can function to display and develop individual and relational identity and thus bond participants; and we have seen that teasing among intimates plays on relational identity and can therefore nip or even bite. While there is room for the nip or bite among some intimates, this is not necessarily true with friends, acquaintances and strangers. An understanding of how conversational joking as a verbal activity functions ought to contribute to our knowledge of how be successful in social talk.

Clearly, while humor is culture-specific, its social function in terms of individual and group identity formation appears to cross cultural boundaries. Works such as those by Hall (1993) on gossip and Le Page (1985) on acts of identity suggest that discourse is fundamental to the development of selfhood. This sense of self and of self as a member of a group can be observed at the micro level in speech events such as conversational joking, where participants display and develop either their individual or their relational identity. Situational humor is one of the speech genres that accomplishes this, and it does so poignantly because it is culture specific; that is, it requires, more than any other speech genre, in-group knowledge. While joking across communities reveals structural similarities, the differences appear in the specific topics, taboos, and ways of establishing bonds. Members of one community might engage in more teasing that bonds while the other does so more in teasing that bites. The universals lie in the notion that Conversational Joking functions on a continuum from ID to RID, and that maximum RID can be accomplished through joking and teasing that bonds.

Certainly what makes for a good laugh differs across societies. The bottom line is, "We all enjoy a good laugh." This study of conversational joking begins to elucidate what makes for a good laugh and why.

3.   Conclusion: Face to face in the social domain

I must confess that upon embarking on this chapter I did not know where to begin. So much has been researched and written about conversational interaction in the social domain that to embark on a discussion of the topic certainly seemed to be opening up "a can of worms." How could one begin to do justice to this broad topic? Thinking about what we actually try to accomplish in much of our social interaction led to a logical beginning: why not commence with a discussion of how such a large portion of this talk is interactional, that is phatic? The bulk of social conversation is just that — it is done for the sake of getting to know others, for not only creating new relationships and friendships, but also for affirming and reaffirming existing relationships.

This chapter has been organized to discuss extant research in the social domain with reference to sociolinguistic variables; speech acts, events and other activities and phenomena; and methodological issues in the analysis of face-to-face interaction in social life. These organizing principles have been used with the intent of covering vast territory: discussing the importance of looking at variables that condition and constrain talk (e.g. social distance, gender); perspectives that influence how we view social talk (e.g. speech acts, speech events); and approaches to data analysis that influence the questions asked and thus the answers obtained (e.g. ethnographic techniques, CA techniques, laboratory techniques).

Talk in social interaction has been analyzed for the sake of explicating not only how we do things with words, but also how this 'doing' reveals aspects of who we are. Language use reflects and perpetuates individual and social identities; moreover, language choices enable us to develop new relational identities, as we have seen in the study on conversational joking. Studying social talk in interaction enables us to learn just what is appropriate or inappropriate; what is collaborative and what is rude; what makes us sought-after interlocutors and what it is about our talk that has the potential to alienate others. This all has to do with being and becoming competent members of our social communities. People who know how to choose topics of interest to their interlocutors draw people into their circle. People who know how to make relevant and insightful contributions to a conversation are people with whom others want to spend time. People who know how to be supportive when support is sought have a wider social network than those who do not know these things. How to greet, how to give advice with content sensitivity, how to overlap without interrupting, how to signal solidarity and identity through in-group discourse markers, how to ask the right kinds of questions, how to be a friend, are all skills of social conversation that distinguish the conversationally inept from the conversationally skilled. Studying social talk can indeed give us deep insights into how to be happier social beings.

Notes

1. Length of audio-tapes ranged from ten-minute segments to longer, two-hour conversations from which joking sequences were taken. Asterisks in the transcription represent segments that were inaudible. Periods in parenthesis indicate partial deletion of segments of the transcription that were not relevant to the analysis of situational humor.

2. "The insights one has into one's native language and into the behavior within one's own speech community permits a level of analysis which is far deeper than that which can be reached in other field sites" (Schneider 1968: vi).

3. Appropriate teasing and joking is culture specific. In many communities or groups joking about God or using profanity in word play might be construed as offensive, in others not. Thus, knowing what one can joke about and how far one can go with the joke is an essential part of being good at conversational joking.

4. The intention might actually be one of disguised aggression. In fact, teasing is frequently used as a form of releasing aggression in a non-threatening way among intimates and in a threatening way among interlocutors who are status unequals as a show of power. We will not deal with this aspect of teasing here, since it has been amply studied in Miller 1986, Eisenberg1986, Schieffelin 1986, and Straehle 1993.

5. The patterning of speech acts in a "Bulge"-like pattern have not, to my knowledge, been carefully plotted out. I contend that when actual data is plotted on a graph of social distance, it will be found that the bulge is always skewed. While strangers do a lot of apologizing (e.g. for clumsy behavior such as bumping into others), intimates typically do not do so.

CHAPTER 4

Face-to-face in the education domain

1. Introduction

This chapter focuses on one aspect of educational discourse, that of higher education. The reason for limiting the discussion to this one area has to do with the preponderance of research in educational discourse generally and classroom discourse specifically. To attempt to include of all of this literature (much of which encompasses classroom discourse of young children and limited English proficiency speakers) in the present chapter would make it difficult to do justice to an overall discussion of the topic. Examining one focused area of adult NS/NS interaction in the educational domain makes it possible to show that analyzing and learning from studies face-to-face discourse can help many people navigate through this important domain of interaction.

A college education and even a graduate education are no longer rarities, as they used to be several generations ago. More and more young people and older individuals are seeking a college degree or an advanced degree as either a credential for career or simply for further learning. Because of this, the educational scene is becoming more and more diverse, with different ethnic and socioeconomic groups, more diverse age groups, and a more even gender distribution evident. This is particularly true in spheres of interaction that have in the past been open to only whites, males, and middle and upper class individuals. Analyzing the discourse of higher education is therefore increasingly important for helping those previously uninitiated into the appropriate norms of interaction in this domain. Knowing how to do the talk of college and university settings can help open doors. Knowing why misfires occur can help prevent them.

The narrow focus of this chapter on face-to-face interaction in higher education is relevant to many readers of the present volume, who are likely to be in some way involved in higher education discourse: as faculty members, graduate or undergraduate students, teaching and research assistants, members of laboratory teams, and study groups. Face-to-face interaction in higher education serves as an example from which we can learn about discourse and interaction in educational settings generally. Much of the research reviewed in this chapter focuses on interaction between members of the academic community outside the classroom: in advising sessions, colloquia series, and laboratory groups, for example. Other research focuses more strictly on discourse within classrooms. This chapter culminates with an in-depth analysis, carried out in collaboration with Jodi Nelms, of the use of sarcasm in the classroom discourse of undergraduate courses at a large state university.

1.1   Face-to-face interaction in higher education

Interactions in the educational domain have potentially great impacts on individuals' apprenticeship into the academy. The work of Karen Tracy and her colleagues, emanating from the discipline of interpersonal communication, is exemplary of how this occurs. Three articles overviewed here (Tracy and Carjuzaa 1993; Tracy and Naughton 1994; and Tracy and Muller 1994) are examples of how face-to-face discourse analysis serves to elucidate the social construction of self as part of the academic world.

Tracy and Carjuzaa (1993) focus on identity issues of becoming and being an academic. They examine this process through analysis of the discourse of questions and responses in a departmental colloquium series, including patterns of talk and silence. The authors discuss two types of "face," the *intellectual* and the *institutional*. Intellectual face is the manner in which people are perceived and want themselves to be perceived in terms of their ability to address colleagues' questions and their presentation of their intellectualism through their own questioning of others. Institutional face, on the other hand, is representative of one's status in the department (e.g. graduate student, junior faculty, senior faculty, etc.). In the analysis, the researchers discuss an almost unavoidable approach/avoidance phenomenon among members of this community: that of desire to present oneself in a favorable intellectual light without appearing overbearing or arrogant. Indeed, the ability of academics to walk this fine line contributes to the success of some and failure of others in displaying their intellectual identity.

The existence of these two types of face, which are often in opposition to each other, leads to issues of how to question others without inappropriately asserting status. For example, a gentle type of questioning is expected of those with lower-status institutional face than those with higher institutional status. An important issue in the conflict between the two types of face is the stress between the community's purported desire for a sense of egalitarianism (yielded through interview data) versus individuals' desire to display their own intellectual identity, which is often done through asserting status superiority. Clearly, the two types of face are not always separable. Higher institutional status is difficult to disambiguate from intellectual status. Though this is not always the case, the expectations are for those with higher status to have achieved such status through intellectual merit. Therefore, the distinction between the two types of face is a fuzzy one.

Participants in the study expressed conflicting views that one's institutional face ought to be irrelevant in colloquia, since equality should prevail in intellectual exchanges. Nevertheless, the data analysis showed that such equality was indeed difficult to achieve. Individuals' intellectual identities based on institutional status necessarily came into play in the discussions. For example, people of higher institutional status felt freer to make intellectually more challenging moves, and visa versa. The researchers found that one way in which intellectual identity was enacted was through speakers' introducing and framing their own work. This served the purpose of instructing colleagues on how to handle their questioning and challenging. Hedges, referring to one' work as "in process," and distancing oneself from one's work, for example, all served to lead others to treat a speaker more gently. This stance is not without its drawbacks, however, since it also has the potential of displaying a speaker's intellectual identity as less able. While warding off criticism is a benefit of such hedging, the tradeoff is opening oneself up to perceptions of intellectual weakness. In other words, a high level of intellectual face goes hand in hand with opening oneself to difficult questioning and challenges. What this means is that even individuals with less institutional status, such as graduate students, should be able to display their intellectual identity as stellar in departmental colloquia, through their presentations, assertions, challenges to others in their field, and the way in which they frame their own work. This, in turn, influences the kind of questioning they get as well as the way they field questions from colleagues. Hence, while it is possible to have strong intellectual face without institutional face, it has the consequence of making the individual vulnerable to challenges.

Not surprisingly, Tracy and Carjuzaa's data showed that talk and silence patterns followed alongside institutional status, despite claims of equality in this context by all participants. Graduate students were less likely to talk at all and less likely to ask questions other than information questions. Moreover, certain speech acts were prevalent only among those of lower status: e.g. asking for help, advice, or permission. Giving advice, help or permission, on the other hand, indicated higher status. "…intellectual discussion among faculty and graduate students cannot escape the tensions between expertise and equality" (189).

No matter how exceptional a graduate student may be, the freedom to be intellectually challenging is constrained by the status of being a student. The constraint is somewhat different for junior faculty, who are expected to display their acuity more formidably. Nonetheless, issues of power and dominance clearly are at work here. All of us who have been in such situations know from experience that students and lower status faculty members (e.g. junior, or untenured faculty) need to carefully monitor the way in which they use language in interaction with colleagues. The issue, then, is how to present oneself as intellectually strong without alienating these colleagues? As long as others who have control over our futures are judging us, we are faced with this problem.

In further pursuit of this issue, Tracy and Naughton (1994) showed how questioning practices reflect presenters' knowledgeability, originality and intellectual sophistication by examining how identity work is accomplished through such practices. They found that intellectual identity is developed and displayed through the manner in which one questions and responds to questions. This conclusion led to their terming of this type of analysis as "identity-implicative discourse analysis." Such analysis takes into account relational identity development, or RID (Boxer and Cortes-Conde, 1997), in that, "the actual situated meaning of the conversational move could change if participants possessed a certain relational history" (Tracy and Naughton 1994: 285). The display part of RID lies in the desire for participants to be viewed as intellectually capable. Thus, expression of originality, sophistication and knowledge are displayed through questioning practices. A perception of recipients' level of knowledgability is displayed in a questioner's formulation. In other words, the way a questioner proceeds indicates how the recipient's knowledge is perceived. As such, questioning that presumes lack of knowledge has the potential to threaten the intellectual face of the recipient. For example, faculty members asking questions of graduate students typically do a lot of face work to make it easier for graduate students to answer questions. The downside of such work is the possibility of displaying the student as lacking in knowledge to the audience: "In sum, through the presence of knowlegeability-limitation markers, or through their absence, question formulations imply whether the recipient is expected to know a particular piece of information" (Tracy and Naughton 1994: 290).

Originality in an academic's work is a sought-after identity marker. Challenges to originality claims are made in several ways: connecting that work to work previously done by others or future work done elsewhere, and implying the similarity of the work to others'. In such a way projects are described as dated. Thus time references are critical in conveying praise or criticisms of another's work. When the level of sophistication of one's work is challenged, there is great potential to problematize a scholar's intellectual framework. In general, word choice, use or avoidance of certain speech acts, and framing, are the foci of this type of identity-implicative discourse analysis.

Along similar lines of analysis, Tracy and Muller (1994) focused on the socialization of new community members into the academy. Their study sought to answer the question, "What do academics believe are appropriate ways to communicate during intellectual discussion? What are the tensions among these beliefs?" (323). Data for this study was a series of open-ended faculty interviews addressing issues of likes and dislikes of the interviewees regarding characteristics of the discussions in the colloquia, concerns of presentation of self during the colloquia, and descriptions of what characterized good intellectual discussion. The authors discovered some contrary beliefs concerning participation expectations of members, ideas and status, and the place of expression of emotionality in these discussions.

Interviewees generally voiced the belief that good discussion must necessarily discount status differences in participants; however, there were obvious status differences that impacted on participation in the colloquia. The opportunity to talk as well as the content of talk is always influenced by rank. This fact is at odds with what people believe must be inherent in good discussion. The reality is that ideas are seen as more credible when asserted by individuals of higher institutional status. Indeed, it was frequently suggested that ideas of graduate students should, in general, be more gently received. As for participation level, while it was believed that all should have equal access to it, it was also believed that participation should be by those who are well informed. Regarding emotional expression, "in a nutshell, participants viewed feelings of passion, caring, and involvement as good and feelings of defensiveness, hostility, and personal attack as bad" (336). Group members' concerns not to hurt feelings were found to be in conflict with the need or desire to challenge as a part of good intellectual discussion.

The research endeavors of Tracy and her colleagues serve as excellent examples of how to apply the sociolinguistics of face-to-face interaction in higher education. Through our oral discourse we display and develop our intellectual identities moment-by-moment in real time interaction. How we question, how we respond to questions, how we frame our work, how we challenge, the speech acts we use or refrain from using, and the mere fact of whether we speak up or remain silent, are all issues to analyze and from which to learn. Without the confidence to participate orally, we run the risk of being perceived as intellectually weak rather than merely shy. Knowing how to ask questions that assert our expertise without sounding unduly arrogant can display an identity that is intellectually keen yet open to challenge without being threatened.

The theme of apprenticeship into the academy is indeed interesting for those of us involved in this world. The discourse strategies of becoming an academic are particularly relevant for graduate students hoping to enter the academic discourse community. Rudolph (1994) describes how apprenticeships between professors and graduate students are constructed during office hour interactions. Through an analysis of the interactions of one graduate student with her advisor, she shows how a positive affective bond is created through expressions of interdependence, cooperation and shared membership in the discourse community. These afford the apprentice opportunities toward socialization into the discourse, which Rudolph (following Gee, 1990) refers to as Discourse, with a capital D. At the core of apprenticeship relationships are both openness on the part of the novice to be guided, and granting (unspoken) permission to the expert to instruct and generally guide the apprentice into becoming a scholar. Thus, the apprenticeship is co-constructed through the linguistic expression of affect between the novice and expert. The result, or product, is the successful completion of the graduate degree. In order to achieve this product, graduate students must be socialized into "a new belief system" (207).

Rudolph's data derives from two audiotaped interactions between one NNS graduate student and her advisor, and a post-hoc interview with the student. The choice of using this particular graduate student may have inadvertently yielded data reflecting cross-cultural miscommunication. The use of a native speaking graduate student might have produced somewhat different findings, since it can surely be assumed that miscommunication of the transfer type occurred that affected the interaction. For example, in order to ensure participation by the student in the office interactions, the professor needed to resort to confirmation checks. This is something characteristic of NS-NNS interaction that may or may not be differently enacted in NS-NS student/professor apprenticeships. The particular professor studied needed to do a different kind and amount of work to mentor this NNS student. Rudolph makes the claim that this work reflected the desire to establish an affective bond with the student. Indeed, Rudolph herself suggests the possibility of idiosyncratic behavior on the part of the student. I assert that in this case it may have been transfer from L1 norms rather than idiosyncrasy. Thus, while evidencing the need to use confirmation checks to empower the student in this data, NS-NS data might give evidence of different conversational moves to indicate desire for positive affective bond and licensing to participate.

Notwithstanding this possible shortcoming, Rudolph's study has interesting implications for mentorship relationships in academic life. Studying advising sessions between students and their mentors can indeed yield insights into the discourse moves inherent in building strong affective bonds that have positive consequences for a student's future. Likewise, negative moves can inform how positive results are thwarted.

A study Bresnahan (1992) focused on advising sessions also, but of a different type. Here the analysis was of interactions between undergraduates and departmental advisors in sessions where the undergraduates were seeking course information and access. The analysis looked specifically at the effects of advisor style on overcoming client resistance stemming from the conflicting roles of undergraduate advisors, who function as both institutional gatekeepers and student advocates at the same time. The study shows how this role conflict can cause infelicitous interactions.

This research differs from those reviewed above in that it does not deal with becoming a member of the academic discourse community per se. Thus, it is discourse rather than Discourse (Gee, 1990; 1999). That is to say, it has less to do with knowing the rules of academia and more to do with knowing how to get what one wants (on the undergraduate's side). For the advisor, it has to do with knowing how to use discourse to get the undergraduate on her or his side while still upholding the rules of the institution.

Bresnahan's study, emanating out of the fields of communication and social psychology, demonstrates the interdisciplinary nature of face-to-face discourse analysis. Using data from 14 recorded advising sessions, she contrasts 'foot in the door' (FITD) and 'door in the face' (DITF) constructs from psychology, analyzing how students ask for help as well as how this affects advisors' stance. We all know that when the outcome of such interviews results in lack of concessions, the students tend to blame the advisor rather than the institution. While a gatekeeping stance on the part of the advisor may intimidate students into public compliance, an advocate stance has the ability enhance private compliance. The former makes use of "power, status, gender, knowledge, and hierarchical difference..." (231). The latter is termed "collaborative/integrative style", and "emphasized the shared nature of decisions and the necessity for both parties to reach agreement rather than for one participant, generally the more powerful, to mandate outcomes for the other." (ibid).

That advisors and students are often at cross-purposes is aptly demonstrated in this research. Advisors who act as gatekeepers cause increased anxiety on the part of the students during the course of the interviews. Advocacy style encompasses a stance toward careful listening and responding to client needs, providing ongoing reassurances. Door in the face (DITF) tactics come from such student speech behavior as asking for exceptions to institutional rules. Hyperexplanation on the advisors part is one' method of DITF. In contrast, FITD tactics exemplify ratifiying students' needs and typically result in assurances to the student. It was found that when students maintained an issue-centered focus, making no attacks on the institution or its representatives, interviews tended to be more felicitous, allowing the advisor to take an advocacy role. Without this, power plays tended to ensue, with conflict resulting in gatekeeping. This also occurred when advisors pushed for quick problem resolution. Bresnahan concluded that students who engage in "cooperative negotiation" get more FITD. When this occurs, advisors are increasingly able to focus on integratively based solutions.

The implications of carefully analyzing the discourse of advising sessions clearly lie in satisfaction on the part of both students and the institution. Advising is a delicate art, particularly when advisors have the dual role of advocacy of students' needs while also representing the institution's needs and requirements (see, for example the work of Agnes Weiyun He on language use in advising encounters, 1998). Advisors can learn how to walk the fine line between both, leading to satisfaction on the part of the student and compliance with institutional norms and rules. Likewise, students can learn how to present their needs appropriately and thereby increase their chances of getting what they want. Through the careful study of fine-tuned discourse strategies, both can benefit.

Thus far I have offered an overview of some of the discourse literature in higher education focusing on contexts of advising and colloquia. Other important existing research deals with small group interaction such as those of laboratory. One such recent piece by Conefrey (1997) analyzes the interactional patterns of a neuroscience laboratory group to ascertain aspects of culture, gender and authority that may cause women to drop out of the sciences. It is a fact that women who have "dropped out" cite one important reason for having done so as experiences with negative verbal dynamics in a laboratory, in which the interactions tend to be male dominated and follow male norms.

Conefrey's data was drawn from a weekly meeting of a lab group in which an undergraduate female team member, Lilly, was put in the role of chairing the meeting. The group was composed of members of varying statuses, from the principal investigator (PI) to postdoctoral fellows, a technician, and several students. All members took turns chairing the weekly meeting, which had as its task the presentation and discussion of a scholarly paper.

The analysis covers the speech acts and moves of the various participants, showing how Lilly becomes disenfranchised by the sarcasm, teasing and sports talk of the male members. This language is shown to cause the young woman to quickly lose control of the proceedings. Interruptions by the PI cause Lilly to be cast as a novice, further devaluing her contribution and ability to lead. Indeed, the author demonstrates how such moves by the male team members lead Lilly to constantly lose the floor, thus rendering her unable to lead the discussion. Along the lines of the work of Tracy et. al. (above), it is shown how the undergraduates of the group, particularly the females, do not make many verbal contributions but typically respond by laughing, or as audience to the teasing, sarcasm and banter. Junior members take very little active role in the discussions, remaining silent unless they themselves are presenting. Thus, despite the overt desire to have an equality of members, status of individuals prevails as the important factor in participation patterns. Indeed, gender comes clearly into play as a factor in the overall status relationships in this group. Gender as a sociolinguistic variable has been demonstrated to be a master status (West 1984). The conflating of low student status with female gender no doubt contributes to Lilly's inability to maintain her leadership role in this particular laboratory group.

One way of analyzing rights and obligations to speak or be silent is the use of certain speech acts. In this study, an important speech act that was performed only by the PI was the issuing of directives. This right was within his status and role as head of the team. Likewise, disagreeing, evaluating, and controlling the topic were done only by senior members. These displays of seniority were shown to be mitigated somewhat by the teasing sequences. However, the teasing was exemplary of documented male speech behavior in North American speech communities (e.g. Maltz and Borker 1983).

> Such a theory would suggest that Lilly loses the floor because she is not expecting
> it to be taken from her, or that she is expecting responses to build on rather than
> detract from her topic development; similarly, that males seize any opportunity to

take the floor from Lilly because this is what they normally do in conversations with each other" (Conefrey 1997: 329).

Male dominance of the speech event is aptly demonstrated by examples of how the male team members operated the teasing sequences and disrupted turn-taking rights. "The women in the group use humor to support others and to establish intimacy, and the men use it to maintain control and dominate others (Ibid)." Likewise, status and gender are confounded, as the more senior members of the team are male. "…it seems likely that given women's traditionally low status in academia, and in science in particular, both gender and status contribute to the dominance of senior, male laboratory group members and the disempowerment of Lilly…" (330).

The analysis reflects the problems that women in science have in becoming socialized into the discourse community where more senior male members function as gatekeepers. The difficulty is so great as to force many women to switch into other fields or to drop out entirely. Indeed, there is a growing literature in the field of female-friendly science (cf. Rosser 1997, 2000). Face-to-face discourse is clearly an important aspect of why women become alienated and turn away from these fields. Analyzing the language and interactional patterns that are prevalent in face-to-face discourse in largely male-dominated fields in the sciences and elsewhere enables us to ascertain just why women choose to leave these fields for other, more friendly spheres of educational and work life. Discourse phenomena such as interruptions, getting and holding the floor, in-group talk, teasing that leaves out women or that makes women the focus, are all examples of the talk of alienation. The alienating features need not be as obvious as negative or sexist remarks. Indeed, as we have seen above, they are often much more subtle.

The present discussion of face-to-face discourse in higher education would not be complete without some discussion of classroom discourse per se. A fine example of a classroom discourse study in higher education is one by Michele Foster (1989). The piece aptly demonstrates how teacher-student interactional patterns in the formal classroom have the ability to affect students' success in higher education. The study, which focuses on an African-American female teacher in an urban community college, shows how when the discourse conventions of the teacher are congruent with the students' expectations, increased interaction ensues, with better comprehension and general success of traditionally low achieving students.

The 33 students in the class in management that Foster studied were mostly African American adults. Foster demonstrates how the teacher's use of performances to interpret texts engages the students in a way that leads them to better participate and learn. The discourse pattern in such performances is similar to rhythmic refrains. Overlapping speech and back-channeling are indicators of a high level of student attentiveness and interest. "She [the teacher] deliberately manipulates grammatical structures, uses cadence and meter, repetition, vowel lengthening, catchy phrasing, figurative language, symbolism, and gestures to underscore her point" (14). These devices serve to draw out the abstractions of the narrative in the texts and assist students to remember the information that they have heard. The performances are moved forward only via the active participation of the students. The most successful performances are those that recall personal narratives, becoming the context through which students make sense out of the academic material. "Performances are participatory, spontaneous, interactive events that require mutuality between teacher and students" (20). In such a way the teacher is able to utilize the behavior, norms and values of the community to lead the students to success. The ethos is group-centered, and learning thus becomes more of a social event than the typically individual endeavor that it is in white communities. The study shows how such a congruence, de-emphasizing competition and status differentiation, can indeed help to improve the academic achievement of African-American students.

We have seen in the review of literature above that face-to-face interaction in the discourse of higher education takes place in various settings around campus: classrooms, departmental colloquia, laboratory groups, advising and mentoring sessions, to name a few. All of these contexts have important implications for individual success or failure in the educational domain. The knowledge of how to talk with individuals of different gender and status relationships affects how to go about achieving one's goals. Whether the desired goal is gaining entrance into a needed course, getting a good grade, becoming a ratified member of the discourse community, or obtaining a stellar reference for a future job, the consequences of knowing how to do face-to-face discourse in the educational domain are far-reaching.

The following study of classroom discourse in a large research university is a detailed example of one speech behavior and its effect on students. Jodi Nelms and I examined the functions of sarcasm in college classrooms. In the analysis, we present the repercussions of its use, both positive and negative, and the consequences for teacher and student satisfaction or dissatisfaction.

2. "Yeah right": Sociolinguistic functions of sarcasm in classroom discourse

2.1 Introduction and background

Sarcasm is generally thought to be a negative speech behavior. Folk perceptions of sarcasm are that it is hurtful, insulting, and generally alienating to the recipient. Clearly, this perception yields the view that sarcasm (and its corollary, irony) have no place in the discourse of higher education specifically, and educational settings generally. The positive uses of sarcasm have rarely been discussed. The purpose of this research is to examine just how sarcasm is actually used in face-to-face interactions in college classrooms and what the repercussions are of its use, as perceived by professors and students.

We distinguish between sarcasm and irony. First, sarcasm is overt irony *intentionally* used by the speaker. Our data shows that sarcastic remarks are not seen as "slips of the tongue" but carefully planned and constructed with clear purposes in mind. Second, only *people* can be sarcastic, whereas *situations* are ironic. Therefore, the firehouse burning down is ironic, but an exhausted teacher is sarcastic when telling a colleague, after having a particularly bad day in the classroom, that she loves teaching. Kruez (1996) has identified at least five cues which may help signal irony: (1) counter factual cues ('what a lovely day!' uttered in a shelter while waiting out a tornado); (2) extreme exaggeration cues ('the service here is really outstanding' said after waiting twenty minutes just to get a menu at a restaurant); (3) tag question cues ('you enjoyed that, didn't you?' said to someone after a root canal); (4) direct cues ('I love this class — NOT.') and (5) kinesic/prosodic cues (rolling of eyes, winking, and an ironic tone of voice). Sarcasm also has a much clearer target than does irony. It is commonly thought that these targets must be human — whether present or not present. However, data from this study shows that these targets can also be inanimate objects or commonly held beliefs. An example of the latter is a situation where a professor walks into a classroom to collect the syntax homework and says to the students, 'I know you all enjoyed drawing trees during the long weekend.' Here, while the recipients of the sarcasm are the students in the class, the 'target' of the sarcasm is the general knowledge that drawing syntax trees is not the preferred form of entertainment for undergraduates during a long weekend. For an in-depth review of sarcasm/irony, along with various definitions of these terms, see Attardo (2000).

2.2   The study

This study was motivated by co-author Nelms' firsthand experience as a graduate student at the University of Florida. She was stimulated by the particular course material, sociolinguistics, and even more so by the individual teaching style of the professor. A few weeks into the course, however, Nelms began to notice that her classmates were not as amused by this particular teaching style as she was. At that moment she decided to become a participant observer of the course, keeping one notebook open for class notes, and another notebook for notes capturing the professor's verbal and nonverbal repertoire. The professor was aware of her intentions. After determining what it was that amused her (the professor's use of sarcasm), she began to discuss the issue informally with her classmates. It was indeed the sarcasm that they believed was hindering their performance in the class. What Nelms had found to be quite humorous was apparently not so humorous to many of her classmates — especially those who were the *target* of the sarcasm.

The aim of this study was to find out who uses sarcasm in the classroom (e.g. what sorts of faculty, male or female, senior or junior); how it is used (e.g. related to content or administrative issues); the purposes of its use as perceived by students and teachers; and the reactions to its effect. Our goal was to ascertain which forms of sarcasm, if any, are appropriate in the classroom, and to draw implications for its use in the classroom discourse of higher education.

2.3   Methodology

Data for the study were collected from videotapes of natural classroom interaction and was triangulated with ethnographic interviews. Eight undergraduate courses were taped during a college semester. There were four male and four female professors who participated in the study. All four of the male participants were full professors; one of the female participants was an associate professor and the other three were untenured assistant professors. All eight professors were native speakers of US English, and ages ranged from thirty-two to fifty-eight. Other variables such as ethnicity, religion, location in which they were raised, academic background, and number of years teaching varied considerably. Over the course of this one academic semester, three to five 50-minute classes per instructor were taped. Subsequently, ethnographic interviews with all eight of the professors (between 2 hours and 3 hours each in length) as well as interviews with 44 students, were conducted, with at least one student interviewed from each class taped. We analyzed the data using interactional sociolinguistic techniques.

2.4   The uses and targets of sarcasm by professors

Of the 48 hours of recorded classroom teaching, the corpus consists of 114 sarcastic utterances distributed fairly equally between the female and male professors, as can be seen in Table 1 (professors' sex is coded as F or M before their designated code letter):

Table 1. Total uses of sarcasm

ID	Total
FA	15
FB	20
FC	5
FE	9
Total-F	49
MD	12
MF	12
MG	29
MH	12
Total-M	65
TOTAL	114

F=female; M=male A-H=professor coding

The overall low number of sarcastic utterances in this study is not surprising, given that the setting is the classroom, where the typical teacher-student relationship is one best characterized by social distance. Sarcasm tends to increase as interlocutor relationships become closer (Kruez 1996).

At least one utterance was classified as sarcastic in each observed class. The average number of sarcastic utterances per class period totaled 3.2. The remarks were aimed as follows (see Table 2): 36 were delivered with the class as a whole intended as the recipient; 37 were delivered with a single individual student as the target (27 male and 10 female targets); 21 were aimed toward a common belief; 7 were aimed at a third party not present; 4 utterances were directed towards a group within the class; 3 were aimed at an inanimate object (e.g. the OHP projector or the computer); and 6 utterances were self-directed.

Table 2. Targets of sarcasm

ID	Class	Female student	Male student	Self	Group of Students	3rd party present	Belief	Inanimate object	Total
FA	9	1	0	0	1	3	1	0	15
FB	6	0	5	2	2	1	4	0	20
FC	3	0	0	0	0	0	1	1	5
FE	3	1	1	2	0	0	2	0	9
Total-F	21	2	6	4	3	4	8	1	49
MD	2	4	1	0	1	1	3	0	12
MF	5	0	0	1	0	0	5	1	12
MG	3	3	18	1	0	2	2	0	29
MH	5	1	2	0	0	0	3	1	12
Total-M	15	8	21	2	1	3	13	2	65
TOTAL	36	10	27	6	4	7	21	3	114

F=female; M=male A-H=professor coding

2.5 Student use of sarcasm and their targets

Student use of sarcasm was minimal; in fact we observed only two instances of sarcasm by students. This is not surprising, given that the majority of the courses taped were teacher-fronted. Students were simply not allowed an equal amount of talk time within such classes. This is, of course, typical of classroom discourse.

A student made a remark to a peer as the peer was presenting. Both students involved were female. One of the students in the audience looked at the presenter's overhead transparency and declared, "I like the way you spelled 'manipulation.'" The presenter had indeed misspelled the word and the student in the audience was joking about the presenter's inability to spell correctly. The class, the male professor, and the student presenting were able to laugh at the situation. This example of sarcasm also served to lighten the atmosphere and to relax the presenter.

The second exchange occurred between a male student and a female professor, and was the sole sarcastic utterance by a student aimed towards a professor. The professor and student had been discussing the fact that the student's name had changed since the previous semester (he was now going by a more 'sophisticated' first name, no longer a nickname). The professor was belaboring the issue and the student finally said to her, "thanks" in an effort get her to stop talking about his name change and to move onto another topic. The professor, fully aware of the tone and the intent of the comment, replied "you're welcome," delivered in a rather harsh tone. A male student interviewed about this particular scene indicated that the professor was probably "playing off his humor." The professor herself had much more to say about the interaction. Before the audio portion of the tape even played, she commented about the student's physical position in the classroom by saying, "See look, he's in his little spot again. In the corner, away from everybody else." She then admitted to giving him "a bit of a hard time." The professor did downplay the exchange, however, by adding "he was obviously being funny so I was just being funny back at him." The fact that both the professor and the student regarded this situation as humorous indicates that the exchange was harmless to those immediately involved.

Some professors indicated that the use of sarcasm is more prevalent among faculty members who feel insecure. In the follow up interviews, three of the four female professors disclosed that they were much more sarcastic when they were new at this than they are now. They indicated that as their jitters in front of the classroom eventually disappeared, they became less sarcastic and less defensive. They felt they no longer had to "prove" their ability to the students. The following comment illustrates:

> I remember when I was an undergraduate that the most formal people were the most new people and the most insecure people. That's just the way it is. I'm getting a lot of pleasure watching these tapes right now because part of what I see is my own progress intellectually which reflects in the ease I have in the classroom. There's no defensiveness or attempt to show off or…I'm just doing my stuff. And that wasn't always the case. I used to have much more…I was definitely more aware of proper engagement and now I'm much more cavalier.

Sarcasm tends to be a speech behavior that requires a lot of energy. We came to this realization while taping each professor throughout the semester. Doing so enabled us to observe on days when the professor was ill or preoccupied by matters other than teaching. On such days few if any sarcastic utterances were employed. One of the faculty participants commented via e-mail (concerning a class in which he appeared to be abnormally tired) that "it takes more energy to be sarcastic — we are a verbally lazy culture." This professor had averaged five sarcastic utterances per class and not one of his utterances on this particular day was classified as sarcastic.

2.6   The functions of sarcasm within the classroom

Sarcasm can be somewhat vague. It has a number of uses and functions that other communicative acts do not have. In this respect, sarcasm can be seen as a communicative polysemy entailing a breadth of different functions as well as attitudes ranging from negative to neutral to positive. It is therefore complex to state rules of the use of sarcasm since "one runs the risk of generalizing too much or creating too limited a scope for the concept" (Myers-Roy 1981: 87).

Our micro-ethnographic approach enabled us to observe the reactions of the students as each sarcastic utterance was performed. In a large majority of the cases (75 of the 114 utterances, or 66%), the sarcastic comment delivered in the classroom was deemed appropriate after triangulating the data. In other words, taking our own "outsider" view of the instance of sarcasm, we cross-checked these perceptions with the views of the teachers and the students in playback sessions during the ethnographic interviews. The sarcastic comments that were deemed appropriate in classroom discourse were delivered in a humorous tone and directed at either an inanimate object or the professors themselves.

Sarcasm as a speech behavior by professors usually elicits strong emotions among students. Within the classroom, we found that sarcasm can have positive, negative and on rare occasions, neutral effects. The positive uses clearly outnumbered the negative in this study. These findings differ from Jorgensen's 1996 study in which she determined that everyday uses of sarcasm served to complain or to criticize the hearer.

2.7   Positive Uses

The most frequent positive use of sarcasm in our data was for humorous intent. These instances functioned to build classroom rapport, lighten the atmosphere of the class (e.g., deflect some type of uncomfortable situation), spark interest in the subject matter, and lessen the gap between teacher and student (e.g. in cases of self-denigrating sarcasm). Sarcasm was also employed positively when professors were trying to make a point, to push students, to respond to minor irritations, and in one case, as an indirect reprimand (see Table 3).

Building rapport in the classroom is typically considered a worthwhile investment on the part of the professor. The amount of effort that is put forth will not only benefit the professor in terms of improving course evaluations and decreasing the number of problem students, but it is also an important factor in ensuring that the class functions smoothly.

Students appreciate when teachers show themselves as human. Self-denigrating humorous sarcasm can create this effect. One example derives from a situation in which a professor was about to show a transparency, but could not

Table 3. Positive functions of sarcasm

ID	Build rapport		Make a point	Spark interest	Push student	Respond to minor irritations	Indirect Reprimand	Total
	Lighten atmosphere	Lessen Gap						
FA	4	2	7	0	1	1	0	15
FB	6	2	2	2	0	0	0	12
FC	3	0	0	1	0	0	1	5
FE	2	3	3	1	0	0	0	9
Total-F	15	7	12	4	1	1	1	41
MD	3	0	3	0	2	1	0	9
MF	2	1	7	2	0	0	0	12
MG	3	0	4	0	0	0	0	7
MH	3	1	1	0	0	0	0	5
Total-M	11	2	15	2	2	1	0	33
TOTAL	26	9	27	6	3	2	1	74

F=female; M=male A-H= professor coding

get the OHP to work. Upon discovering that it was not plugged in, she said, "well, that would help a little." Clearly, such comments are widely heard and serve to humanize the professor. A student commented on the professor's use of self-denigrating sarcastic remarks: "If you make fun of yourself it's an easier response than having the kids go, 'oh…she's an idiot' or whatever."

A comment made by a male professor to a student when the student did not bring in a transparency for a presentation illustrates an attempt to lighten the atmosphere. When the student said he couldn't afford to buy a transparency (as an excuse), the professor's reply was to ask him to write it all on the chalkboard. The professor then said, "Did you calculate in the cost per data point of the chalk?" The entire class showed an appreciation of the humorous intent of the remark by their robust laughter. While the student who was the focus did not reply, it was clear from the videotaped interaction that he felt comfortable proceeding with the presentation. Indeed, the professor's comment served to relieve some tension.

The following example also illustrates a situation where the professor employed sarcasm in order to deflect some type of uncomfortable situation for the student:

[uttered by a male professor to the class as a student had just finished presenting for the first time in his class. She was anxious to sit down, but he wanted her to remain at the front of the class and answer questions. X refers to the student presenting.]

"Ok, class, ask away. X is *dying* to entertain you."

The student interviewed concerning this situation reported that the professor was "jokingly harassing her, like, 'ask her questions and make her sweat a little.'" This student also reported that the professor laughed when this exchange was taking place, showing that a serious matter such as making a classroom presentation can be handled in a tongue-in-cheek manner. It was apparent from the videotape that the presenter herself felt much more comfortable beginning her presentation after the professor uttered his comment: the redness in her face began to abate and her body seemed much less tense. This situation also illustrates the notion that humorous sarcasm can be completely serious. The professor was in fact encouraging the students to ask her questions, and he did want her to 'sweat a little' so that she would be able to learn from the experience and be better able to handle the situation when presenting her work outside of the classroom setting. The professor in this course commented that the student was "scared stiff" and that he was "just being facetious." The word 'just' in his comment implies that he did not intend harm to the student and that he was indeed teasing her. He realized that the student did not want anyone to ask her any questions. At the same time he was acknowledging the fact that the rest of the class also realized the presenter's desire not to be asked questions. The students knew that they would be presenting themselves soon and that they were all nervous about being challenged by their classmates. Hence, although the professor was indeed encouraging questions from the audience, he was fully aware that it would not be easy to encourage a lively dialogue.

Sarcasm was also used positively when employed in expressing indirect reprimands. While this latter function seems counterintuitive, an example should serve to clarify: A professor was putting transparencies on the overhead during a class lecture. She had just changed transparencies when a frustrated student asked if the professor could leave the last one on the overhead a little longer. The professor had been reviewing the material from the previous class so had gone over the transparency quickly. The professor reacted to the student's request by saying, "Start writing fast" in a joking tone. In the follow up interview the teacher said that she was upset at having to waste class time for this student, who had been absent the period before. The professor stated in the interview, "I was chiding them, but yet I'm doing it in kind of a laughable way cuz I don't want to humiliate them." This use of an indirect reprimand, in the form of sarcasm, can serve as a face-saving strategy. Sarcasm often serves to soften the recipient's negative feeling toward the speaker or the situation. This kind of use serves to makes the professor seem fairer and more concerned for the students. A more direct/literal comment (e.g., "you missed the previous class so I shouldn't give you more time to copy the lecture notes") might give the appearance of rudeness or thoughtlessness and perhaps be seen as a lack of concern for the students' success in the course.

Jorgensen's suggestion (1996: 629) that "hearers in real life frequently do not recognize speakers' motives," rings true. In the student's interview concerning this situation, she laughed after viewing this scene and said, "she's really good about going with our pace and answering questions and things like that." The student clearly missed the fact that the professor intended this comment to be a reprimand for missing the previous class. While the instructor was able to save face and did not damage the rapport in the class with her use of sarcasm, this instance highlights a possible drawback in using an indirect speech behavior in order to serve the purpose of a reprimand. That is, if the students did not realize her intentions, then the instructor's effort to change students' attitudes towards classroom attendance may have been in vain.

The inability of students to recognize the intent of the sarcasm may also be due to other factors. Students may be focused so closely on the course content that they miss these cues, preventing their processing the remark as sarcastic and therefore missing the underlying meaning of the utterance. Several of the professors shared in the interviews that sarcasm requires a certain amount of "sophistication" and "mental dexterity" to process, which, according to them, most of their undergraduates lack. The professors felt that their sarcasm was most successful when the students were unable to detect the sarcastic tone. This calls into question the fact that if the sarcasm was not detected, then the actual intention of the utterance may have gone undetected as well. We may question the motivation for the sarcasm in such cases. That is, the intended outcome cannot be realized if the utterance is not recognized as the speaker had intended it. We can assume that the payoffs (e.g. saving face) in using sarcasm outweigh the desire to make changes in students' performance.

Table 4. Targets of positive sarcasm

ID	Class	Female student	Male student	Self	Group of students	3rd party absent	Common Belief	Inanimate object	Total
FA	9	1	0	0	1	3	1	0	15
FB	5	0	1	1	1	0	4	0	12
FC	3	0	0	0	0	0	1	1	5
FE	3	1	1	2	0	0	2	0	9
Total-F	20	2	2	3	2	3	8	1	41
MD	0	4	1	0	0	1	3	0	9
MF	5	0	0	1	0	0	5	1	12
MG	2	0	0	1	0	2	2	0	7
MH	2	0	0	0	0	0	2	1	5
Total-M	9	4	1	2	0	3	12	2	33
TOTAL	29	6	3	5	2	6	20	3	74

F=female; M=male A-H=professor coding

The sarcasm found in this corpus also served to 'make a point.' The majority of these cases resulted in positive reactions from the students (only two were classified as not being positive; one negative and one neutral). Professors used sarcasm with this purpose on 29 occasions. For example: Professor D's class was discussing abnormal human behaviors, and the professor had just asked a question. A student had provided 'lip licking' as an answer, but was not correct. The professor responded to the student by repeating his statement, and adding to it slightly, by saying, "hey, that was good lip licking there." Repeating the wrong answer, using a sarcastic tone, was this professor's way of making it clear to the class that the student had not provided the answer that he was looking for, and that others were still invited to attempt to answer the question. The student who was the target of the comment confirmed that Professor D had been successful at making his point when, without prompting, he offered the following about this particular utterance, "It's just to prove his — make his point. To put it in such a way that we can understand it — in the context of the social setting." Even though the student interviewed was in fact the target of the comment, he did not respond negatively to the use of this speech behavior. When directly asked about how he felt, he responded, "I don't know. It didn't hurt. It kind of relieved — instead of him saying, 'That was a stupid comment.'" In this case, a more literal statement may have been too direct and interpreted as more hurtful for this particular student.

The data in the corpus also shows that when sarcasm was used humorously, it had the effect of sparking students' interest in the subject matter. Students commented that the use of sarcasm was employed to "catch our attention" and "making it [the point] stand out in your mind." As an example of a professor using sarcasm to spark student interest, Professor E was discussing rape and male paternalism. She had just said, "Don't go outside at night because the rapist will get you." One of the female students inferred from this comment the intended meaning of the utterance: "I don't think that women need to be protected at night." In this sense the sheer absurdity of the remark, which was in apparent direct contrast to the actual belief of the professor, helped the comment to stand out in the minds of the students. This student continued this notion in a lengthy narrative:

> It's just the way she says it. It just makes it sound so ridiculous. Just these things we take for granted. And 'Ahh, women shouldn't be outside at night [said sarcastically]' and she goes on to talk about how we need to change the discourse in order to change thins like that. Just at first when she says it, like when she says it, she let's you know in this way that she thinks it's absurd and we should talk about this. It's like she's subtly implanting the things in your head. But she doesn't even, not that she's planning to do it, but it's like she's not going to come out and say, 'You know, I wanted to talk to you today about how women should feel comfortable at night and you should be able to walk alone to your car' or something like that, and then outline why. She's going to make it in a way that makes it SEEM absurd and then start to talk about it.

The above student indicated that this style "worked very well." Another female student indicated that it "sparks your interest. It's stupid. It's like, if you thought like that, that's wrong." These student insights suggest that by making a claim that is contrary to what they believe, that these comments stand out in students' minds and, while tapping into their curiosity, spark their interests in the content material.

2.8   Negative Uses

Negative functions of sarcasm were realized in several ways: shaming the students, pushing the students to perform, and using a sarcastic remark defensively. Sarcasm was also used negatively when a professor was responding to minor irritations (see Table 5). Of the more than 55 hours of audio-taped data from student interviews, all but three professors received positive reactions to their sarcastic remarks. The sarcasm employed by these faculty members was classified as negative after triangulation through the student interviews. In many of the cases, the sarcastic remarks were humorous and served to entertain the class as a whole; however, the *target* of the sarcasm served as the "butt of the joke." In these cases, where the comments were directed toward an individual student with a clear negative semantic load, the sarcasm was deemed inappropriate in the triangulation data (see Table 6 for distribution of the targets of the sarcasm).

Table 5. Negative functions of sarcasm

ID	Ridicule	Indirect reprimand	Push students	Self defense	Respond To Minor irritiation	Make a point	Total
FA	0	0	0	0	0	0	0
FB	0	3	0	1	2	0	6
FC	0	0	0	0	0	0	0
FC	0	0	0	0	0	0	0
FE	0	0	0	0	0	0	0
Total-F	0	3	0	1	2	0	6
MD	0	0	0	0	0	0	0
MF	0	0	0	0	0	0	0
MG	16	1	4	0	0	1	22
MH	1	0	2	3	0	0	6
Total-M	17	1	6*	3	0	1	28
TOTAL	17	4	6	4	2	1	34

*all six instances were cross-classified with 'ridicule'
F=female; M=male A-H=professor coding

Table 6. Targets of negative sarcasm

ID	Class	Female student	Male student	Self	Group of students	3rd party absent	Common Belief	Inanimate object	Total
FA	0	0	0	0	0	0	0	0	0
FB	1	0	4	1	0	0	0	0	6
FC	0	0	0	0	0	0	0	0	0
FE	0	0	0	0	0	0	0	0	0
Total-F	1	0	4	1	0	0	0	0	6
MD	0	0	0	0	0	0	0	0	0
MF	0	0	0	0	0	0	0	0	0
MG	1	3	18	0	0	0	0	0	22
MH	3	1	2	0	0	0	0	0	6
Total-M	4	4	20	0	0	0	0	0	28
TOTAL	5	4	24	1	0	0	0	0	34

F=female; M=male A-H=professor coding

One of the male professors (professor G), who used most of this type of sarcastic utterances, was indeed disliked by the students. At one point in a student interview, the student who was the focus of the sarcastic remark violently tossed his pencil case and book at the TV. The comment was "And now that you've solved the great problems of the 20th century…" Clearly, this comment showed the professor's negative assessment of the work that the student had just done. At stake here was the student's sense of pride, as he was standing in front of the classroom facing his peers.

The sarcastic comments delivered in this classroom seemed particularly hurtful, without regard for the students' feelings or well being and without interest in their learning of the course material. In the interview with this professor, he asserted that he was using sarcasm to entertain himself. Students' perceptions did not appear to be of concern, as the following comment illustrates: "You know, I don't care what happens in there — as long as I'm having a good time."

Sarcasm of this type can be extremely entertaining for those who are not the chosen targets (similar to the shock value present in a daytime talk show in which the guests become enraged and verbally abuse each other). However, the use of sarcasm in this manner can be particularly damaging to the targets when they are undergraduates. Negative uses of sarcasm in the form of cynicism often served to discourage these students. The ability to receive sarcasm entails a type of toughness with which not all individuals have had experience. One student indicated that "some people are really shaken up" by the professor's use of sarcasm. This has serious implications for pedagogy.

The use of negative sarcasm also appears to stifle student involvement in the class. In the course described above, where most of the negative instances of sarcasm were present, the professor did the majority of the talking in the class. When asked about this, a student commented, "I always hide, not wanting to get picked on. I always sat behind that pole."

Professor G seemed to use sarcasm negatively in order to shame/ridicule his students. An example of sarcasm used for the purpose of ridiculing students, which occurred during a class presentation, will illustrate: A male student had used a newly learned word while giving a presentation in front of his peers. The professor interrupted the presentation, remarking to the class, "The boy learn'n some Vocabulary." There seemed to be no reason to interrupt the flow of the presentation other than to draw the entire class's attention to the observation that the professor had made concerning the student's newly acquired lexical item. It appeared that the professor was astonished by the fact that the student could add new words to his repertoire, and thus he felt compelled to share his lack of confidence in the student's abilities with the class. The student rolled his eyes in disbelief after the comment was made and then continued with the presentation. The professor viewed this scene as light banter, while a student remarked "I have no idea the purpose." While this type of comment could have been innocent outside of the classroom, it seemed potentially damaging to the student.

Scolding students, a much harsher form of the indirect reprimand discussed above, was also found in the form of sarcasm. Professor B, for example, used sarcasm in this manner in order to make changes in a particular student's behavior. The students had been asked to form a circle prior to the start of their panel. One student, however, insisted on staying outside the circle, hence he was not physically a part of the panel. The professor remarked, "I just wanna make a circle. It's not that hard." In fact, it was not that difficult to arrange the desks in a circular fashion; however, the frustration in which the professor expressed her opinion and the tone of her voice clearly made the remark sarcastic. The intended meaning (directed towards the "problem student") was something like, "Come on. Just make a circle so we can get on with the panel." She was in fact scolding him for wanting to be different and for not conforming to the rules that she had prescribed for creating a circle. The discourse continued as the student refused to join the group. The professor first said to the student, "Do you want to be an island?" and then followed up with a comment directed towards the entire class, in frustration: "If X wants to insist on being different…" However, a student's take on the situation was insightful. The student said, "I just think it was because he wasn't doing what she said, personally. Because she's such an anal person and because she is such a 'right out of high school' teacher. You know, very particular and just how she wants him to do. Cuz she kept getting mad about it. I think she just wanted to get her way [laughs nervously]. She's the authoritarian figure [said in a harsh tone]. I think she should run the class more, more content oriented." The student is frustrated at the 'wasted' class time that was spent while the professor attempted to change the student's behavior, which was ultimately to no avail. The professor's reflection of this scenario follows:

> "My gut instinct would be that he felt a little insulted having to sit in a circle, you know, that he was trying to make a statement being up there in his own little space. I was just giving him a little crap about it. [laughs] But it's important. As you notice, I'm not looking at him. If you sit there and plead, then they're going to weight it too much. They're going to think, 'oh, she really wants me to circle and I can show my

*independence.' It's not about me. That's my bottom line. When I was a new teacher, I
took everything so personally. If they screwed up on an assignment [pretending to cry]
'Why are you doing this to me? Didn't you listen to what I said?' I'm like, it's not about
me. It's about them. He's not going to get any participation points if he's sitting outside
the circle and can't participate in it."*

From this elaborated comment, we can see that the professor is acutely aware
that the student is responding negatively towards her. She has temporarily lost
control of the individual and is noticeably frustrated. The professor is also
losing sight of the fact that the interaction *did* seem to be about her, contrary to
her debriefing narrative comment.

Another way in which sarcasm was used in the classroom was to push the
students to perform better. This may intuitively seem like a positive use of this
speech behavior since the end result would be a higher quality of student
performances. The data, however, show that all but three of the eight utterances that were classified as pushing the students had negative reactions. This
was confirmed through the students' interviews. One African-American professor, Professor G, employed sarcasm in this manner quite frequently. In fact,
four out of the six utterances in this category were produced by this one
professor alone. Targeting a young African-American man in the class, the
professor said, completely unrelated to the context of the class, "What are you
going to do if you graduate, IF you do?" It was clear that the professor had been
pushing this particular student throughout the semester. It was also clear that
this young man would indeed graduate soon and that the professor was aware
of this. His comment seemed to convey the idea that he wanted to *make sure*
that this student stayed on course and did actually graduate as planned. A
student interviewee commented, "That was my first and last class that I will
take with him. Yeah, he constantly pokes fun at X [the target of the utterance in
question]. Maybe he's trying to push X to be a better student or a better person
because he is Black. Or maybe he [the professor] sees himself in X. But
comments like that, I don't understand why he would say that. He's one of
those teachers, you either like him or you hate him." In the professor's interview, he was adamant that his use of sarcasm to push students was not ill
intentioned. The discrepancy in this course between the students' views and
the professor's view is salient.

Sarcasm was also found to have a negative effect on the students when the
professors used it defensively. Professor H used sarcasm in this manner when
he was attempting to put the test answers on the overhead projector. He asked
the students if they could see the answers, and one student replied "no, no" in

a harsh tone. Professor H replied, "Well, I'm sorry." His reply was delivered in a sarcastic tone. After viewing this sequence, the professor commented:

> *"I was responding to the way they said they couldn't see. I was playing fun of it. Not that I meant any disrespect. I said, 'could you see?' and somebody said 'no, no' [in a harsh tone]. Like they were angry. So, that when I said, 'I'm sorry'...I was just playing. In the sense that, whatever I heard, whether they intended it to be disrespect — I was just playing. I can tell you that if they say it in the most disrespectful manner and it wouldn't make any difference to me. I would just — 'oh, ok' — -I'm just playing. I could have not said anything. [laughs] But I'm just playing."*

In reviewing the videotape, it was clear that the professor was not 'just playing.' This illustrates vividly that although a professor's intentions may not be disrespectful, students often perceive them in this manner. It was unfortunate in this case that the professor chose a negative sarcastic comment, which only increased the anxiety that the students were feeling. One student explained:

> *"He kind of like — I don't know if he was being sarcastic or what. I don't know. He kind of always has that little edge to him. So, you really can't figure it out. Like sometimes he'll say something hilarious and he'll say it in that tone. Not meaning towards anybody or making fun of anybody — he'll just say it in that tone. And other times he'll be like, 'you bunch of dumb asses — I'm sorry — get it?' You know, it's like a smart-ass way. So, I don't know...I think he was just like frustrated with all the equipment because he couldn't figure it out. I don't think he meant it towards anybody — like in particular. Because he's always having problems with the equipment. He needs some technical help."*

2.9 Neutral uses

We classified sarcastic utterances as neutral when they did not seem to have either an adverse effect or a positive effect on the students. Comments concerning minor irritations fall into this category, as well as instances of indirect reprimand and of making a point (see Table 7). Two male professors (Professors D and H) provided the data for the four male uses of this type of sarcasm, while one female professor (Professor B) provided the data for both of the female utterances.

When calling roll at the beginning of a class, Professor B remarked about a student who was absent who had asked for special permission to be allowed to attend the class by saying: "This is great...you gotta love students." In a follow-up interview with a male student from this class, the student: "She's not surprised, maybe, that we're irresponsible and lazy. I'm sure she loves students,

Table 7. Neutral functions of sarcasm

ID	Indirect reprimand	Respond to minor irritations	Make a point	Total
FA	0	0	0	0
FB	1	1	0	2
FC	0	0	0	0
FE	0	0	0	0
Total-F	1	1	0	2
MD	2	1	0	3
MF	0	0	0	0
MG	0	0	0	0
MH	0	0	1	1
Total-M	2	1	1	4
TOTAL	3	2	1	6

F=female; M=male A-H=professor coding

but not then." The teacher, upon viewing this segment, said: "My policy is that if you're not there, I can make fun of you. I was just making a joke, you know, how dare she not come when so many people were trying to get in the class." Uses of sarcasm such as this example were classified as neutral in large part because the target of the sarcasm was not present in the classroom. Table 8 illustrates the distribution of targets of neutral sarcasm.

Table 8. Targets of neutral sarcasm

ID	Class	Female student	Male student	Self	Group of students	3rd party absent	Common Belief	Inanimate object	Total
FA	0	0	0	0	0	0	0	0	0
FB	0	0	0	0	1	1	0	0	2
FC	0	0	0	0	0	0	0	0	0
FE	0	0	0	0	0	0	0	0	0
Total-F	0	0	0	0	1	1	0	0	2
MD	2	0	0	0	1	0	0	0	3
MF	0	0	0	0	0	0	0	0	0
MG	0	0	0	0	0	0	0	0	0
MH	0	0	0	0	0	0	1	0	1
Total-M	2	0	0	0	1	0	1	0	4
TOTAL	2	0	0	0	2	2	1	0	6

F=female; M=male A-H=professor coding

2.10 Student reactions to sarcasm

Although most studies have investigated sarcasm from the point of view of the speaker, this study has triangulated the data involving the interpretation of sarcasm by the hearer as well as a non-participant third party. This allowed for the exploration of the various interpretations that non-speakers derived from the sarcastic comments. It also investigated the opinions that the hearer and audience had formed in relation to the perceived intentions of the speaker, specifically in regard to the receiver of the sarcastic comment.

Interpreting sarcasm and reacting to it involves highly tuned communicative competence and cultural competence. Students have certain expectations of their professors in the classroom. Knowing the cultural expectations in both the larger speech community as well as a particular undergraduate class, for example, can be vital to the success or failure of classroom interaction between student and professor. Some individuals see instances of sarcasm as humorous/ positive, while others may analyze the same utterance as negative. In most cases in this study, the participants saw sarcasm as a sign of intellectual wit or as an elite verbal art form even when the comment was directed toward them in a negative manner. However, recall that when students interpreted the sarcasm as negative, it had serious consequences. In the case of courses that were obligatory for students to satisfy major requirements, withdrawing from the class was not an option. One student allowed the negative verbal behavior in the course she was taking to affect subsequent course choices, saying that, "This was my first and last class I will take with him." She felt a sense of frustration and resentment in the course and did not wish to subject herself to this in further semesters. However, just as negative uses of sarcasm can have a strong influence on whether to register for a course with the same professor again, positive uses of sarcasm can have an equally strong effect. For example, a student enrolled in one of the courses in which only positive sarcasm was utilized compared this to her other courses and said, "…I don't mind coming to her class, whereas other classes, I'm like, 'God. It's not Wednesday again, is it?…She's the first professor that I have been disappointed that she won't be teaching another class next semester."

2.11 Topics that trigger sarcasm

The topics most often found to trigger the use of sarcasm included: student participation, grades and individual abilities; the research being discussed; the course itself; and the instructor's teaching style or personality (see Table 9). The largest category of sarcasm was the students themselves. An example comes from Professor D's class. One of his female students was drawing a less than skillful chart on the blackboard. Giving her time to finish her work, he moved on to another student's research by saying, "While artist Eileen is working…". The student's lack of artistic ability was the focus of the sarcasm, which produced laughter from the class.

Table 9. Topics that trigger sarcasm

ID	Student(s)	Research	Class	Professor	Total
FA	6	6	2	1	15
FB	7	5	6	2	20
FC	2	1	1	1	5
FE	0	5	1	3	9
Total-F	15	17	10	7	49
MD	7	4	1	0	12
MF	1	9	0	2	12
MG	18	5	5	1	29
MH	3	1	3	5	12
Total-M	29	19	9	8	65
TOTAL	44	36	19	15	114

F=female; M=male A-H=professor coding

Utilizing the class in general also seemed to be a topic for sarcasm. For example, as Professor A ran over the allotted time for her class period, she suddenly said to her students, in a sarcastic tone, "you didn't tell me that class was over." This was classified as sarcasm since her intended meaning was quite different from her actual utterance. The message was a clear apology, something like this: "Oh no, I'm sorry I ran over time. I had no idea what time it was." In addition, it was obviously not the responsibility of the class to help her with time management issues, yet she was attempting to place the blame on them, albeit in a teasing manner.

The professor as the topic of the sarcasm was found in fifteen cases. One example comes from the beginning of a class, as the said to the students, "…speaking so eloquently last Thursday." He was using himself as the topic of the sarcasm, as he had noticeably (according to the professor and students) rambled during the previous lecture. The students seemed to enjoy his remark as it set a more relaxed tone for the rest of the class period.

The topic of students was referred to more frequently than the topic of professors. Male professors referred to the topic of students three times as frequently as to the topic of professors. Female professors show a similar pattern, referring to students twice as often as to professors. This may illustrate how status emerges as a strong variable in this study.

2.12 Timing of sarcastic utterances

The distribution of sarcasm throughout the semester appears to have been random (see Table 10).

Table10. Number of sarcastic utterances per taping

ID	Taping 1	Taping 2	Taping 3	Taping 4	Taping 5	Total
FA	4	3	6	1	1	15
FB	4	6	4	1	5	20
FC	1	1	3	X	X	5
FE	1	4	1	3	X	9
Total-F	10	14	14	5	6	49
MD	1	5	2	3	1	12
MF	3	3	2	2	2	12
MG	9	5	1	7	7	29
MH	3	1	3	5	X	12
Total-M	16	14	8	17	10	65
TOTAL	26	28	22	22	16	114

X= no class taped F=female; M–male A-H=professor coding

Professors tended not to employ sarcasm early in the semester, prior to gaining the students' trust. The issue of tenure versus non-tenure may have an effect on the verbal choices that professors make in the classroom. For female professors, fewer sarcastic utterances were found in the very first taping for two professors (C and E). This was also the case with one male professor (D). Again, this may show that professors are more consciously aware of their verbal behavior in the classroom before relationships have been negotiated and the class structure has been established. They may be less likely earlier in the semester to employ speech behaviors like sarcasm, that are prone to misinterpretation.

In addition to examining the use of sarcasm throughout the semester, we thought it important to look at the distribution of sarcastic utterances within each particular class period. For the purpose of this analysis, class time was divided into three different phases in order to analyze the use of sarcasm in each one. Phase I corresponds to the warm up/administrative portion of the class; Phase II consists of the body of the class; and Phase III is the wrap up/ wind down time.

From Table 11 we can see that an overwhelming majority of the sarcastic remarks were found throughout Phase II. This is not surprising, given that neither Phase I nor Phase III typically take up more than five minutes out of each class period, whereas Phase II comprises the remainder of the class period[1]. Due to this difference in length, it is not appropriate to compare Phase II with Phases I and III. However, a comparison between Phases I and III is appropriate. There was a difference in the frequency of the use of sarcasm between Phases I and III. Female professors employed sarcasm more than twice as much in the warm up phase than they did in the wind down phase, and males produced sarcasm more than four times as much in the warm up phase than in the wind down phase. Several professors commented that they used sarcasm to get the students' attention. There may be more need for this at the beginning of a class period than at the end. For example, when time is running out and the students are beginning to pack their bags, sarcasm is less likely to occur, given the energy required to produce a sarcastic remark and the effect that the comment might have on the students at that point in the class.

Table 11. Sarcasm per phase

ID	Phase I	Phase II	Phase III	Total
FA	1	11	3	15
FB	5	15	0	20
FC	1	3	1	5
FE	1	8	0	9
Total-F	8	37	4	49
MD	2	10	0	12
MF	0	11	1	12
MG	5	22	2	29
MH	6	6	0	12
Total-M	14	48	3	65
	22	85	7	114

F=female; M=male A-H=professor coding

There were several instances of sarcastic "spurts." That is, sarcasm did not occur consistently throughout the class period. Sarcasm would appear, for example, at times when a professor was emotionally charged and had a lot invested in the discussion at hand (e.g., protecting their own self identity when they had done something foolish). There tended be long time lapses before the next sarcastic remark appeared.

In summary, the data shows that there is not a clear pattern for the use of sarcasm throughout the semester. With regard to the phases within a given class period, the comparison between the phases of similar length (Phases I and III) showed that sarcasm was used more frequently in Phase I than in Phase III.

2.13 Responding to sarcasm

Students do not respond to sarcasm with sarcasm. The notion that sarcasm is not typically responded to with more sarcasm is discussed in Nelms, Attardo, Boxer (2000). That study, based on a corpus of 395 sarcastic utterances, showed that individuals responded *literally* to sarcastic comments 93% of the time. In the present study, only one sequence showed a professor and a student interacting sarcastically with each other. The fact that students responded to sarcasm with sarcasm in less than one percent of the data is telling. More common responses to sarcasm include: a zero response (81/114 or 71%), laughter (17/114 or 15%), a literal response (8/114 or 7%), and laughter followed by a literal response (7/114 or 6%). These findings are represented in Table 12 below.

Table12. Responses to sarcasm

ID	Zero	Laughter	Literal	Laughter+Literal	Sarcasm	Total
FA	1	4	3	7	0	15
FB	19	0	0	0	1	20
FC	3	2	0	0	0	5
FE	1	7	1	0	0	9
Total-F	24	13	4	7	1	49
MD	7	2	3	0	0	12
MF	12	0	0	0	0	12
MG	26	2	1	0	0	29
MH	12	0	0	0	0	12
Total-M	57	4	4	0	0	65
TOTAL	81	17	8	7	1	114

F=female; M=male A-H=professor coding

That students do not respond to their professors' uses of sarcasm with sarcasm appears to contradict the findings of Gibbs (2000). The difference between

Gibbs' work this study, however, is one of speech event. Gibbs'(2000) involved 149 undergraduate students and their friends in social talk producing 289 utterances, of which 28% were classified as sarcastic. He found several examples within this 28% that involved addressees responding to sarcasm with more sarcasm.

However, classroom discourse is a distinct speech event. One-upsmanship by students vis-à-vis professors is rare. The class atmosphere simply does not allow for students to respond to sarcasm with sarcasm. In terms of responses to the sarcasm, the principal difference between the outcomes of this study and that of Gibbs is clear: Gibbs investigated face-to-face interaction of a close group of friends, while our study investigates a much different population, that of individuals socially distant from each other and in a context where one individual (the professor) has power. Given the power difference, students may be unwilling to jeopardize their grade or even the relationship that they have already established with the professor by contributing a risky response.

With regard to student responses to sarcasm in classroom discourse, the fact that the camera was focused on the professor in each class taping allows us to report only on the data collected in the form of field notes. Based on these field notes, only four types of responses to sarcasm emerged: zero response; laughter; literal response; or (as in the one situation discussed above) another sarcastic utterance. From student interviews, it became clear that much of the sarcasm was met with nonverbal responses. One student disclosed that he "just smile-laughed" when he heard his professor using sarcasm. First, the professors often embedded these utterances within a larger context so there was no room for a response; and second, responding in many of these situations would not have been fruitful. In the cases of the negative uses of sarcasm, for example, the students learned early in the semester that responding to it would not have affected the outcome of the situation. Thus, they remained silent and allowed the professor to continue. It does not appear, then, that sarcasm requires a verbal response.

2.14 Conclusion

The norms for classroom discourse are relatively fixed in terms of the expectations of the students and of the teaching profession. Thus, deviations can be readily identified. Classroom interaction is controlled by a set of unwritten rules that are not present in other domains such as social conversations between friends at the dinner table. In other words, professors may use sarcasm (and other more indirect linguistic strategies) to convey messages that can be handled in a more direct manner in ordinary social conversations.

The data from this study suggest that sarcasm has multiple functions in the classroom. Some of the more frequent uses are to build rapport, to make a point, and to ridicule. The data also suggest that these uses of sarcasm can be perceived as positive, negative, or neutral by the students. The most important factor in creating this perception was the particular target chosen by the professor. That is, when the target of the sarcasm was an individual student, the comment was more likely to be perceived as negative. However, when the target was not a specific student (e.g. the class as a whole or a common belief), sarcasm was more likely to be perceived positively. In the present study, *students* served as the topic most likely to trigger sarcasm. The student interviews showed that this use of sarcasm is risky.

Professors (and teachers generally) need to make a conscious effort to ascertain how their speech behaviors are perceived by others. What seems humorous to the powerful group may have a negative effect on the listeners, particularly in situations where students are attempting to display their intellectual identities in front of their peers. As this study shows, there are clear positive as well as negative uses of sarcasm. Negative uses of sarcasm in the classroom obviously need to be avoided; nevertheless, positive sarcasm may serve useful purposes in classroom discourse. Building rapport in the classroom is a worthwhile investment on the part of the professor.

Why should speakers choose to be sarcastic? Why consciously make an effort to say something sarcastic? Bearing in mind sarcasm's evaluative edge, we begin to wonder what the benefits of sarcasm are for the speaker, as this speech behavior certainly elicits emotional responses from hearers and targets. Giora (1995) suggests that sarcasm prevents speakers from sounding boring. She points out that using sarcasm for a "surprise effect" allows speakers to be viewed as funny and witty rather than dull and boring. This could be a useful teaching strategy.

Folk perceptions of sarcasm is that it is a negative speech behavior. Indeed, in the domain of education generally and in classroom discourse specifically, sarcasm is thought to have no place. We have seen, however, that certain uses of sarcasm can have a felicitous effect on the interaction, creating a rapport between professors and students and functioning to make the subject matter more engaging. These positive uses of sarcasm are related to humor in the classroom. While conversational humor can be a double-edged sword, so too can sarcasm be, especially in the educational domain. When used to make light of a situation, to banter, to put oneself down (as opposed to others), and to lighten the atmosphere of a class, sarcasm not only has a place but can be used to the benefit of learning and teaching. Viewed this way, sarcasm does indeed have a positive role to play in higher education.

3.   Conclusion: Face to face in the educational domain

Education is a domain in which most members of western society spend a great deal of time until reaching adulthood (and well into adulthood for many). Because of this fact, the study of face-to-face discourse in educational settings is critical. The preceding discussion of oral interaction in the educational domain serves to illustrate how members of the academic discourse community gain entrance, keep others out, and either succeed or fail. Discourse savvy is basic to one's ability to negotiate the pathways to educational attainment. For faculty members, knowledge of how to talk the talk of higher education can lead to good teaching evaluations, tenure and promotion, and general success in one's teaching and scholarly career. For students, knowing what to say and when to say it can help them successfully display their emerging identities as learners and scholars. This talent is no small matter. Gaining knowledge, attaining degrees and credentials, achieving status in the academy, are all goods that are rewarded. However, the rewards are not only tangible, financial and concrete. They are also intangible. Succeeding in the educational domain means access to knowledge — an endeavor that must, in our modern society, be a lifelong process.

Note

1. Some classes met for a total of 50 minutes, while others met for a total of three hours.

CHAPTER 5

Face-to-face in the religious domain

1. Introduction

The domain of religion has seen a relative paucity of sociolinguistic research over the past decades. This would seem somewhat surprising, given what appears to be resurgence and increased involvement in religious life in recent years among people across North American communities. People move from place to place much more frequently in modern life than ever before. Most of us no longer have the security of remaining in our communities to continue close relationships with family and friends throughout our life span. In a culture of mobility such as present-day US society, people are increasingly turning to religious groups for their sense of community as well as for fulfillment of spiritual needs.

The reason for this reliance on religious groups to offer a sense of community lies in the human need for a network that substitutes for family ties and that offers new social bonds. Like it or not, in our modern society young people are leaving home more often than not to pursue higher education. People with careers in business and industry are likely to be transferred several times over the course of their work lives. Moreover, we are now a culture in which mid-career changes are more ordinary than extraordinary. Changing jobs frequently entails moving to new places. How do people find new communities when moving around so much? One common way to do this is to join a religious community. Knowing how to become a member of a religious community means learning new ways of interaction. Within any specific religion, there are variations in approaches, ranging from more traditional and conservative to more recent, modern, or simply different.

Becoming a member of any new community entails acquiring the communicative competence needed to participate in that community. Religious groups and congregations require special sorts of competence, both verbal and nonverbal. Even when joining a religious community that is the same denomination as one of which one has already been a member, variations in practices from place to place and congregation to congregation necessitate learning how to become a member of a new speech community. Recent research by Prieto (2001) on Spanish-speaking Protestant communities in the US, aptly illustrates just how important is religious in-group identification for individuals far from home.

The present chapter gives an overview of important research that has been published in the literature on religious discourse. The chapter culminates with an in-depth ethnographic analysis of language use of the "bar and bat mitzvah," a coming of age rite of passage ceremony in Judaism.

1.1   What do we know about religious interaction?

Perhaps the earliest sociolinguistic analysis within the religious domain was Kenneth Pike's 1960 piece on "Glimpses of a Church Service." The chapter, which formed part of a unit on "The Structure of Behavior Illustrated," analyzed the segments of an evangelical church service from *emic* and *etic* points of view. Pike's goal was to illustrate just how segments are bordered within a hierarchical structure. In so doing he was able to give an account of the various sub events of the larger service and connect this with how verbal behavior is generally structured across speech events. Indeed, he compared this church service with a sports event to highlight the structural distinctions. Pike's study was the first to take a close look at religious life from a sociolinguistic perspective. Later studies took this early work as a jumping off point for further analyzing verbal interactions in religious life.

One of these was an early published volume edited by William Samarin (1976) that specifically focused on sociolinguistic examinations of the *language* of religious interactions. Samarin's goal was to explicate how sociolinguistics could bring a unique perspective on religious studies, allowing us to glean something of how religious practice relates to other aspects of cultures and societies. Samarin states: "… we discuss some of the functions, ends, or goals that language serves in religion, the various kinds of linguistic resources that are exploited, and some of the social processes that characterize the use of language" (Samarin 1976: 5). An important assertion in Samarin's introduction is that religious communities reinforce social identity. Samarin offers examples of how identity emanates from such experiences as conversion and initiation rites. Religious registers and styles distinguish a member of one community from another and give force to one's identity. A good example is the testimony-giving style among Pentecostals, reflected in rapid speech with high pitch.

Since becoming a member of any new religious community entails learning new and specific norms of interaction, it is worth exploring what it means to have communicative competence in any such community. The fact is that frequent usages in the religious domain tend to be rare in ordinary talk (e.g. genres such as recitations, magical formulae, prayer and songs). Learning and practicing these new norms must necessarily have an effect on one's linguistic repertoire and social identity. From a social psychological perspective, group cohesion is encouraged by norms that are part of an in-group repertoire that distinguishes a group from others. Samarin notes that in some churches cohesion is achieved by allowing new members, early on, the possibility of reading part of the service, thus demonstrating their communicative competence as an in-group member. This, in addition to such practices as learning how to pray aloud in public, for some religions, encourages group solidarity.

Ferguson (1986: 205) reiterates this important function of religious discourse in that it "affirms the group identity of speaker and audience and reinforces shared beliefs and values." The author took three types of religious services for his analysis: (1) an evangelical service analyzed by Pike above; (2) an old order Amish church service; and (3) his own analysis of a Sunday mass on the Georgetown University campus. Following Pike, Ferguson notes the segmentation of each of the three services into differentiated speech events, or smaller sub-units of the larger service. The knowledge of the boundaries of these segments is an important part of the communicative competence of members of each congregation. He discusses the existence of what he terms "formatted discourse, in which the texts are composed or produced on the spot but within quite rigid guidelines or formatting..." (Ferguson, 1986: 206). This piece by Ferguson is indeed a thorough sociolinguistic analysis, in that it encompasses the analysis of such formatted discourse in juxtaposition to free texts such as the social talk surrounding the more structured genres (e.g. greetings, background explanations, apologies and other speech acts). Ferguson discusses here the phenomenon that he terms the `one-many dialog' (Ferguson, 1986: 209). I refer to this same phenomenon in this chapter as the `face-to-faces' structure that is in opposition to face-to-face discourse. The greater part of religious ceremonial discourse is indeed in this one-many dialogic format, as we shall see in the in-depth study of a bar mitzvah that forms the second part of this chapter. To talk about face-to-face interaction in religious discourse is to include only some of the speech behavior that forms part of talk in this domain. Ferguson aptly states:

The people praise God, they hear the messages of their faith, they make requests of God, they feel repentance and are reassured, they feel the spirit at work, and so on. It is the task of the discourse analyst to investigate just how the words of the service accomplish these things for the participants, and in general what the underlying assumptions of the community must be as to how language in this particular activity can mediate so powerfully (Ferguson, 1986: 211).

The language of religious interactions is sometimes used to convey to fellow worshipers the feeling of human/divine communication. Such is the type of interaction described by Szuchewycz (1994) in a description charismatic prayer meetings within a Catholic community. This study analyzes the use of specific linguistic devices by participants that function to create a sense that all are part of special interaction with each other and, more importantly, with the Almighty. Schuchewycz shows how this is accomplished through the use of evidentials in the personal narratives told in the prayer meetings. The marked use of evidentials "creates, reinforces and sustains religious conviction" (Schuchewycz, 1994: 389). In the spontaneous talk of prayer meetings within this community, participants try to attribute their contributions to spiritual authorship and authority, thus transforming the contribution into a spiritual message. In so doing, the individuals demonstrate that it is possible to communicate personally with God, and that through the group activity the divine enters into the interaction, helping to solve some of the problems inherent in the issues under discussion.

Prayer meetings are spirit-led events in the sense that the Holy Spirit is seen to work through the 'hymns,' 'sharings,' 'teaching,' 'readings,' 'prophetic words,' and 'silences' of the meeting to communicate a specific message to the prayer community on each occasion that it gathers together (Schuchewycz, 1994: 391).

The author shows how this spiritual message is socially constructed through participants' contributions. The participants themselves attribute spiritual leading of their participation through the use of linguistic devices such as confirmations, linking through lexical repetition, and evidential markers in their story rounds (e.g. stating that one has a 'strong urge' to tell something, or that one is 'being led' to share something). These markers clearly indicate divine agency to the group. In this way the public sharings conform to co-constructed norms of interaction. The establishment of a sense of divine/human communication is central to the discourse of these charismatic prayer meetings and serve to distinguish this type of sub-community from the more traditional Catholic community.

Through the study of various types of religious discourse, it becomes apparent that specific speech behaviors are employed to conjure up a sense of spirituality. Such discourse gives credence that linguistic contributions are guided from above, and it creates a sense of group cohesive activity that can only be accomplished in the context of the specific spiritual context.

Indeed, language of all sorts is utilized to accomplish spiritual tasks. In some contexts it is language that approaches the "magical." The work of Leilani Cook (1995) is an in-depth analysis of magical language from a linguistic perspective. Cook demonstrated how meaning, sound and performance all form an important part of the language of magic in carrying out the functions of communicating with supernatural forces. Synonymy, metonymy and homophony are all essential elements. For example, metonymy is employed to enhance power. Consider the following charm:

Charm Against Epilepsy and the Fever

What manner of evil thou be
In God's name I conjure thee
I conjure thee with the holy cross
That Jesus was done on with force.
I conjure thee with nails three
That Jesus was nailed upon the tree.
I conjure thee with the crown of the thorn
That on Jesus' head was done with scorn.
I conjure thee with the precious blood
That Jesus showed upon the rood (cross).

From Middle English Lyrics, Luria and Hoffman, (eds.) p. 112.

In this charm, the objects used (a cross, nails, blood, a spear, etc.) not only represent the power of Jesus but symbolize that which brought Christians eternal life, the Crucifixion. "For a formula which must protect the user against life-threatening epilepsy and fever, this is a powerful schema to access" (Cook, 1995). Also extensively employed in magical language are alliteration and onomatopoeia. The latter imitate the sounds of nature. This allows the speaker to access whole schemas of reference through the images the sounds suggest.

Performance, as well as thought and word, are paramount in magical language in that it serves to reinforce cultural values that gave rise to the incantations. Rhythmic chanting, for example, is an earmark of magical delivery: Christian, Jewish, Buddhist and Islamic traditions all make use of cantors to deliver their sacred words. Finally, magical language utilizes performative speech acts to alter reality (e.g. I conjure thee, I trample upon the evil eye, I lie down this night with the nine angels, etc.). As Cook states, the language of magic needs to be powerful, taking from creative, intuitive and powerful uses of language to effect forces such as "charming the skies and quieting the seas" (personal communication).

A discussion about the use of talk and its absence in the religious domain would be incomplete without including descriptive work on Quaker norms of interaction and the value that this religious sect places on silence. Indeed, sociolinguistic research on the functions of silence in Quaker services dates from the work of Bauman (1974), which explicated the important role of silence in the ethnographic study of language use. For Quakers, revelation is not through the word of God, but is an ongoing process that every person is capable of realizing: "The faculty through which this direct personal experience of the Spirit of God within oneself was achieved…was the Inner Light" (Bauman, 1974: 145). In order to achieve the Inner Light, Quakers strove to suppress the earthly self; the manifestation of this suppression was thought to come through silence. Early Quakers of the seventeenth century rejected the prevalent formalism of other branches of Christianity. The value placed on silence reflected their distrust of speaking. The task of the Quaker minister (which could be any member of the congregation at any time so moved) was to bring other members of the congregation "to the desired spiritual state" (Bauman, 1974: 147).

Later work by Alan Davies (1988) further explores the functions and uses of silence in Quaker services, in which everyone has equal access to "ministry" in that the right to speak comes from being moved by a higher force. Indeed, as the author notes, "Quakerism has always had a tension between speaking and silence" (Davies, 1988: 106). For Quakers, silence is a necessary and creative part of worship. Out of deep silence emanate spoken contributions that arise from the personal experiences and beliefs of speakers. Thus, the ministry is open and free for all to participate, and there is "readiness for dialogue in a setting of silence" (Davies, 1988: 110). Silence in Quaker meeting for worship encourages or gives rise to divine inspiration. Other scholars of religious interaction (e.g. Samarin 1976) contrasts this with the Pentecostal propensity toward noisiness as its defining characteristic. According to Maltz (1985: 118) "Quakers look inward while Pentecostals look outward." Thus, becoming a member of these speech communities clearly necessitates inculcating different norms as a part of developing communicative competence.

Davies (1988: 118) asserts: "The holding of a Meeting for Worship as a felicitous speech event requires that participants maintain this delicate balance between speaking and silence." Because of this tension and because silence is the unmarked category, Davies likens the Meeting for Worship speech event less to a formal speech event and more to a "continued state of incipient talk" (Davies, 1988: 119). Norms for turn taking differ from that of other formal speech events (e.g. classrooms, meetings, etc.), where one person typically has the privileged role of allocating turns. While Meeting for Worship is a formal speech event, the priesthood is present in all participants, and turn allocation is thus not explicit. Moreover, certain speech acts relevant to other more commonly known formal speech events are absent in Meetings. These include formal greetings and closings by the ordained to the congregation.

Davies reports on a study of 14 Meetings for Worship that he audio-recorded, encompassing 72 speakers. As would be expected, the majority of speakers were men (41 to 31 women). In general, the contributions were simple and brief. The language use was deemed "religious" in that most lexical items referred to God. The typical pattern was to start with the personal and move to the divine. In the ministry, topic has utmost importance, since the first topic leads to subsequent contributions by other members who are moved to speak. The discourse generally is located in the here and now. Speaking is of a sort that does not encourage questions requiring answers. Constraints include the unspoken agreement that people do not speak more than once, nor monopolize the speaking.

That religious interactions make fertile soil for sociolinguistic investigation is also asserted by Jonathan Webster (1988: 86): "the sociolinguist is endeavouring to discover the system of rules underlying the sociolinguistic competence of members of a socially defined group." Webster, like others above, takes the perspective of religious community interaction as linguistic solidarity, where there is tacit agreement on rules of appropriate speech and style for its expression. Religious groups have distinct modes of expressing their mutual interests, and this distinction is reflected in special vocabulary reflected in a register unique to the group. As for style, he finds repetition to be paramount in religious expression, as in sermons, testimonies and prayers. None of these speech behaviors are interactional. On the contrary, they are transactional, characterized by one speaker speaking to either the congregation or, as in prayer, speaking directly to a higher power. The interactions are by and large in the form of one-many dialog, or face-to-*faces* rather than face-to-face. That is, even in Quaker contributions, they involve one individual speaking to the rest of the congregation.

A rare study that did focus on face-to-face interaction in a religious community was Sequeira (1993). This was an ethnographic study that took place over a period of 18 months, studying 49 church members with a range in age, sex, roles in the church, and length of membership. The focus of the research was an analysis of personal address in a church community in the Pacific Northwest. Building on early research on address terms by Roger Brown and his colleagues (e.g. Brown and Gilman 1960; Brown and Ford 1961), Sequeira studied the social meanings of various terms of address, demonstrating that members draw on their communicative competence within the specific speech community. The study demonstrated choices to be constrained by context, public vs. private meanings, and interlocutors' beliefs. She presents this community as taking negotiational approaches in choosing forms and patterns for particular goals, given their interpersonal relationships and the context.

The research site was an Episcopal congregation with roots in Anglicanism. The interesting fact in this particular community was the split between the traditionalists (Old Church) and those representing renewal (New Church). Among the researcher's findings was that most members used first name (FN) to address each other, despite differences in professional and social status. It appears that membership in the community overrides other status indicators. Only with more senior members of the congregation, such as elderly widows, were titles and last names (TLN) used. Children, of course, were the exception, using TLN with adults until they reached a certain age or role in the community. Kinship terms, such as *brother* and *sister*, were used as terms of endearment between adult members. Reasons given for the preponderance of FN usage were expediency and friendliness. However, when a visitor entered the scene, address usage reverted to more formal TLN when referring to another. Thus, solidarity was demonstrated in this community by the in-group phenomenon of difference in address terms.

When clergy interacted with each other there was evidence of fluidity in address terms, particularly when junior clergy interacted with their seniors: "changes in address reflect changes in the perceived role relationship and visa versa" (Sequeira, 1993: 272). Indeed, address terms reflected feelings about personal relationships even in this context. Commitment to community was evident throughout. Such commitment was reflected in knowing which address terms carry the appropriate force in different contexts. For example, T only was used exclusively in reference to the clergy. Here, there is a distinction between those that adhere to Old Church norms and those of New Church leanings. While the former see authority as attached to the role; the latter see it as attached to the person. Those with Old Church leanings used the term "father" in direct address, seeing more importance in the role as opposed to the interpersonal relationship. Conversely, "those congregational members and clergy who have a single, personal allegiance to renewal view their roles as equal with no hierarchical distinction" (Sequeira, 1993: 280). Thus, the norm is FN, and "father" is a vestige of Old Church belief. Sequeira aptly demonstrates that the linguistic choices of these community members are fluid and open to negotiation, and this is reflected in address term choices. The use of address terms in this religious community is discursive rather than determinate.

In general, the existing sociolinguistic literature on religious interactions demonstrates some consistent findings: most of what is truly part of the religious domain is face-to-*faces*. The aspect of face-to-*face* interaction in the domain of religion borders on social interaction. Indeed, it is sometimes difficult to disambiguate the social aspect of religious groups with the religious aspects. People participate in religious groups to satisfy many needs: spiritual, intellectual and social. This last need is not mutually exclusive from the others. Our sense of belonging is not only social but derives from an inner need to satisfy the mind and the soul. Becoming part of a community, especially a religious community, affords the individual the opportunity to take on the norms of interaction of an in-group distinguished in many ways from all other groups. Knowing how to speak or maintain silence privileges membership. Thus taking on the norms of a religious group transforms one's individual, social, and relational identity. We have seen that a religious community is a speech community par excellence, privileging those members who abide by the agreed-upon norms of conduct and interaction. One can integrate into such a community only by taking on the rules and ways of speaking or patterns of maintaining silence. The intellectual and social are thus interwoven with the spiritual.

Let us now turn to an in-depth analysis of one such type of community and one speech situation within it. I analyze next the event of the bar or bat mitzvah in North American Judaism. This analysis demonstrates how the spiritual, intellectual and social spheres interact.

2.   An ethnography of a Bat/Bar Mitzvah

2.1   Introduction

The bar or bat mitzvah is a Jewish ceremony and celebration of a youth's coming of age rite of passage from childhood to adulthood at age thirteen. The ceremony is a formal welcoming of the youth into the religious community. Traditionally, this rite of passage was for males only, as women's functions in Orthodox Judaism was of an auxiliary nature. In fact, in Orthodox Judaism, women are not allowed to make up any of the ten persons required for a *minyan*, the minimum number of people required for a prayer group. While Orthodox women are allowed to pray, they are not required to (Rabin 1976). The Bar Mitzvah denotes the blessing of the son, *bar* meaning son in Hebrew. It is only in the past several decades that young girls have had the privilege of going through this rite, and thus the term Bat Mitzvah emerged (*bat* denoting *daughter* in Hebrew).

> Modern westernizing Orthodoxy permits parents to celebrate a girl's reaching the age of twelve, at which she is under Jewish Law bound to keep the commandments. These celebrations (called Bat — Mitzva) are modeled on the Bar-Mitzva celebrations of boys at thirteen, and the girls often will give a learned lecture. In Reform synagogues and in many Conservative synagogues she will be "called up" to have a part of the weekly portion of the Pentateuch read to her (Rabin 1976: 143).

In present day North American communities, the Bat Mitzvah is celebrated upon a girl's thirteenth birthday rather than at age twelve. I analyze here a Bat Mitzvah and a Bar Mitzvah in two different North American Conservative congregations.[1] The Bat Mitzvah took place in November, 1999 in Baltimore, Maryland; the Bar Mitzvah occurred the following month in Gainesville, Florida. The goal of this study is to provide a descriptive analysis of the speech situation in Judaism, and in so doing to ascertain the norms and rules of speech behavior and interaction.

2.2   Methodology

My intention in observing both a Bar Mitzvah and a Bat Mitzvah is that the two events would allow for a comparison between the rituals, indicating any possible differences in gender expectations between the two. Moreover, observing in two different US congregations, far apart from each other geographically, would allow for variations in the norms across different communities of conservative practice. Ideally, one would have to observe more than two such events to realize any generalizable assertions about these religious rituals. Nonetheless, ethnographic case studies such as these allow for in-depth analysis that are descriptive in nature.

Data for the study are in the form of field notes taken during and/or immediately following the two events. The use of electronic equipment is forbidden on the Sabbath, the holy day of rest in Judaism. Because of this restriction, neither audio nor video recording was possible. Extensive field notes also needed to be surreptitiously obtained, given that another Sabbath restriction in Judaism is a ban on writing. This is not necessarily strictly adhered to in Conservative congregations. Nevertheless, writing in the synagogue is, while perhaps not 'forbidden,' negatively sanctioned by the community members. Field notes were therefore written down immediately following the ceremonies, with attempts to recall significant aspects of the speech events.

Ethnographic interviews are an important source of data for this type of study. These were conducted with the Bar Mitzvah boy in Gainesville, with one of the Bat Mitzvah girls in Baltimore, and with the parents of both of these children. In addition, I carried out an in-depth interview with the rabbi of the Gainesville congregation. These interviews served to triangulate the data by enabling me as the analyst to share my perceptions with the actors themselves, and to compare the insights of the celebrants and parents, for example, with the insights of the spiritual leader, who added important information about the rituals themselves.

A few words are in order here regarding studying the speech behavior of a community of which one is a part or not. Traditional ethnographers of speaking tended to focus on societies and speech communities alien to their own. More recently, however, analysts have taken to studying speech behaviors of communities in which they themselves participate. This is the aspect of what Wolcott (1987: 41) referred to as making "the obvious obvious or the familiar strange." The advantages of studying one's own community are outlined in Schneider's (1968) study of kinship:

> We speak the language fluently, we know the customs, and we have observed the natives in their daily lives. Indeed, we *are* the natives. Hence we are in an especially good position to keep the facts and the theory in their most productive relationship (Schneider, 1968: iv).

While I am not a member of either of the congregations that are described here, I am by birth a member of the more generalized religious group of Jews.

The fact that I am not a member of any congregation makes me somewhat of an outsider; the fact that I know something about the rituals and the languages (Hebrew, Yiddish) gives me insider insight. This state of being neither an insider nor an outsider is worthy of extensive methodological discussion; however, suffice it to say here that the dangers inherent in this state point to the necessity to cross check one's intuitions carefully through interviews with the participants in the speech events. Given this, the ethnographic interviews in this study are an important part of the data collection process and serve to illuminate aspects of the Bat and Bar Mitzvah that may have seemed clear on superficial analysis, but that required further insight on the actual speech interactions.

2.3   Background

The Jewish Sabbath begins at sundown on Friday evening. The rites of passage of the Bar and Bat Mitzvah always take place during the Sabbath and usually on Saturday, though the ceremonies may begin during the Friday evening services in the synagogue. Typically, the youth that is undergoing the *mitzvah* (blessing) participates to a greater or lesser degree in the services, especially those on Saturday morning. These services usually commence between 9 and 10 a.m. and last for two to three hours. The Sabbath service has several parts. A short (typically averaging one hour) service welcoming in the Sabbath takes place on Friday evening, commencing at sundown. On Saturday morning there is an initial preliminary segment, the Bat or Bar Mitzvah portion, mourning for the dead, giving prayers for healing of the sick, and rejoicing in God's allowing for another Sabbath to be celebrated.

The Bar or Bat Mitzvah is normally something that the youth has anticipated for some time, preparing for the service by studying in Hebrew School for many years, participating in youth activities of the community, and learning her or his part of the Torah reading for that particular Sabbath. Thus, the initiation of the youth into the community is a process that begins at an early age and is typically many years in the making. The process is linguistic, spiritual, intellectual and social, depending on the particular congregation. Some communities take more of an intellectual approach to the learning, arguing points about what was meant in the holy texts. Others take a more social approach, involving the youth in activities of the community such as camping trips. Regardless of the approach, the goal is always to bring the youth into the fold. An important part of this initiation process is the inculcation of the norms and values of the community, including linguistic and cultural aspects. The learning of biblical Hebrew is clearly an important part of the agenda. To a greater or lesser extent, depending again on the congregation, students in the Hebrew School are taught to read the language and to decode its meaning. These are two quite separate skills. Indeed, many of my own generation learned to read but never knew the meaning of what they were reading. It was sufficient for these youth of the fifties and sixties to merely decode. Nowadays it is more common for the students to learn the meaning of what they are reading. A large portion of the Mitzvah ceremony involves reading in Hebrew, even in the non-orthodox congregation. The parts of the service that are conducted in English focus mostly on the giving of directions (e.g. for the page to turn to, to stand, to read silently); the announcement of special celebrations among the congregation (e.g. anniversaries); and the speeches and sermons.

Let us turn to descriptions of the actual ceremonies in the two communities, beginning with the Bat Mitzvah in Baltimore. I describe here the Friday evening service, the Saturday morning service, and the *kiddush,* a light luncheon which takes place immediately subsequent to the service on the Sabbath. A party is always part of the celebration at some time subsequent to the Sabbath morning ceremony. This may take place in the afternoon, evening, or on the Sunday following the day of ceremony. A few words will also be mentioned about the party, but the discussion here will be brief, as it constitutes more of a social rather than religious occasion.

2.4   The Bat Mitzvah

In this suburban Baltimore community, the rabbi began promptly at 9:30 with the preliminary prayers. The full congregation was not yet seated, with people streaming in during a major portion of the opening segment of the service. While the commencing of the service should signal silence and order to the congregation, it seemed to have little such effect on this group. There was no directive from the pulpit for people to be seated. The Rabbi simply commenced the formal service, employing Hebrew throughout. As for the congregation, the speech act of greeting predominated. While the rabbi began leading the congregation in prayer in Hebrew, the people welcomed each other in English, Hebrew (*Shabbat Shalom*), or Yiddish (*Gut Shabbes*). They waved to each other and walked up to each other, kissing and conversing despite the fact that the formal service had already begun. The societal value of social interaction was reflected in the language and behavior of this speech community. The use of codes other than English reinforced the social identity of Jewishness for these community members, as outsiders present would be unable to share in such a greeting ritual in these languages.

As the service was commencing, young children were running around with parents running after them to prevent them from climbing up to the pulpit. Another societal value, the importance of family and children and their well being as superordinate, was evident. The formal service proceeded during these unofficial goings-on, with the rabbi incanting and with the congregation reciting in chorus certain segments of the prayers. This is ritualized to the extent that worshipers know where and exactly at what points to recite cho-rally, or, as Ferguson (1986) termed it, to follow the 'formatted text.' In the Baltimore congregation, the rabbi led and congregation followed his lead.

The Bat Mitzvah segment took place during the middle of the morning service, after the preliminary prayer service. Two young girls were performing the rites that particular morning, having to read pre-designated parts of the Torah that coincided with the dates of the ceremony. For this week's service the segment focused on the story of Jacob. The first celebrant gave a summary of the story from the bible in English. She then proceeded to read it in Hebrew. After the reading she gave a short speech in which she related how this story had a personal meaning for her — teaching her about honesty and moral values.

The Bat Mitzvah event is a formal one, with rehearsed parts to be conveyed to the audience. Giving the short speech, a sub-event of the larger Bat Mitzvah, entailed prior preparation. In my interview with the Bat Mitzvah girl she indicated that she had begun preparing her speech months in advance of the actual occasion. This is an important part of the ceremony, as the girl's family and friends are all expecting to hear the relevance of the particular biblical story to the girl's life and experience of becoming a Bat Mitzvah. The event is normally new to these young celebrants; indeed, for many it is the first time in their lives that they are addressing an audience and talking about their own spiritual growth. It is a moment for all to be proud of this culminating achieve-ment of the child after years of preparation.

Subsequent to the speech, pre-selected members of the girl's family or family friends took turns at an *aliyah*. This term literally translates to "going up" or "ascending." An aliyah signifies a turn at stepping up to the pulpit to either read a part of the Torah or to perform a ritualized service. Examples of such services are carrying the Torah around the hall, folding it up, or opening/closing the ark. The readings necessitate a level of initiation into the rituals of the service, and/or the rehearsing of the part read, unless the individuals are versant in reading biblical Hebrew. Recall that many who are able to read in Hebrew do so as a transliteration exercise only, being unable to ascertain much of the meaning of what they are reading. In this congregation, given that two young people were celebrating their Bat Mitzvah on the same day, the verbal *aliyot* (plural of aliyah) needed to be shared between the families of the two girls. Thus, these were special parts played by the parents and grandparents. The segment in which the Torah was carried around the perimeter of the congregation celebrates the fact that the community has the Torah. It is a joyous segment. Aligned with this joyous feeling, the sub-event was an opportunity for the audience to begin to greet each other, converse, and generally talk to each other. The social aspect of the service was once again evident.

The second Bat Mitzvah girl then took her turn reading, first in English and then in Hebrew, the part of the Torah for that particular Sabbath service. She also followed her reading with a short speech about what this day meant to her. For this girl, the lesson was to be a good member of her community, to continue to always have faith in God, and to serve her world in humanitarian deeds. The community values of in-group solidarity and working to make the world a better place were reflected in this speech. In-group solidarity takes several forms. first is the initiation of the child into the religious code, the Hebrew language. Second is the teaching of the children about the history of the Jewish people and their struggles throughout the ages, from ancient to modern times. Third is the inculcation of societal values through formal interaction in the school, informal interaction in community activities, and modeling of appropriate norms of speaking and interaction during the actual religious services. Knowing the rules of the Sabbath, as one example, is important for any initiate into the adult religious community.

The continuation of the service ensued, with the female Cantor (person who sings part of the service) singing parts of the prayers throughout. The service ended, as is typical form on Shabbat, with a sermon in English delivered by the Rabbi, the topic of which was how Conservative Judaism fits into Israel and the world. The sermon was both philosophical and political. This event of speech-giving differed sharply from the speech of the Bat Mitzvah girl. While the latter served as a reflection of the day's meaning to the youth, the rabbi's sermon served a teaching purpose for the congregation. Thus, the topic was not congruent with the Bat Mitzvah. The sermon here was a separate part of the morning service that was more connected to the Sabbath services in general than the Mitzvah portion of the whole service.

In summary, the Bat Mitzvah celebration is embedded in a normal Sabbath service on Saturday morning. While for some congregations the youth's rite of passage is a large part of the service, in others it forms only a smaller part, as in this Baltimore synagogue. It seemed clear that many of the speech events and acts of this service were not necessarily connected to the rite of passage. The Bat Mitzvah girls participated in only a small segment of the whole service, reading their parts of the Torah and giving a short, five-minute speech on the day's meaning for them. The remainder of the service was that which ritually occurs on Shabbat: welcoming in the Sabbath and celebrating its meaning for the congregants. This was despite the fact that a large portion of the audience this day was family and guests of the Bat Mitzvah girls who do not necessarily attend the services regularly.

In-group linguistic and behavioral norms prevail across North American Jewish speech communities. That is, any Jewish person brought up in any congregation, regardless of region, ought to be familiar with the formatted texts, that is, the rituals, speech events and speech acts that prevail during the Shabbat service. The differences in norms of speaking and interaction for conservative congregations are slight. Larger differences exist between these and other types of congregations (Orthodox or Reform). Thus, Conservative Jews ought to have some ease in moving from one conservative congregation to another. Jews with backgrounds in the other traditions have some norms for the Sabbath rituals that differ from those of the Conservative approach. Thus, they are not insiders to the extent that members of other conservative congregations are. Non-Jews and secular Jews (i.e. those with little or no religious training) are clearly the outsiders. Hence, the in-group norms are narrow, applying best to those of the same denomination, next to all other Jews, and least of all to outsiders.

The morning services were followed by a light luncheon to which all members of the congregation were invited. Here, the predominating speech act was congratulatory to the Bat Mitzvah celebrants and their families.

2.4.1   The celebration

The evening party began with a formal candle-lighting speech event to celebrate the girl's thirteenth birthday. Thus, there were thirteen candles to be lit. This is an opportunity for the Bat Mitzvah celebrant to honor special people in her life by calling them up to light one of the birthday candles. The girl proceeded to a reciting of an original poem for each person, couple or group to come up to light a candle. This Bat Mitzvah celebrant had spent many months writing an original poem for each person or group who lit a candle. In our interview, she indicated that her goal was to reflect on her relationship with the candle lighters. Moreover, she sought to make each poem sound as clever as possible, something joyful to listen to but yet meaningful. The following is an example of a welcoming poem to the candles and cake (addressed to me, as the girl's aunt, and to my family):

> Over the years your family's grown,
> Three of the six of you for my whole life I've known,
> I have fond, happy memories of our visits to Philly,
> Walking on South Street where the people looked silly.
> When you moved to Florida our visits grew less,
> But the distance didn't serve as our relationship's test,
> Instead, in the past two years, new relatives I've found
> An uncle and two more cousins — all around.
> Thank you for coming from so far away
> I can't believe yesterday you were in Paraguay
> I know our relationship is strong down to the core,
> Please come up and light candle number four.

Clearly, quite a bit of ethnopoetic preparation is evident in the poems for each of the thirteen individuals or groups who lit a candle.

Following this toast to the special guests by the Bat Mitzvah, there is a speech event that precedes the serving of the meal. This is the blessing of the wine and the bread, carried out in Hebrew by a special person present that is typically an elder fluent in Biblical Hebrew. In this case, the elder was one of the grandfathers. Once the blessings were completed, the party began in earnest.

In sum, the linguistic and cultural manifestations of the Bat Mitzvah are multi-layered. first, there is the preparation, in Hebrew, of the reading from the Torah and the other parts of the morning service in which the celebrants participate. Then there is the preparation, in English, of the short speech that forms a part of the Bat Mitzvah celebration. This is not to mention the numerous preparations for the social part of the event, the party and all of its activities, including a form of "toast" to special guests that is entailed in the lighting of the candles, and the blessings in Hebrew that precede the meal. In all, the Bat Mitzvah is indeed a special day in the life of the individual and her family and a special celebration for the friends and relatives as well as the entire community. Increasing the size of the in-group by adding a new, officially adult member is indeed a *mitzvah* (blessing) in Judaism.

2.5   The Bar Mitzvah

The bar mitzvah that took place in Gainesville, Florida was also a conservative service. Recall that this celebration is of a boy's coming of age into the religious community, the more traditional type of rite of passage. In this case, the bar mitzvah boy took over virtually the entire morning ceremony, leading the service and prayer welcoming in the Sabbath, leading the mourners in the *yahrtzeit* (prayer of mourning), and reciting his reading from the designated portion of the Torah. The service began at 10 a.m. and continued until 12:15. As with the Baltimore community, this service also was somewhat informal, with people entering the sanctum late and sporadically, all the while greeting each other with the Yiddish *gut shabbes* (good sabbath). As in the Baltimore congregation, children were heard throughout the service, and the congregants generally ignored their outbursts.

During the course of the interview with the rabbi of this congregation, he outlined in depth the various speech events and acts of the morning service:

> The service itself has several preliminary or warm-up aspects to it. First come the morning blessings, which relate to the physical of the body; then the verses of song, or chantings of psalms, which gets to the emotional level. So it goes from the physical to the affective. From there, after those warm-ups have taken place, the central part of the morning service itself is the recitation of pre-biblical passages known as the *sh'ema*, followed by prayers on particular themes. So it begins with recognition of the divine as the source of nature, God as creator; from there moving from creation to revelation; God as source of Torah, God as teacher. Torah is expression of divine love for us. So, from creation to revelation and then the expression of God's one-ness, the biblical paragraphs themselves, they're quotations (e.g. from Deuteronomy, etc.), acceptance of God's sovereignty; accepting the commandments; then making the segue from creation to revelation now to redemption — seeing the divine as that which has helped us in the past, helps us in the present and will be connected to a sense of a messianic hope of future salvation as well.

The only part of the service that is different when there is a bar or bat mitzvah is that all of the above parts, at least in this congregation, are led by the bat or bar mitzvah youth. In other words, the mitzvah does not substantially change the normal events and acts of a typical Shabbat service.

While both services were highly ritualized, in this one there was more evidence of the congregation's familiarity with the formatted texts, or routines of the morning service, with community members knowing exactly where to pray silently, in chorus, and in song. Hence, there was a more serious nature to this service. The difference seemed to be due primarily to the regularity of attendance of the audience. In other words, there seemed to be great overlap between regular congregants and people celebrating the Bar Mitzvah. The ethnographic interview with the rabbi of this congregation indicated that the Bar or Bat Mitzvah is always integrated seamlessly into the regular Shabbat service. In this congregation, the celebrant plays an important role in the prayer, singing, and even giving directions.

The interaction was face-to-face, face-to-faces and faces-to-faces, on the pulpit and off. The informal greetings during the official goings-on were examples of social face-to-face interaction, replete with hugs and kisses, similar to those of many Latin American cultures. The rabbi-led and Bar Mitzvah-led prayers were face-to-faces. The rabbi indicated that he typically tries to make the entire Shabbat service one in which he does not lead but all face each other. He accomplishes this by setting up lectern in the middle of the sanctum, so that he is not facing the congregation but in the middle of it.

> The theological choreography is not that God is on the stage up there. It's that divinity wells up from the center and it's all coming together. It's classic in Judaism. What began to happen 150 years ago is that we tried to get Protestant. It's more of a sense of a holy happening from the midst of the community, from the people who are there.

Thus, this is an attempt to make the service truly one in which the community participates together in a faces-to-faces format rather than is led by the rabbi in a face-to-faces format. The *aliyot* (calling individuals up to the pulpit) were also examples of faces-to-faces. Code mixing was evident, with prayer in Hebrew, instructions in English, and greetings in Yiddish. Individuals knew how and when to chant, recite in chorus, and read silently, even without instructions from the rabbi. Thus, the rabbi needed not be the leader, for the event was indeed a communal one.

The bar mitzvah boy indicated in the ethnographic interview that he had participated in the Saturday services for many years, and thus was familiar with the sequences, language use, and prayers. Because of this, he was able to fully lead the service. Indeed, he had learned most of the service before actually preparing for the Bar Mitzvah. Because of his advanced preparation and knowledge, at the Friday night service the boy himself, rather than the rabbi, as in Baltimore, welcomed in the Shabbat.

In my questions about what is learned in the schooling that is preparatory to the Bar Mitzvah event, the boy indicted that the Hebrew school merely teaches Judaica, that is, about the Bible and cultural themes in Judaism. "You learn to read Hebrew there, but not the meaning of the reading." In other words, the reading is decoding alone, without knowing the translation of the words. This Bar Mitzvah boy, however, had attended the Hebrew day school until fifth grade, and therefore was not only able to read the prayers in Biblical Hebrew, but was also fluent in conversational Hebrew. He was unusual in that his preparations went far beyond what is typical in North American Jewish communities. His attendance of Hebrew day school gave him the ability to utilize all of the language skills in this special day of his coming of age.

The portion of the Torah for this week was a story that continued from that of the last *Shabbat*. Despite the seriousness with which the congregants took the service, there was a pervasive joyous atmosphere throughout. This was evident in such activities as the blessing of one couple that are members of the congregation on their 50th anniversary. Clearly, this couple was attending the service as regular celebrants of the Sabbath, not as guests of the Bar Mitzvah. The community members displayed their group identity as a tightly knit in-group, with such actions as singing in Yiddish of *Mazel Tov* (congratulations) and clapping for the couple.

In the two and one half-hour service, sub-events fluctuated between the congratulatory and the serious. For example, following the congratulations of the golden anniversary was a part of the service intended for prayers for the sick. People were invited to line up to tell the names of those in need of healing, and they received a special prayer for recovery. Following this, the Bar Mitzvah boy once again came up to read and lead in Hebrew. This was followed by a concluding event in which the boy's friends threw confetti at him, and from which he ducked in order to feign worry. At this point, all clapped and sang *Mazel Tov* again, but this time to the Bar Mitzvah boy.

Like the Baltimore celebrants, the boy here also made a speech about the meaning of his Torah reading to his own life. Preparations entailed some consistent face-to-face interaction with the Rabbi in a sort of mentoring relationship. The boy and Rabbi had met once per week for several weeks prior to the Bar Mitzvah to discuss the boy's participation and prepare him for the service and ceremony. Regarding the preparation of his speech, the boy indicated that he spent some time doing research on the internet to see how people commented on that portion of the Torah, the literal meaning and what was actually happening. "I looked for lines that I could use as analogies to real life. I think that's really important, because not everyone understands all of the Hebrew. I mean, it sounds nice, it's a nice tune, but not everyone understands what's going on. So I feel that the Torah reading is very important because everyone can then, you can show everyone what's really going on."

In contradistinction to Baltimore, in this congregation the rabbi's speech focused directly on the boy's life in relation to the reading's teaching. The speeches of the Bar Mitzvah boy and the Rabbi in this service were coherent with the Bar Mitzvah celebration. From the ethnographic interviews conducted for this study with the celebrant, his family, and the Rabbi, it emerged that the Rabbi of this congregation looks for ways to make analogies to the Bar Mitzvah in his sermons. The boy commented, "It's nice that he does that at all the Bar and Bat Mitzvahs. It shows that he actually cares."

Only upon completing his sermon did the Rabbi say a few words of a political nature, when he offered a prayer for the US leaders to bring peace to their international dealings and negotiations. Indeed, such a prayer focusing on issues in the larger world forms a regular part of the final portion of the service in this congregation. This alerts the community members that they are part of a wider community that, despite not sharing in the in-group norm for the conduct and interpretation of speech and behavior, remains an important part of their lives. It reminds the members that they are part of two civilizations: Jews first but also Americans. Indeed, the Rabbi's intention is to connect the individual's lives to the lives of others in the community and the planet.

2.6 Conclusion

The Jewish celebration of a youth's coming of age is an important rite of passage that initiates the individual as a full-fledged member of the adult religious community. The structure of the Bar or Bat Mitzvah varies according to the type of congregation (e.g. Orthodox, Reformed, Conservative) and the demographics of the particular community. A consistent sociolinguistic fact is that the celebration of the mitzvah is embedded within an ordinary, typical Shabbat service, forming but a part of that service. In some synagogues, the celebrant conducts the service in almost its entirety, as we saw above in the Bar Mitzvah. This has nothing to do with the gender of the celebrant. Indeed, Bat Mitzvahs follow the same structure in that congregation, with the girls conducting all or most of the Shabbat service. The extent to which the youth leads is more dependent upon individual abilities than general policy. Demographics play a role in the variation of extent participation from one congregation to another. In the Baltimore community, which has a rather large Jewish population, it is often the case that more than one Bar or Bat Mitzvah takes place on the same day. When a congregation has so many youth going through the rite of passage each year, it is only logical that the celebrants play a more minor role in the regular service, lest the services be rendered "pediatric," according to the Gainesville Rabbi. In a smaller community such as Gainesville, with a Jewish population of only some 650 Jewish families among a population of 150,000, the youth are able to play a more major role, given willingness and readiness.

In sum, the Bat and Bar Mitzvah form a part of the services to celebrate the Shabbat. The service as a speech situation has many sub events and predominating speech acts that range from the spiritual (e.g. blessing, praying, chanting), to the social (e.g. greeting, congratulating) and intellectual (e.g. debating). The youth's initiation into the adult religious community entails a process of many years of enculturation, with formal training, face-to-face interaction with the spiritual leader, and social participation. The process of becoming a member of the in-group is one in which the acquisition of communicative competence is paramount.

3.   Conclusion: Face-to-face in the religious domain

Talk in religious interaction has up to now been sparsely studied. From a sociolinguistic perspective, such talk is an important part of the lives of many in North American speech communities. Becoming a member of a religious in-group entails acquiring the norms and rules of interaction of that group. Communicative competence in religious interaction encompasses knowing the structure of services, knowing when and how to perform speech acts or be silent, knowing how to appropriately address, greet and congratulate fellow members, and generally knowing when and how to pray, recite, worship, rejoice, chant, bless, and thank God. The norms differ greatly from one religion to another, from one denomination to another, and, even within the same denomination of a religion, from one region or speech community to another. In an increasingly alienating world, religious interaction, whether it is face-to-face, face-to-faces, or faces-to-faces, is an important part of finding a sense of belonging to a community. Without this sense of belonging, we are left with isolation.

Note

1. Conservative Judaism is an approach to the Jewish religion that is neither Orthodox (traditional) nor Reform (modern).

CHAPTER 6

Face-to-face in the workplace domain

1. Introduction

Face-to-face interaction in the workplace has great importance for career success, harmonious interactions with co-workers, and satisfactory encounters with personnel in service and institutional encounters. While there has been a great deal of research published in the past decade on this aspect of discourse, much of this work emanates out of fields other than linguistics: sociology, psychology, and social psychology, for example. Because of this, some of the research that focuses on workplace interactions has more to do with behavior other than language. In the past several years, however, new studies have appeared on talk in workplace interactions, many of these specifically focusing on institutional and service contexts.

The research overviewed in this chapter is thus divided between three types of interactions within the workplace domain: (1) service encounters; (2) institutional encounters; and (3) workplace encounters. The two former categories are included here since they have great relevance for day to day well being in the work world. For example, the work of Gumperz (1982) outlines in microanalytic detail the pitfalls of infelicitous communication in institutional and service encounters, focusing particularly on *cross-cultural interactions*. I review here other work on institutional and service encounters that deals with face-to-face interactions among people of the same or similar speech communities in mostly North American contexts. My intention is to demonstrate that the pitfalls are found not only in cross-cultural interactions where individuals do not share the same norms of speaking and interaction. Indeed, differing expectations of such encounters exist even *within* a speech community and are often at the root of interactional dissatisfaction.

An important text on workplace talk among native speakers who ostensibly share norms of speaking is Drew and Heritage's *Talk at Work* (1992). This edited volume contains many important studies that exemplify conversation analytic approaches to talk in institutional settings. Most of them analyze data in British and European contexts, including news interviews (Greatbatch; Clayman); job interviews (Button), court and legal proceedings (Atkinson; Drew), medical and psychiatric encounters (Heath; Bergmann; Maynard; Heritage and Sefi), to give some examples. Indeed, the volume is seminal in that it is one of the first to take talk in institutional interactions as its sole focus.

Participation in institutional and service encounters comprises an increasingly large part of our everyday lives. When these take place face-to-face, as they often do, they are likely to result in varying degrees of frustration depending largely upon the interactional skills of the participants involved. There is often tension in such encounters, for the variables of institutional power and status are at work when there is inequality of power behind one of the interlocutors. This frequently creates a situation in which the person in the role of requesting service or attention may need to find some interactional way to "grease the wheels" in these sorts of encounters. This is not true of all types of service encounters. Indeed, where a service is being provided for which the customer pays, the old adage "the customer is always right" may still in many cases prevail. In such interactions, it is the task of the person in the role of server to grease the wheels so that the customer is satisfied and therefore builds loyalty to the provider (e.g. restaurant or retail establishment) and thus spends more disposable income.

It should become clear, then, that workplace encounters offer examples of face-to-face discourse in several different types of contexts, not all of which focus on solidarity with others for the simple sake of solidarity. Indeed, in some contexts roles are specifically adversarial. Whether it is to get ahead in one's career, to sell more of a product, or simply to "get one's way" when dealing with bureaucracy, this type of face-to-face interaction is an important aspect of everyday life. Why is it that one person is able to move ahead in the career sphere when another of equal background, training and capability is stifled in doing so? The answer often lies in the realm of interactional skills. The same is true of bureaucratic encounters. There are those who arm themselves for a "fight" when anticipating dealing with red tape, or even a simple matter of returning merchandise for refund. There are others who deal with such situations with equanimity of spirit, and often get what they want more easily. As for institutional encounters, we can learn much from the study of talk in this sphere. How to get the information we need to make informed decisions, how to present our case in a favorable light, how to present ourselves as we wish, are some examples of the importance of knowing what we as speakers can do to achieve our goals. The aim of this chapter is to offer to the reader some insights into how communicative competence in workplace and institutional encounters can help us greatly in this important domain of our day-to-day lives. The chapter culminates with an example of face-to-face interaction in a specific workplace setting, a brokerage house.

1.1   Talk in service encounters

Sociolinguistic research on service encounters dates back at least to the work of Marilyn Merritt (1977), with several published pieces that derived from this larger research project. One of these, published in that very year, described what the author referred to as the "playback." The playback move is done by the server in order to reiterate the name of a requested item, and is typically accomplished with interrogative intonation. As such, it serves as a confirmation check. This playback provides an opportunity for the customer to correct any error in uptake on the part of the server, thus contributing to a satisfactory service encounter in that the customer obtains what s/he set out to. Analysis of one type of move such as this in a service encounter is microanalytic analysis par excellence. While it is true that we rarely think about such small pieces of language, applying sociolinguistics brings to our attention the functions of such moves. Knowing that a confirmation check in a service encounter can help to smooth the interaction helps to accomplish the goals of the service.

Other small units within the service encounters further illustrate how small pieces of discourse can have big impacts. Merritt (1984) is a well-known piece focusing on the use of "OK" in service encounters. In service encounters, she notes, OK is normally not approbative but rather signals that an action requested by the customer is about to commence. Likewise, on the customer's part the use of OK does not signal approval but rather that she or he has satisfactorily examined the requested item or considered the requested service. Moreover, Merritt demonstrates that this expression is also used as a bridging device, releasing the server from current obligation.

Merritt's pioneering work on service encounters serves to inform us of the uses and functions of micro features of talk. Such understanding is particularly relevant to cross-cultural communication. Native speakers ought to know the functions and uses of service encounter moves and recognize them for their communicative value. This knowledge is normally below the level of consciousness. Miscommunication occurs when the norms for their use differ across speech communities. Even from one region to another, small nuances may change the valence of meaning for small expressions. Merritt's ethnographic analyses of the discourse of service encounters are useful in examining the use of small moves in a stretch of service encounter discourse.

Other early research on service was carried out by Butler and Snizek (1976) focusing on waitress-diner interaction. The primary goal of this research was to study how servers work to increase the tab and thereby increase the tip. This type of study has important implications for both servers and customers that are particularly relevant to present-day life in the US, as more and more people take their meals in restaurants. First, the authors note that status differentiation is made salient in such types of service encounters via the titles and address terms utilized by the participants: customers are addressed as "ma'am" or "sir" while servers are not. Given the status differential between customer and server, one of the few if only ways that servers can exert control over the reward structure of the job is to participate in a certain communicative activities that result in "tab building" (p. 210).

The researchers utilized a quasi-experimental design along with observation of talk that enabled comparison between the treatment group and the group receiving no treatment. The experimental group participated in manipulative strategies such as suggesting appetizers, increased alcoholic consumption, and dessert. When asked for a recommendation, the server's strategy would take the form of suggesting the most expensive item. Results showed that the mean tab of the experimental group was significantly higher than that of the control group. "In short, it would appear that the waitress is able to influence diners' consumption by means of initiation ('getting the jump'), suggestion, recommendation, or a combination thereof" (221).

This research is relevant to our discussion in two ways. First, it makes salient techniques that restaurant servers can employ in order to make more money. Second, it illustrates for those of us who dine in restaurants some of the implicit mechanisms used so that we can recognize attempts to manipulate our choices in ordering food and beverages. Thus, it is clearly very relevant to people in modern urban societies where home dining is an increasing rarity.

These research studies have a common thread: the customer and server or sales associate, whether it be in a department store, hairdresser or barber shop, or restaurant, have face needs and desires that may be in competition with their need and desire to make money. They may want to increase their commission or tip by establishing rapport with their customers; however, they also wish establish their credibility. These two needs are often in conflict: their wish to display their expertise (and thus their status superiority in this specific realm) is often incompatible with establishing solidarity. Sales personnel thus walk a fine line between these competing needs. The knowledge of how to accomplish both goals at the same time can greatly aid in felicitous service encounters for both customers and sales associates.

Examples of these competing needs are highlighted in three studies on interactions having to do with haircuts and makeup. Hamilton (1997) analyzed how we communicate what we perceive as desired results in interactions at the hairdresser or barbershop. The goal of the study was to ascertain how we negotiate meaning of what we want in a haircut, accurately conveying our intentions to the server. Hamilton videotaped six segments between hairdressers (both male and female) and clients of different genders and ages. Her findings indicated that repetition was the most important discourse device in maintaining involvement and keeping attention. Moreover, the negotiational uses of repetition and reformulation helped to achieve a common conceptualization of the cut or style desired by the client. The reformulation of the initial utterance to an increasingly more specific utterance was found to be vital to achieving a common understanding of what the client wished the hairdresser to do.

Another study on hairdresser encounters, Jacobs-Huey (1996), focused on hair negotiations in an African-American beauty salon. The researcher here analyzed how such negotiations in this setting reflected identity display and development. Studying the discourse strategies of typical encounters in this particular salon in this speech community, Jacobs-Huey noted that clients and hairdressers attempt to build a relationship of trust through conversations that focus not only on hair but also on personal issues. In the hair negotiations, both client and server negotiated expertise, co-constructing the co-expertise of the client. Clients often discussed their concerns, based on past negative experience, with hair damage due to caustic chemical treatments for perms that led to scalp burning and hair loss. These conversations gave evidence of client knowledge that aided in the negotiation of hair treatments to avoid such dangers. When this occurred, the server also engaged in strategies to build up her/his professionalism. Expertise was thus bandied back and forth between the interlocutors:

> I have observed hairdressers do the "certified expert thing" in several conventionalized ways. As one black hair care specialist noted at an educational seminar for hairdressers: 'sometimes you have to lay hair science on them [clients] so that you can get your clients to see your vision' (1996: 333).

The discourse strategies that predominated in the hair negotiations in this beauty salon were indirectness, signifying, and he-said/she-said, all used to maintain harmony and balance of the expert/novice statuses. In such a way not only hair treatments, but more importantly perhaps trust, were negotiated.

Hamilton's and Jacob-Huey's studies are examples of seemingly insignificant but important moves in service encounters that have the ability to teach us what to do to get what we want. This kind of research shows how we can use talk-in-interaction to achieve the type of haircut or hair treatment we envision. From an ordinary communicative perspective, knowing how to use such strategies as he-said/she-said, indirectness, repetition and reformulation in may indeed be below the level of consciousness of most speakers. However, when this kind of knowledge is brought to our awareness, as it is in this research, we benefit. While it is true that haircuts may not be life-or-death phenomena, they are important everyday activities for many, both women and men. Many of us no doubt recall at least one instance in our lives in which a visit to the barber or hairdresser resulted in tears.

Along the lines of this research is a very interesting study on cosmetic service encounters. Sniad (1998) analyzed face-to-face interactions in purchases of cosmetics at in a department store. Her study, aptly entitled, "Games with Face," examined the ways that women, in the context of department store cosmetic counters, perceive and express their social identities and how those identities are affected and often even defined by cultural concepts of beauty. The findings suggest that customers and sales associates frequently experience a sense of competition with each other on the basis of beauty (or knowledge of beauty products) which tends to clash with their intentions to build solidarity. Specifically, the sales associates recognize that building rapport with customers could potentially boost sales and earn repeat customers. At the same time, however, establishing their status as cosmetic experts is very important to them, and asserting their knowledge and expertise can either boost sales or adversely affect the sales. The customers seem to see solidarity with the associates as a means of improving the service they obtain. At the same time, they have a need to be recognized as a customer, which inherently deserves a certain level of respect.

In the sales encounters, both the customers and the associates employed common discourse strategies to indicate either their desire to build solidarity or assert status (i.e. increase or decrease their social distance). This approach/avoidance struggle between the women in their different roles is what Sniad referred to as "face games." Throughout the interactions, both women expressed and interpreted the relationship they desired, the perceived desire of the interlocutor, and the social identity they wished to project. For example, the associates might suggest an interest in building rapport through the use of inclusive pronouns, compliments, commiseration, repetition, and/or accommodation. Assertion of status was achieved by their failure to redress face, their use of bald on record utterances, and their use of inclusive pronouns and in-group terms to designate other sales associates that kept the customer in the position of outsider.

The findings of this study in no way suggest that all women are affected by or concerned with the same appearance issues or in the same ways. The participants' willingness to invest time and money in order to meet certain societal expectations for female beauty, however, was a commonality among all the female participants in the study. It may therefore be argued that these women were more vulnerable to the face games in these interactions and that the same women may engage in different interactional strategies in other types of sales encounters.

Rhetorical strategies of service encounters, particularly those used to ascertain the purposes of the customer in store purchasing, are the focus of a study by Lamoureaux (1988/89). An important aspect of the discussion focuses on embeddings, or instances where sales personnel address the needs of a new customer while still serving a previous customer. This phenomenon has always been of interest to me, as it certainly must be to many. For example, an issue is why is it that servers often they take phone calls as a priority over live customers? This type of interruption of service occurs so frequently in modern service encounters as to be frustrating. One cannot help but wonder if it is easier to accomplish the service encounter by phone, since phone callers often take priority.

An issue brought up by reading Lamoreaux's study is how to get a server's attention, while not appearing to interrupt or be rude, when s/he is still serving another. Clearly, the norms for accomplishing these tasks differ regionally as well as idiosyncratically. One would certainly find differences in the propensity to interrupt between New York and Midwestern cities, for example (see Beebe, 1995 on rudeness in New York City). What is considered rude in one place or by one person may indeed be typical and accepted face-to-face interaction in another community. Lamoreaux's study merely scratched the surface of probing these differences. Since that study, internet service encounters have become a normal, accepted way of obtaining goods and services. Service encounters are thus rapidly losing their face-to-face nature, rendering some of the issues discussed above moot.

1.2   Talk in institutional encounters

Service encounters are similar to institutional encounters but with distinctions that render them different in interlocutor expectations. Karen Tracy (1997) outlines this very clearly in her work on emergency 911 calls. She highlights how interactional troubles in such calls stem from differences in frame expectations between callers and call-takers, with callers expecting a customer service (service encounter) frame while receiving a public service (institutional encounter) frame instead.

> A service encounter of any type could be framed as customer service, but historically some services have been treated as different in kind. Emergency service, I would suggest, is one of them. It differs from most services we think of as customer ones in that the served person does not pay directly (320).

911 callers frequently feel anger, frustration and exasperation when their perceived needs are not met. This is to a large extent a result of call-takers' requests for information about location and other details to determine both the urgency of the call as well as whether the caller is within the geographic limits of the particular 911 service. Tracy asserts that emergency service is not only committed to helping citizens, but also to creating a safe way for its officers to help and to catch offenders. Interactional troubles most often occur in reaction to call-takers' questioning. Callers, on the other hand, expect fast service as well as an estimate of the speed of service, as they would in such service encounters as ordering takeout food.

Implications of this research reside in changing the expectations of both the callers and call-takers. First, callers can learn the constraints of call-takers and emergency service providers, and be ready with such information as location and supporting details of the situation. Conversely, call-takers might benefit from some further training in how to calm callers and treat them politely within the constraints of their information gathering.

Another good example of institutional discourse that has great potential to go awry is McElhinny's (1995) research on female and male police officers' handling of domestic violence. Through analysis of two scenes involving a female and a male officer, she demonstrates that female officers may take on traditionally male characteristics of interaction, such as coolness and "all business." "Emotion is a limited commodity and using it means losing it." (227). Thus, both female and male officers in such scenes exhibit impartiality and objectivity. Complainants, on the other hand, expect more sympathy from female officers than they get. McElhinny aptly demonstrates how such situations cause what she terms "facelessness" in face-to-face interactions. When personal comments do come at or near the end of these interactions, they show a marked shift in frame from the official goings on. Thus, both female and male officers employ the same linguistic strategies when taking down the accounts and writing their reports: lack of emotional response, absence of backchannels, long silences, absence of expected responses in adjacency pairs. "The cost of professionalization to citizens (female and male) may be the absence of freely offered sympathy at some of the most stressful moments of their lives" (239).

We have the ability to learn a great deal from the study of institutional encounters in our day-to-day lives. We are increasingly dependent upon individuals who are unknown to us and who serve in capacities to provide needed help, whether it be police, legal, medical, or otherwise. Many of our daily face-to-face interactions focus on dealing with such personnel. Our ability to know what to do with language can greatly facilitate how smoothly these interactions are accomplished and how quickly we achieve what we set out to do. Indeed, it may be a life or death situation.

Knowing the expectations of institutional encounters can help us through some of the most challenging of such encounters. I noted earlier in this chapter that Drew and Heritage's 1992 volume on institutional encounters, *Talk at Work*, offers many fine examples of just how true this is. One of the few articles in that text that analyzes North American discourse data is Drew's own analysis of courtroom cross-examination in a rape case. His ethnographic approach to the data analysis informs us of linguistic strategies used to discredit a witness as well as how witnesses can prevent being discrediting despite having relatively less power in this context. Drew focuses on how attorneys produce inconsistencies in witnesses' testimonies through specific types of questioning. He also notes that witnesses have the ability to counter this goal by answering in such a manner as not to deny but to give a different version of what the attorney is trying to present. By knowing this, a witness is able to subvert the attorney's attempts to manipulate the unfolding of a full account of events leading up to the crime.

It should be very evident by this point that there is much to be learned by reading sociolinguistic analyses of talk in institutional encounters. Power may be inherent in the position of one of the interlocutors (i.e. the attorney as opposed to the witness); however, this power can be expertly manipulated or even subverted with full knowledge of how to do things with words. In the case of medical emergencies, criminal actions, or legal interactions, such knowledge is not only important, it is crucial. Without it we are left unable to present ourselves as we wish and/or unable to get the help we need.

1.3   Talk at work

We turn now to research that exemplifies workplace encounters in which co-workers and colleagues communicate with each other. There is a rather abundant literature on the subject, perhaps most notably the work of sociolinguist Deborah Tannen, in her best-selling book, *Talking From Nine to Five* (1994). Gender as a sociolinguistic variable is salient in a fair portion of research on face-to-face interaction in the workplace. That gender takes such a prominent place in sociolinguistic studies of the workplace is no doubt due to the fact that status and power differences are inherent in workplace contexts, where they are built into organizational hierarchies. The study of gender in the workplace has been undertaken from various perspectives. Tannen and others highlight how gender is confounded with status and power precisely because female/male differences in linguistic style constrain how women and men are perceived and thus how status and power are achieved. The fact that Tannen's work has been made accessible to a lay public has opened up to non-linguists the potential importance of studies in face-to-face discourse in building more harmonious workplaces. This is not without its controversy, however, as we have seen previously (in the chapter on social interaction). Sociolinguists who take the stance of male dominance as opposed to female/male difference take issue with Tannen's viewpoint. These scholars hold that women's style is undervalued and should be venerated. Before giving the reader an overview of the counter-arguments, let us first turn to a short piece by Deborah Tannen that serves as a very good overview of her research on workplace talk.

Tannen (1995) was written for the *Harvard Business Review* in order to explicate aspects of misperceptions of male and female ability in the workplace due to different communicative styles. Several of these communicative mismatches are shown to affect female ability to move upwards in the career ladder. Tannen asserts that female/male differences are due to differences in child socialization, affecting judgements of competence, confidence, and getting heard. These style differences are well documented in the literature on gender and language (e.g. Maltz and Borker, 1983). While girls tend to focus on affiliation in early relationships, boys focus on status and hierarchy. Girls learn from early on not to sound too self-confident. This is particularly problematic when male managers judge female employees by their own norms. Women differ from men in several aspects of linguistic style: "...directness or indirectness, pacing and pausing, word choice, and the use of such elements as jokes, figures of speech, stories, questions, and apologies" (243). Women's style of politeness and indirectness makes us seem less self-assured. Women are more likely than men to ask questions, making us vulnerable to perceptions of lack of knowledge. Moreover, women say, "I'm sorry" more than men to indicate commiseration and as a simple politeness device. These seeming apologies are not apologies at all; however, they do serve to make women appear weaker and less competent. Talking up or down their achievements is another salient difference between the two sexes. Male style of talking up is likely to negotiate their moving up. When women take on these traditionally more male features of talk we are deemed "bossy" or even "bitchy." Women, as opposed to men, have the desire not to sound boastful.

Recall that Tannen has been criticized by feminist linguists as taking too strong a "difference" point of view, ignoring issues of power and dominance of men over women through language and non-verbal behavior. Senta Troemel-Ploetz has been one of her severest critics. Troemel-Ploetz (1991) pointed out that while males have power in the workplace, women's management style is perceived as preferable by both female and male workers. She asserts that until women achieve some sort of power in their personal and professional lives, they will continue to be subject to male domination via language use that is of the male style. The problem, according to her, is not to understand these differences but to venerate female linguistic style as preferable, so that perhaps men can learn from it and adopt it.

Troemel-Ploetz (1994) illuminates just how this female style is preferable in a sociolinguistic analysis of female/male conversational strategies in the workplace. The author maintains that women in leadership positions succeed by using a strategy she terms 'camouflaging a dominant speech act" (200). Some ways of doing this are: calling a request and invitation, convincing and persuading rather than ordering, positive mirroring, sharing power rather than asserting authority, suggesting rather than criticizing. Both Troemel-Ploetz and Tannen discuss the female use of the pronoun 'we' as an inclusive gesture, showing a concern for reducing status differences. However, in keeping with the 'women's style as preferable' theme, Troemel-Ploetz summarizes by stating:

> [this style] is a more egalitarian, more democratic and in the end more humane way of dealing with people…it would be preferable to the command-and-control style, simply because it is more ethical; it is preferable because the values that underlie it are more humane values. (1994: 209).

Hence, while Tannen's approach is to have the sexes come to an understanding of each other, Troemel-Ploetz's approach is a call to learn from women's style so that women, indeed all, can benefit.

Many other female sociolinguists have analyzed gender differences in language use of the workplace. One example is Statham's (1987) study of women managers. Statham found women to be more people-oriented, leading to more satisfaction by their subordinates. Her data indicate that women are also more task-oriented. Women's increased concern for their employees was found to be motivating for their subordinates. The men interviewed by Statham focused on the importance of their jobs. She called this orientation 'image engrossment.' Men delegated more than women did and in a different way. Men's delegation led to less involvement with their subordinates. When women delegated, they were perceived as more involved with the task. Women and men both seemed to prefer their own styles. "Men who truly used the person-investment style with women subordinates were very appreciated" (424). The author concludes that these differences in style make it difficult for women and men to work together happily.

The body of research on gender differences in workplace interactions leads to the conclusion that women's styles have positive implications for the workplace. In order to get ahead and achieve career success, many women have thought it necessary to take on typically male interactional styles. This situation is unfortunate, given the findings that women are perceived aggressive at best when doing so. Moreover, it is unfortunate that women's leadership styles still prevent women from gaining access to more leadership positions. If the findings of the above studies are any indication, women's affiliative style is indeed a positive one in the workplace. Rather than try to become something that we are not, we ought to be able to lead in a different way. Indeed, men can and should learn something from women's style in the workplace. There is clearly a mismatch when workers claim to be more satisfied with the styles of women leadership and management, while at the same time the world at large and the business world in particular remain hostile to this style. Clearly, that which is associated with women's language and behavior remains derogated. Until women achieve more power in the workplace, the situation is likely to remain unchanged. Therein is the catch: in order to move up and ahead, women need to become more powerful. On the other hand, as long as women speak like women we are denied power. Studying face-to-face interaction in the workplace is the first step in coming to terms with this quandary.

There are many other studies relevant to workplace face-to-face interactions that deal with issues other than gender differences. An interesting example of a speech behavior that has important implications for workplace success with superiors and colleagues is a study by Hall and Valde (1995) on 'brown-nosing' in organizational life. The authors outline the problem with perceived brown-nosing in the workplace: "The idea of the brown-noser going beyond necessary requirements of politeness or the job itself is consistently linked to the ulterior goals of getting attention or advancement" (399). Excess seems to be the operational difference between ordinary politeness and brown-nosing. Persons who engage in such verbal behavior expect to maximize their personal value to their superiors. However, the perception of falseness is what characterizes the speech behavior as extremely negative. The implicit perception of interviewees in this study is that workplaces ought to be meritocracies. Brown nosers are portrayed as two-faced, artificial, and selfish. Getting along with colleagues is thus impeded if one is perceived to be a brown-noser. Cultural values that are revealed in the study of brown-nosing are (1) the importance of being a team player; and (2) valuing honesty and straightforward competition.

One of the most studied aspects of workplace discourse has been the use of humor. Humor can serve many purposes in work life, from getting employees on your side to smoothing over the necessity of asserting power relationships that may otherwise be resented, or at least not appreciated. Vinton (1989) analyzed the functions and uses of humor in a small, family owned business with only 12 office employees, where working as a team is emphasized. She documented several different types of humor: "teasing to get work done, joke telling, bantering, and teasing to get across a criticism to a higher-status person" (154). The first of these, teasing to get work done, was most prevalent along with self-deprecating humor and banter. Indeed, punch lines of jokes tended to poke fun at the joke teller. Teasing occurred within and between the different status jobs. For example, one function of teasing by a higher status employee of one of lower status was to get that individual to do a job, but the directive voiced humorously was more pleasant, of course, than a bald-on-record directive. Indeed, in such a small organization, everyone was found to tease and banter with everyone else, to the extent that such workplace humor was perceived as a "great leveler" (161).

Vinton's conclusions are that humor served to socialize members into the organization. Indeed, those who did not invite joking and teasing were not well socialized into this workplace. The author concludes that humor in this context served many important functions, perhaps the most important of which was to create an atmosphere of teamwork and cooperation, even with the owner and CEO. The bonding aspect of these speech behaviors is important. Implications are that lighthearted humor in the workplace can create high levels of employee satisfaction.

The use of humor in a homeless advocacy organization in the US is the focus of a study by Yedes (1996). The workplace relationship here is distinct from the traditional types of organizations described above, in that it is composed of mostly volunteers doing work for a community in need. Thus, rather than a for-profit business, this was a non-profit, more egalitarian organization dealing with intense issues. Everyone was open to being teased and to being the teaser in such a stressful workplace context. Humor served as a means to release the tension of the seriousness of the work of dealing with hundreds of homeless individuals on a daily basis. Yedes analyzed teases that reflected tensions in enacting social justice. She notes that joking enabled the staff to bond and thus better deal with these tensions and further enabling them to negotiate with each other and still maintain harmony. Humor in this workplace allowed for an atmosphere in which work was equally divided among staff; in which staff set their own deadlines (thus humor has a diffusing function); in which differences were noted but egalitarian relationships maintained.

Humor has been amply studied in various domains, particularly in social interactions. While much of the research on humor has been found to serve the purpose of establishing rapport between interlocutors, there are types of humor that can serve to bond members of an in-group while excluding those who are outsiders. Such is the case of the workplace that is described in the following study, researched collaboratively with Andrea DeCapua.

2. An in-depth analysis of workplace speech behavior: Bragging, boasting and bravado: Male banter in a brokerage house

This study is an ethnographic analysis of male boasting behavior in the workplace setting of a brokerage firm. The spirit of competition inherent in this context is reflected and maintained in social interaction among white male colleagues both in and out of the office setting. The men whose language is studied here attempt to establish and reinforce their standing within a continually fluctuating hierarchical order via a form of boasting and banter that emphasizes sexual prowess and athletic abilities — traditional male domains. In these verbal exchanges, the brokers make constant use of profanity. Selnow (1985) points out that profanity plays a unique role in groups in that it may serve to provide linguistic bonding among members of an in-group while at the same time intentionally or unintentionally alienating others. Recent media attention has, in fact, noted that colorful and profuse profanity is one of the hallmarks of verbal interactions among brokers: "At many brokerage firms, 'traders can't go through a whole sentence without the f-word'…. Profanity is part of the patois" (Siconolfi and Auerbach 1996: 1). We examine such banter in terms of the performance and construction of social identity (e.g. Goffman 1967; 1974; Erickson and Schultz 1982; Hamilton 1995) and its consequences for in-group bonding and out-group alienation.

2.1 Background

Bragging and boasting are typically defined as synonyms of each other. To brag is to use arrogant or boastful language. To boast is to speak with exaggeration or excessive pride, especially about oneself. Boasting subsumes proud or vainglorious speech — "tall talk". Bravado is defined as a swaggering display of courage. Banter is an exchange of light, playful teasing remarks; good-natured raillery. It also includes making fun of people, or holding them up to ridicule (Oxford English Dictionary 1971; Random House Dictionary 1987). The speech behavior described here reflects all of these elements.

Linguistic studies of boasting as a speech behavior are scant; that which has been carried out tends to investigate the speech act/event with reference to gender as a sociolinguistic variable. Miller, Cooke, Tsang and Morgan (1992) distinguished between "positive" and "boastful" disclosures. In contrasting these disclosures they found that boasting embodies competitive language typically associated with masculinity; positive disclosures were associated with feminine speech behavior. Likewise, Rodriquez and Ryave's 1995 study of competitive management of face among mentally retarded male adults noted that aggravated disagreements included bragging and fabrications. These were tools for the establishment of personal inferiority and superiority.

Little research has been carried out on bragging and boasting per se; nonetheless, much work has been done on conversational humor that is relevant to the present discussion (See, e.g. Apte 1985; Attardo 1994; Boxer and Cortes-Conde 1997; Davies, 1986; Drew 1987; Johnstone, et. al. 1992; Kotthoff 1986; Long and Graesser 1998; Norrick 1994). This literature suggests that humor can function to "facilitate in-group interaction and strengthen in-group bonding or out-group rejection" (Attardo 1994: 32).

While humor that incorporates wit is highly valued in our society, it is also a means for social control. Drew (1987) clearly illustrates this mechanism in his focus on the manner in which teasing functions as a response to complaining, extolling or bragging. A study by Johnstone, Ferrara and Bean (1992) further corroborates the notion that joking and teasing function differently for women and men. The authors compared female and male telephone interview talk, finding male respondents less compliant and more eager to subvert the interview with teasing or banter. Moreover, Kotthoff (1986) found that for women humor establishes "intimacy" while for men humor is often realized as a form of aggression and domination (p. 22).

Humor, including teasing, is certainly valued by the members of the speech community studied here. The ubiquitous workplace banter is not only a primary bonding tool but at the same time an important exclusionary mechanism. This study builds on previous research in conversational humor by (1) focusing on a certain type or subcategory of humor (i.e. boastful humor), and (2) by analyzing the gender consequences of such humor within a workplace setting.

Thirty sequences of bragging and boasting were taken from spontaneous conversational interactions in the brokerage house and after hours in outside settings where colleagues socialized. The data consist of audio-taped transcribed sequences as well as field notes. In addition, five ethnographic interviews were conducted with four of the male brokers and one with the female office manager. Categories emerged from the analysis.

2.2   The workplace

The brokerage firm is located in suburban Washington, DC. This is an office setting where compensation is pure commission; the brokers receive a percentage of sales of stock and they must reach a certain gross production per month in order to remain in the company. Daily and monthly totals are posted. As one informant stated, "Everyone's aware of how everyone's doing; it's sometimes like a contest. It's a peer thing, a decent motivational tool. Intelligence has nothing to do with it. It's pure sales — excitement." In essence, a good stockbroker is a good salesman and monetary reward is everything.

The office consists of a large room filled with desks on which sit computers and phones. The only division between the brokers is low partitions about 2–3 feet high. Everyone is easily visible and audible to everyone else. There is minimal privacy and the workspace is called "The Bullpen," a standard industry metaphor derived from the sport of baseball.[1] As described by Pete:

> You're less than three feet away from the guy sitting next to you, so everyone hears everyone's conversation, both business and social.

All of the brokers are male, and all but one are white North Americans between the ages of 24–35. They all have college degrees, played athletics in college and were members of fraternities. They come from various parts of the East Coast and have worked together for the past two to four years. The one male who does not fit this profile is Isaac from Nigeria, and thus is not included in our data. Isaac, although well liked and respected, is not a member of the in-group and does not socialize with the other brokers after work. As a born-again Christian, he is very involved in his church and religious activities, and does not drink, dance or engage in mating rituals.

The two women who work in the office with the stockbrokers also have college degrees. Debbie, although a licensed stockbroker, works as the boss's (Bill) assistant; Pam is the person in charge of trades and making sure the necessary paperwork is completed. These women are salaried; however, Debbie also receives a 5% commission based on Bill's sales. When male informants were questioned as to the absence of female stockbrokers, they indicated that the high level of stress and competitiveness of the field were unattractive not only to females, but to most people. As Sam put it, "99% of the population can't do what we do, and only 10% of the other 1% make it after 5 years. If I were a woman I wouldn't work here." Accordingly, women are even less likely than men to enter this field and stay in it.

The members of this speech community participate regularly in a speech event we term here "intense bantering" or "jousting." Jousting derives from the notion of engaging in mock combat where winning is a matter of besting rather than terminating one's opponent. In verbal jousting the loser either has no effective repartee or listeners (overhearers/audience participants) laugh at the victor's last response.

The men are under a great deal of pressure to sell stocks. One informant, Pam, indicates that the bragging, boasting and bravado we describe here are outlets for stress: "It's sometimes fun, but it's sometimes tense". Brokers' productivity is governed by the vicissitudes of the stock market. Based upon our analysis of the data we contend that these bantering exchanges are attempts by the brokers to display themselves as competent and powerful individuals. Furthermore, because humor functions as a release valve for the tensions as well as a means of social control, the humor inherent in the bragging, boasting and bravado serves two functions: first it acts as a mechanism for establishing a hierarchical or "pecking" order; second, it serves to bond the members of the group.

2.3   Findings

In this workplace setting social identity display is often "performed"
(Erickson & Schultz 1982). It subsumes sexual bravado and innuendo, display
of quick wit, put downs and one-upsmanship (Maltz & Borker 1983). As we
noted above, profanity is indeed one important component of the performance. Identity is not only displayed and performed on an individual basis, but
as part of the process of "relational identity development" (Boxer & Cortes-
Conde, 1997) or male bonding. This is accomplished through the use of
metaphors of current events, sports, and sex and is constant, contributing to a
"locker-room" atmosphere.

The categories that emerged from the analysis of the data indicate that
bragging, boasting and bravado perform the individual and relational identities of the speakers vis à vis (1) displays of superiority; (2) expressions of sexual
bravado; and (3) quick wit, one-upsmanship and verbal dueling. These are
clearly not mutually exclusive categories.

2.3.1   *Display of superiority*
The brokers spend a considerable amount of time boasting about how and why
each one is superior to the others in the firm. Example 1 was spoken in the
context of Bill bragging to the rest of the office about being the number #1
producer in terms of dollar amount of sales. He uses a favorite topic, the male
sex organ, as a metaphor for success in selling:

(1)   Just picture yourself on top of the Empire State Building with your dick
hanging out, watching yourself peeing down the street.

Although not usually associated with *human* behavior, the need to mark
one's territory among males of certain other species is accomplished by
urinating around the perimeters of the claimed area. Bill is clearly drawing
on theetaphors of being on top of the world and staking out his position to
proclaim his superior status in the brokerage house hierarchy. In the next
example (2), Sam complains that he hasn't been chosen to open a new oYce
in the Tampa area. In the process he expresses his superiority as a broker
through a boast regarding his productivity.

(2)   I'm #1 in the Wrm, I'm kicking butt and they're churning and burning &
Ted is such a frigging whiner that they just don't get along for shit. I'm
not a manager, so they can't send me; I've made more in one transaction
than Ted did all last month, so there are some problems.

This excerpt illustrates another favorite topic in this community — money. Although Sam has been extremely successful in terms of sales and is recognized as being number one among the members of the bullpen, at the time of the data collection he did not have the title of "manager." Hence, Sam felt he was being denied an opportunity open only to those within the next group or class (i.e. managers).

Recall that the most important element in determining prestige is monetary compensation. Because compensation is completely based upon performance, how much brokers earn determines their rank within the bullpen hierarchy. Given the Xuctuations of the stock market and the nature of sales, this hierarchy is in a constant state of change, and anything that improves a broker's standing is cause for celebration — or at least making it public knowledge. Our female informant, Pam, related the following story of an incident that had occurred just a few hours prior to the interview:

(3)   A guy made a couple of trades, made a $1000, stands on his chair, scream ing at the top of his lungs, 'I MADE A THOUSAND DOLLARS!'

Pam indicates that theirs is an oYce of big egos and "macho" behavior: "These men think the world revolves around them."

Personal superiority is not only expressed by boasting of one's sales ability; indeed, the data contain numerous examples of references to physical prowess. All the informants stressed that the men in this Wrm are sports fanatics. They spend a great deal of time both playing and watching all kinds of sporting events. During their lunch hour the brokers often gather in a lounge area to watch sports as they eat. Quite a number of them play together on hockey, softball and basketball teams after work and work out at a nearby gym. For these brokers, sports serve both as bonding and as competition. Moreover, physical prowess, strength, and endurance are prized. One of our consultants, Sam, in introducing sequence 5 (which he overheard) inadvertently bragged about his own capacity for physical abuse:

(4)   Sam: When I play hockey, I'm a very physical guy. I try to block the puck with my body, so it's not so unusual for me to be covered in bruises, you know, you just get used to dealing with the pain; you do what ya gotta do.

Those who don't measure up are subject to ridicule or derision as illustrated by the following example:

(5) Dave: Shit, I got this fucking bruise on my leg from blocking that shot.
Burt: What'd ya want, ya play the game and if ya gotta get physical, ya block the shot with your body. Ya know, you're such a wimp I'm gonna call you Merlot.
Dave: What the fuck're you talking about?
Burt: That's because you bruise like a grape.

Burt not only ridicules Dave for complaining about his 'sports injuries', but in so doing displays his quick wit with his reference to bruising grapes and wine. This has been shown to be an important component of performed social identity.

2.3.2 Sexual bravado

Physical prowess is often equated with sexual prowess. The better athlete is the better lover; in this culture the man in good physical shape is believed to be more likely to attract women. Consider the following excerpt, which takes place in the bullpen:

(6) Dave: You going to the gym today?
Merl: (loud enough for everyone in office to hear) Right now I'm going to get a shirt that says "Under Construction" and in a couple of months I'm gonna get another T-shirt (does flexing pose, everyone is now watching him) "Open for Business".

Clearly Merl's bragging reflects current trends in North American culture that place a premium on well-developed upper bodies in males and their (perceived) attraction for women. This boast is the expression of what Merl considers his own physical superiority; therefore, it is a display of sexual bravado.

Sexual bravado is expressed by these brokers more directly and graphically in their narratives about personal sexual exploits. These are related to the group in an embellished style with vivid exaggerated imagery. Sexual swaggering is salient in (7):

(7) Dave picked up a girl in a bar the previous night while with some of the brokers. Morning after:
Jack: [loud enough for everyone to hear very clearly] So how did it go with Amy?
Dave: [directs himself to others in office who are now listening]. Got this piece last night; you know, the one Ron & Mark picked up last month? Went well.

Jack: So what'd ya do?
Dave: everything.
Jack: So was it different? . . .
Dave: I didn't notice anything different. (laughs). Hey guys, get this. We're just lying there in the morning & the phone rings and it's my mom.
Greg: So what'd ya say?
Dave: I told her I couldn't talk: Ma, I got some girl in bed with me I picked up last night. [everyone laughs].

Jack and Greg set the stage for Dave's narrative by questioning him very loudly about his sexual adventures of the previous night. The attention-getting device creates a public context for Dave's performance. Dave's identity display is a collaborative effort where audience effect is assured (Bell, 1984). Jack and Greg appear to be playing "the straight man" to Dave's narrative in that they ask all the necessary questions leading up to the punch line, "Ma, I got some girl in bed with me I picked up last night." Not only was Dave able to express to his audience that he and Amy did 'everything', but the tale goes beyond the expression of sexual prowess to reveal his flouting of social conventions when he tells his mother why he can't talk. Exaggeration in the performance is a clear case of swaggering; i.e. it seems highly unlikely that Dave really told his mother what he claims to have told her. He expresses his fictitious flouting of social convention in order to enhance his status among his peers. The appeal of a 'rebel against society' has covert prestige in American popular culture, celebrating the sentiment that really tough guys can get away with, or are above standard social conventions.

Examples of breaking social and ethical rules abound in the data and in the ethnographic interview narratives. The purpose of such bravado is to heighten the force of the teller's identity display.

(8)   Over drinks after work, Rob recounts a story about cheating his way through a college course.
      I cheated like a fucking motherfucker in that thing. Every single test I cheated. The final exam comes and I'm like fucking — I have no idea what fucking thing is on there [In the background another broker is panting heavily]. There's this old, old lady [the professor] and she's mean and she's like this business lady and I'm like 'fuck it.' And I see her look at me and I'm like, 'she fucking caught me.' And I'm like, 'fuck it, fuck it'
          [laughter].
      And I go up and hand in my test and she says, 'I want to see you in my

office tomorrow.' I'm like fucking scared shit. The next day I go and she tells me, 'Thank you for being such an asset to the course.'

The thrust of Rob's story is that not only does he successfully cheat, but that he is in fact honored by the professor for his class performance. The prosodic features evident in the oral rendition of the narrative greatly enhance the delivery and thus the identity display. This display of identity is further enhanced by his use of obscenities. Rob's display can be likened to that of a type of tricksters among oral cultures in different societies:

> ...there are trickster figures who are particularly involved in various forms of gross and unreasonable behavior which affront the rules and norms of their society...They violate even the strictest taboos....Thus, one type of trickster is concerned with melting the glue that holds society together, the other with using the system to his own best advantage (Hewitt,1997: 41).

We contend the sort of flouting behavior described here is contrary to how interlocutors typically display themselves in public settings as competent and socially acceptable members of a speech community. The rules in the brokerage house community are clearly different from those of ordinary social conversation (e.g. Drew & Heritage, 1992; Hewitt, 1997; Kiesling, 1997).

2.3.3 Quick wit, one upsmanship and verbal dueling

It is widely agreed that quick wit is a prized talent across many speech communities (Apte, 1985; Attardo, 1994; Kotthoff, 1986; Chiaro, 1992). People who can "think on their feet", particularly using humor, are admired. While this is certainly true in this brokerage house, the topics that are acceptable here go beyond traditional boundaries and transcend ordinary taboos. We see this illustrated in (9) and (10).

(9) Greg and Burt are shooting the breeze after hours in the office. Other brokers are still around.
Greg: So Jane [his girlfriend] wants to visit this weekend, but I'm seeing Sharon, so I gotta figure out how to avoid Jane coming down.
Burt: Look, you can't have your cake and eat it, too. You gotta make a choice at some point. It's not like you get a lot of action anyway.
Greg: Are you kidding me — I've had more women sit on me than a toilet seat at a rest stop on the New Jersey turnpike. (All laugh & sputter)

(10) A group of the office guys are in a bar on Saturday night.
Jack to Pete: . . . like you're Jewish.

Pete: I'm not orcadox!
(group laughs)
Dave: Pete you idiot, don't you mean orthodox?
Pete: No, I mean orcadox. Orca as in your girlfriend and "docks" as in
where she hangs out.
(Group laughs hysterically)

Maltz and Borker (1983) characterize male speech behavior across North American speech communities as filled with verbal posturing, insults and put-downs. We clearly see such jousting in the above sequences. Both (9) and (10) contain put-downs:

(9)   It's not like you get a lot of action anyway.
(10) Pete you idiot
      And both examples contain examples of wit:
(9)   I've had more women sit on me than a toilet seat at a rest stop on the New
      Jersey turnpike.
(10) Orca as in your girlfriend and "docks" as in where she hangs out.

In addition, both sequences include one upsmanship. By this we mean that the quick wit of the addressees diffuses and indeed turns the tables on the speakers' put-downs. Consequently, the addressee comes out ahead not only by having "the last word," but also by demonstrating his ability to think on his feet. In this brokerage house community he who gets the laughs gets status. As has been noted in the literature, scoring points in verbal dueling entails dominating the floor, coming up with ever stronger and better put downs, and having the last word (e.g. Cameron, 1997; Siconolfi and Auerbach, 1996; Tannen, 1990).

The wit in both instances makes reference to a sexual topic, again a favorite subject among these brokers. A difference between (9) and (10) lies in the face-threatening nature of the characterization in (10) of the girlfriend as a fat prostitute. The put-down or even "attack" is no longer centered on the recipient but has now moved to his significant other, typically a more sensitive focus of insult. Regardless, no long-term animosity results. Kotthoff (1996) suggests that "good friends are especially likely to overstep the boundaries of politeness… despite clear impoliteness, many humorous provocations…still have a relationship-affirming character" (p. 299).

As already seen, the brokers engage in verbal dueling, a more developed and extensive form of quick wit and put-down. Example (11) further demonstrates how one-upsmanship develops into verbal dueling:

(11) Dave and Jack have just overheard Brad misspell something to a client over the phone. When Brad finishes the call, they tease him about his poor spelling.

Dave Ya can't tell Pete anything — the guy is just beyond it.

Jack: He's so far gone, he won't ever get it. He's lucky that when he's with women it's his balls and dick that get to do the talking.

Dave: They're not doing him much good either the way I hear it.

Pete: Would ya all shut the fuck up? I make BIG money so who the hell cares how I fucking spell.

Brad: That's right, women don't care about what ya got up there but what ya got between here (stands on desk and points to head and crotch)

Jack: Yeah but ya gotta have something down there or you're a goner

Dave: (to Pete) We're gonna have to start calling you Secretariat cuz you go through life with blinders

Pete: What the hell're you talking about?

Dave: You can't see anything except what's in front of you, Secretariat.

The first quip in the duel is Jack's put-down of Pete, which equates his inability to spell with a lack of verbal ability. This put-down leads to sexual innuendo, sexual insult, reference to earning capacity, and more sexual innuendo, culminating in a final put-down incorporating a witty sports allusion, i.e. equating Pete with a racehorse wearing blinders. Not only is this a witty sports allusion, but it is also a somewhat obscure one in the scheme of sports knowledge trivia. Consequently, we can argue that Dave has won this round in the joust not only by using his wit against Pete, but also by demonstrating his superior sports knowledge.

2.4 Discussion

The competitive spirit of this particular workplace setting ensures that the brokers who participate successfully in the verbal exchanges or duels bond into a cohesive group. The norms of speaking manifest a fraternity or locker room-like atmosphere. In essence, a fraternity is a group of young college men bonded through similar interests and initiated through adversity, e.g. rites of passage commonly known as pledging, hazing and hell night. It is a highly competitive, hierarchical organization; only certain men are chosen as members based primarily on how well or how much they exhibit the qualities or attributes valued by that particular fraternity. The degree of standing and influence a fraternity brother has over the other members resides in large part in his ability to project or present a competitive, successful, confident identity (Kiesling, 1997).

Members of a fraternity often live together in a communal house on or near a college campus. This house is frequently the setting for boisterous parties and other events, sexual, athletic and scatological, that build and maintain a sense of camaraderie. All four of the male informants also commented on the fraternity atmosphere prevalent in the brokerage house. In Sam's words:

> …it's like a fraternity atmosphere. It's mostly men and there's no need to worry about social pleasantries; you can just basically do or say what you want and not offend anyone except maybe the women.

Indeed, it is well known that fraternity and locker room talk is replete with ego grandstanding. The language displays on locker-room topics such as sexual prowess and athletic abilities as well as the use heavy swearing are markers of the social identity of those who belong. While such verbal behavior may be the norm in those settings, overt grandstanding of this sort is certainly inappropriate in office settings.

Much recent sociolinguistic research has focused on the function of language displays in the construction of social identities. Eastman and Stein (1993), for example, state the following:

> Language display requires a context in which people share beliefs about desirable foreign attributes and recognise associated languages as symbolic expressions of identity. Where one interpretation reigns, there is no power struggle. The message of display is understood (p. 189).

One interpretation has the ability to reign when there are few outsiders. Likewise, those interlocutors who do not adhere to the same rules of speaking either by choice or due to different background knowledge or life experience will have difficulty becoming members of the in-group. It is only those in the in-group who even possess the ability to compete by virtue of who and what they are. The outsiders in this group, the few women and the one foreigner, do not participate in the banter nor do they socialize outside of the office, as they do not share the prerequisite background schema.

Their possible interpretations and participation are therefore marginal, and in this marginality rests their powerlessness. What often occurs in such situations is that the out-group chooses to seek employment elsewhere. Another male informant, when questioned as to the lack of female brokers at this particular firm said :

> My particular office is a locker room. It's a freaking locker room here. If I were a woman, I wouldn't work here.

The competition that is so blatant on the surface has an underlying subtext of symbolic expression.

Our female informant, Pam, refers to the surface interactional nature of the speech community as macho, egotistical, and immature. She says:

> They rag on each other, ride on each other, and don't let us females in it as much. It's like a big fraternity. The men are allowed to rant and rave about the smallest things and nothing happens. Women, on the other hand, are expected to maintain their composure at all times — they can't yell, get upset or use foul language, otherwise they will be considered a bitch.

Research on sex differences in profanity (e.g. Thorne and Henley 1975; Selnow 1985; Beers 2000) underscores that men are more inclined to perceive the use of profanity as a demonstration of social power. Both power and control are inherent in the linguistic strategies utilized by the brokers, which are not only employed to boost their competitive edge but have an underlying strategy of controlling who gets to compete in the first place. In other words, linguistic expressions of ego aggrandizement are exclusionary to the out-group while at the same time directly linked to monetary reward: ego equals money. Our consultant Pam states, "some of the guys will be very nice and considerate, then get new clients, do business and then get egotistical."

Egocentrism appears to be built into the nature of the interactional space of many brokerage houses. A former bond salesman at Salomon Brothers (Lewis 1989) describes how "in every office of Salomon [there is] a system-wide loudspeaker, called the 'hoot and holler' or just the 'hoot.' Apart from money, success at Salomon meant having your name shouted over the hoot" (p. 165). Recall how examples above expressed precisely such public announcement of large dollar sales. These are meant to be both rewarding and motivational. Thus, the system inherently encourages boastful expressions of achievement.

The question that arises is what it means to have full communicative competence as a member of the speech community. In order to fit in at these brokerages houses, it is clearly necessary to share in some of the schema of fraternity life and athletics that is so prevalent in the everyday talk both in and out of the office. Without such a background, initiates might either struggle to adapt or look elsewhere for work. The attempt to fit in might readily result in failure, both pragmalinguistic and sociopragmatic (Thomas 1983). Those unable or unwilling to participate in the everyday talk of the brokerage house are necessarily outsiders. Women may be most obviously excluded due to their different patterns of socialization (c.f.. Maltz and Borker 1983; Goodwin 1993; Tannen 1994). For example, a Lehmann Brothers Holdings employee indicates that he himself, once known for his obscene language, has changed his tune: "We want female employees to feel comfortable — and a lot of them are less comfortable working in a locker-room type of environment" (Siconolfi and Auerbach, 1996).

2.5   Conclusion: bragging, boasting and bravado

Relatively few individuals achieve long-term success in this field. Our infor-mants attribute this to the pressure cooker environment. We contend that the reasons that so few people "make it" in this arena goes beyond the mere fact that there is high stress and competition. The pivotal factor is how the compe-tition is manifested linguistically.

In some brokerage house cultures initiates go through rites similar to those of fraternity pledges. Lewis (1989) describes how in such brokerage firms an initiate is termed a 'geek': "A person immediately out of the training program and in a disgusting larval state between trainee and man" [sic] (p. 153). One can progress from geek to man only by developing the requisite communica-tive competence. This includes both mastering the rules of speaking and being an effective salesman. The rules of speaking include knowing how to sell and how to boast about one's sales ability.

The popular literature on how to succeed in sales urges people to focus on winning and on being #1: "Just be positive and tell yourself that you are the greatest . . . Say it out loud . . .I am the greatest! Say it again . . . make the walls shake (Girard and Casanove, 1992: 21). A popular book on selling (Auer, 1989) stresses that salesmen, like athletes, are "fighters, determined to win" (p.5). Furthermore, participation in competitive sports teaches men "how to deal with competition, how to lose well and win well. . ." (Salmonsohn, 1996: 89). Many readers may remember how the boxer Mohammed Ali rallied himself and his supporters (and rattled his opponent) by reciting a personal poem of encouragement before a bout:

> I'm going to knock him down in five,
>
> He's going to take a dive,
>
> I'm going to sting him like a bee
>
> So he won't see (quoted in Girard, 1992: 21)

This is not unlike the bragging, boasting and bravado in this brokerage house speech community. The brokers boast to "psyche themselves up" for their sales pitches; to generate new business they must constantly place "cold calls," i.e. contact people they don't know in order to sell them stocks. Recall that to remain with the firm brokers are required to sell a certain minimum dollar amount of stocks. Two months of below minimum sales and the broker is asked to leave the firm. Low or no sales and the broker is "broke."

It is clear that the brokers in our study have learned their lessons well. Those who have not are not as likely to succeed in this highly competitive and stressful environment. The boasting, bragging and bravado among the members of the in-group "serve as screening procedures and also help define and redefine the boundaries of differentiated social groups" (Apte 1985: 55). This clearly creates an inhospitable work environment for those not acculturated. This type of sales attracts a certain kind of individual who has the requisite background and experience. Without them, one would need to become a certain type in order to succeed in this setting. If you can't lick them, you can try to join'em, but new social identities are difficult to acquire. Furthermore a fundamental question arises given what we have seen in the data presented above: Why would most of us want to?

3.   Conclusion: face to face in the workplace domain

We have seen in the above review of literature on workplace talk, and in the in-depth analysis of boasting, that talk in the workplace has important repercussions for career satisfaction. We have also seen, in the discussion of service and institutional encounters, that knowing how to interact in such encounters can smooth our ability to accomplish what we wish. The knowledge of how to present ourselves in such a way as to conform with interlocutor expectations can help us not only to achieve our goals in these types of interactions, but also to make everyday communication more pleasant. We do so much of our daily talk in workplace encounters that it behooves us to learn from studies of how to talk in these contexts.

Communicative competence in workplace and institutional interactions means knowing how to utilize talk-in-interaction for our own benefit and for the benefit of others. We have seen that humor in the workplace, in service, and in institutional talk can serve to lighten a serious atmosphere, motivate people, or merely to vent frustrations in a positive manner. We have also seen how some types of humor can serve to exclude individuals who are not members of an in-group. Understanding the consequences of participating in various types of speech activities can greatly improve our everyday lives.

Gender and language has been the focus of much of the material in this chapter. This seems logical, given that women have entered the workplace in great numbers over the past several decades. Women have many talents to offer workplaces; however, the devaluation of 'woman talk' has been at the root of much of women's inability to advance in their careers. The assessment of woman talk as powerless talk has negative consequences for women's ability to successfully interact in workplace and institutional encounters. The careful study of appropriately assertive speech as opposed to weak speech or aggressive speech can demonstrate that women's style may indeed be a more humanitarian style. This style can serve as a model for effective management affording women the opportunity to successfully manage people in their places of work. This knowledge is important not only for career mobility but, perhaps more importantly, for one's own job satisfaction as well as the job satisfaction of our co-workers.

The worth of studying talk at work has numerous positive consequences that go far beyond that which can lead to financial benefits. Aside from such as increasing the tab if one is a restaurant server, sell more goods if one is in sales, or make more money in general, knowing how to talk in work and institutional interactions can make the world a better place in which to live. Even the female police officer discussed above (McElhinny 1995) could benefit by knowing that using a more female interactional style with female emergency callers might yield more interactional satisfaction. It would certainly benefit the caller, and it would make the officer-caller interaction a more humanized one. This is but one example, in the many discussed above, of the importance of knowing how to use talk for making the world a more humane place.

Note

1. Earlier references refer to the Bullpen as a place where boys could horse around without any rules. In the US midwest, it also refers to a holding pen where yearling bulls were contained in preparation for castration.

CHAPTER 7

Face-to-face in cross-cultural interactions

1. Introduction

The study of face-to-face interaction in cross-cultural encounters is an especially important endeavor in modern times. The reason for its importance lies in the great potential for miscommunication and misperceptions based upon differing norms of interaction across societies and speech communities. In a world that is increasingly smaller insofar as peoples from different societies interact with greater and greater frequency, felicitous cross-cultural face-to-face interaction is essential. This part of applied linguistics is usually termed "cross-cultural pragmatics," or "interlanguage pragmatics." In my view (and this is not necessarily shared by all) these two research foci differ from each other in essential ways: interlanguage pragmatics forms a part of the sub-field of applied linguistics that focuses on *second language acquisition*; in contrast, cross-cultural pragmatics is applied *sociolinguistics*. It does not assume that the non-native speaker is progressing along an interlanguage continuum toward some "target language" norm. The distinction is a fuzzy one, and involves subtle differences in perspective. I would characterize the difference between the two as viewing cross-cultural communication from either a two-way perspective (cross-cultural pragmatics) or a one-way perspective (interlanguage pragmatics). Let me clarify.

Cross-cultural pragmatics (CCP) takes the point of view that individuals from two societies or communities carry out their face-to-face interactions with their own rules or norms at work, which often results in a clash in expectations and ultimately, misperceptions about the other group. The misperceptions are typically two-way, that is, each group misperceives the other. Notwithstanding, the consequences of such a situation are scarcely two-way, since inevitably one group wields societal power at the expense of the other. For example, the work of Twitchen, Gumperz, Jupp and Roberts (1979) on *Cross Talk* aptly illustrates how speakers of English from two different societies, British vs. Pakistani/Indian, have different sets of expectations for how to talk to each other. In this British setting, it is the South Asian group that gets into trouble by not following the norms of interaction of the host society. Subtle contextualization cues (e.g. intonation, volume, repetition, lexical choices) make the British speakers perceive the South Asian speakers as inappropriate and even rude. While it may be true that this perception goes the other way as well, with the South Asians perceiving the British negatively also, the consequences are felt only by the minority group.

The view that cross-cultural pragmatics is a two-way communication phenomenon with the burden of understanding falling on *both* sides is aptly explored in a piece by Davis and Henze (1998). The authors explicate the role that ethnographic analysis can play in the study of CCP, requiring thick description of both sets of norms to illustrate how cultural clashes stemming from differing pragmatic schema occur. In their view, ethnographers do precisely this kind of descriptive analysis in order to adjust the power differential so that it is not only the powerless who must acquire the norms of the powerful. In other words, in this sort of ethnographic perspective it is incumbent upon both interlocutors or sets of interlocutors to come to an understanding of each others' norms: "Ethnographers would lean toward making all parties aware of the miscommunication and seeking a shared understanding of why it happened" (416). I will return to Davis and Henze (1998) in further detail below.

Work by Keith Chick on intercultural communication between whites and blacks in South Africa takes precisely this perspective. Chick's work illustrates the serious consequences of cross-cultural pragmatic differences for the powerless group. In South Africa, where the vestiges of apartheid are still felt, miscommunication typically results in a cycle of negative perceptions causing stereotyping. Chick's work (e.g. 1985, 1989, 1996), most of which focuses on the domains of education and workplace interaction, illustrates the mismatch of cultural frames and schema that lead to discrimination against and stereotyping of South African blacks. The aim of the body of research is not to have the powerless group conform to a target set of pragmatic norms, but to educate whites and blacks alike about what happens, on a micro level, when norms clash. Indeed, in a society such as South Africa, such research is critical.

Because cross-cultural face-to-face interaction has the potential to cause stereotypes, prejudice, and discrimination against entire groups of people, research in CCP has the potential to ameliorate these consequences. For this reason, this type of work is applied sociolinguistics par excellence.

Where CCP takes the perspective of developing mutual understanding, interlanguage pragmatics (IP) typically takes the perspective that it is the task of the newcomer to conform to the norms of the host community. Here the focus is on language learners, or individuals engaged in formal or informal study of a second or foreign language. The assumption is that these learners, especially those in a *second* language context (as opposed to a *foreign* language context), are learning the rules and norms of interaction of the host society along with the phonology, morphology, syntax, and semantics of the L2. Until quite recently there has been little effort to teach the pragmatic level in formal classroom L2 instruction. Indeed, it is only in the past two decades that any effort at all has been exerted to make learners aware of pragmatic differences between L1 and L2. Because of this, the field of interlanguage pragmatics is still in its infancy.

A host of research studies have contributed greatly to our knowledge of IP issues (see, for example, work by authors such as Cohen and Olshtain 1981; Olshtain and Cohen 1983; Kasper and Dahl 1991; Kasper and Rose 1999; Blum-Kulka, House-Edmondson and Kasper 1989; Beebe et. al 1985; Eisenstein and Bodman 1986; Bardovi-Harlig and Hartford 1993). With some exceptions (e.g Bardovi-Harlig and Hartford), studies carried out by these researchers have focused on speech act realization and have by and large *not* used spontaneous face-to-face data, preferring instead to elicit large amounts of data through role-plays or Discourse Completion Tasks (DCT). This is not surprising, given the difficult task of collecting natural data on miscommunication. There is a debate on this issue in the literature, begun by the late Nessa Wolfson (cf. Wolfson, Marmor and Jones 1989) and thoroughly outlined in Beebe and Cummings (1996). One can see by the first and second dates of these papers that discussion initiated in the mid-eighties on this methodological debate has continued over the years. The fact remains that there are relatively few IP studies using data from spontaneous face-to-face interaction.

While Wolfson asserted that the only good data is that which is captured in natural communication, her own work on speech act realization was not specifically interlanguage data, but baseline data on how speech acts are realized among native speakers, in her case native speakers of American English. Thus, her studies on the speech acts of complimenting and inviting, for example, were not specifically cross-cultural studies, and they were definitely not interlanguage studies. They were descriptive analyses of speech act usage among native speakers of US English. These types of studies are indeed important for IP research, since they provide necessary information on just how certain groups of native speakers realize speech acts. They do not, however, provide information that gives clues to potential miscommunication pitfalls. In order to have this sort of information, we need to also have baseline data on how these same speech acts are realized in other languages. In other words, baseline studies on native speech behavior in one language needs to be coupled with data on the same speech behavior in other languages and speech communities. For example, if we are studying the cross-cultural realizations of apologies between US English and Japanese, we would need to collect data in a US speech community and also in a Japanese speech community and then compare these two sets of data to ascertain where the differences occur. This type of contrastive pragmatics can then help us avoid miscommunication. Without using a DCT instrument, this can be a very cumbersome process.

A good example of how to collect valid data for research on interlanguage pragmatics is a recent dissertation on apologies in Korean and American English. Dukyoung Kim (2001) researched this topic by using spontaneous speech data from American apologies and Korean apologies (This data is partially drawn from natural conversation and part from TV dramas in Korean). To study Korean's use of apologies in *English*, however, Kim has employed an oral role play task. Consider what would happen if he had decided to collect the interlanguage data from spontaneous speech. The issue at hand here is: how infrequent are apologies in English by Korean speakers? How long would the researcher have to wait, listen and record before amassing a sufficient corpus for a study of this kind? The answer is: a very long time. In fact, collecting spontaneous speech data for such research is probably not reasonable at all. By having three sets of data, two of which are relatively spontaneous, Kim was able to compare the US and Korean data to pinpoint the areas of contrast. One immediate difference is the use of honorifics in Korean apologies and their absence in most English-speaking communities. The sociolinguistic variables of age and gender condition apologies differently in the two languages. Where the third set of data, the role-plays, enters into the picture is to see if the differences will indeed cause problems. In such a case, DCT instruments, whether they are written or oral, can be quite useful.

As one can easily see, there are ways to collect data for research on interlanguage pragmatics that captures spontaneous speech; however, it is not always an easy task. Much depends on what one is studying and the kind of information sought. Because so many types of speech behaviors occur infrequently in ordinary talk regardless of domain, the majority of studies in this subfield of applied linguistics have relied on data collected through DCTs or some variation of this method.

This chapter focuses principally on cross-cultural pragmatics (as opposed to interlanguage pragmatics) for two reasons. First, consistent with the rest of this volume, the aim is to zero in on studies using data from spontaneous face-to-face interaction. Second, the bi-directional view of CCP gives us a good sense of applying sociolinguistics to solve real world communication problems in a shrinking planet. The attempt to strive for bi-directionality is consistent with the aims of critical discourse analysis, i.e. the raising of consciousness about discourse and power.

The research overviewed in this chapter emanates by and large from sociolinguistics. As before, the literature review that follows is by no means meant to be exhaustive. The literature discussed here is intended to be illustrative of the important kinds of things we are able to learn from studying face-to-face interaction in cross-cultural encounters. The domains included are social life, educational life, and workplace life. To my knowledge, there is a virtual absence of research on cross-cultural religious interactions, perhaps because members of specific religious communities have a built-in shared schema for the norms of interaction. This is true for family interactions as well. Family members typically constitute an in-group with shared norms for the conduct and interpretation of speech behavior. One could easily imagine designing studies to ascertain what happens when a visitors from different cultures stay with host families in which another culture and/or language predominates. Another interesting study would be to investigate the face-to-face interactions of family members (e.g. in-laws) from different ethnic, regional, racial or linguistic/cultural groups. Likewise, one could design a study to research what happens when newcomers enter a new religious congregation with an aim to track the miscommunication stemming from different norms of religious language and behavior. Given the paucity or even absence of research of this kind, the present chapter focuses on three domains only. The culminating in-depth study of this chapter, within the domain of higher education, is a study of cross-cultural interaction in university gatekeeping encounters that I carried out in collaboration with my colleague Christina Overstreet.

1.1 Cross-cultural interactions in social life

Much of the existing work in cross-cultural face-to-face interaction has centered on Japanese/US encounters in all domains, including social life. This is perhaps the case because of the vast differences in norms of social interaction between the two societies. Indeed, sociolinguistic norms differ so drastically between Japanese and US English to make cross-cultural communication a true challenge (see, for example Barnlund 1975; Lebra 1984; Maynard 1986; Wetzel

1988). My own work on complaining in conversations between speakers of US English and speakers of Japanese (1993c) is illustrative of this problem. In that study, I employed tape-recorded data of conversations between ten pairs of native speakers of English and Japanese. This sort of data enabled me to study instances of complaining sequences (or their absence) by both sides. Indeed, it was the preponderance of complaints by the native speakers and the virtual absence among the non-native speakers that showed up as a striking difference. Without knowing Japanese, I had to rely on what I saw occurring in the English data, which was that the Americans did a great deal of griping while the Japanese did almost none. Moreover, it was not the presence or absence of the speech act per se that was so important, but the perceptions of the speakers of both groups about what the other group was doing or not doing.

This is a good example of the fuzzy distinction that I have drawn above between CCP and IP. While the study did indeed focus on learners of English as a Second Language in social talk with native speakers (NSs), the intent was not to conclude that the non-native speakers (NNSs) should learn how to realize the speech act appropriately. Certainly, when we teach language learners about norms of interaction, we do not necessarily want to teach them to behave in ways that are incompatible with their own rules. Imagine teaching students to complain! However, having said this, we do want learners to recognize and understand what is going on with certain speech behaviors and respond accordingly, and likewise we want the NSs to understand the NNSs speech norms. In that study, comments by the NSs yielded such frustrations as, "I sit here going on and on and you just say, 'uh huh.' It's like I'm in an interview or something" (Boxer, 1993c: 292). In other words, the Japanese speaker was overusing backchannel cues, which are ubiquitous in Japanese but interpreted somewhat differently in English. While in Japanese these cues are seen as encouraging, they are not always perceived this way in English, particularly when the backchannels are not occasionally interspersed with a full turn at talk. Thus, what the Japanese needed to learn was not that they needed to complain more, but that they needed to make more substantive response comments. Instead of repeatedly replying with "uh huh" or "hmmn" they could just as easily have replied with "oh no!", or some such response.

What the Americans needed to know was that the Japanese were just following their own norms, which work for them in their own language and society. Knowing this, they could modify their expectations and/or help their Japanese interlocutors to take more substantive turns at talk. As for the Japanese, without an understanding of the rapport-inspiring function of griping, these interlocutors must have thought their conversation partners to be extraordinarily negative. Knowing how complaining works for some groups of native speakers of US English can help Japanese speakers of English respond accordingly. For the English-speaking interlocutors, knowing that griping is rare or even taboo in Japanese social conversation might suggest using different rapport-inspiring speech behavior. This ought to be a two-way understanding; nonetheless, since the Japanese were the language learners, the burden was on them (unfortunately, perhaps) to understand the norms of interaction of the host community.

A study by Hayashi (1988) deals with another important discourse phenomenon in Japanese/American face-to-face interactions, namely that of simultaneous talk and its relationship to differential floor management between the two groups of speakers. Using many hours of audiotaped face-to-face interactions in the social domain, Hayashi found that the Japanese tend to employ simultaneous talk much more than Americans, who abide by the rule of one speaker at a time. In fact the Japanese did twice as much simultaneous talk, termed "sync talk," as the Americans, regardless of whether they had the floor singly rather than jointly. For the Japanese, this "sync talk creates ensemble and comfortable moments" (281).

One very important speech act whose realization differs cross-culturally is refusing, and this is particularly true with respect to Japanese society vs. many Western societies. In Japanese, direct refusals are rare, as they are considered extremely face-threatening. A very interesting early study (Ueda 1974) discussed how to avoid refusing in Japanese society. Silence is merely one of "Sixteen ways to avoid saying 'no' in Japan." The title of that article clearly conveys the importance of not threatening an interlocutor's face in Japan by issuing a direct refusal. In order to do this, there are many ways to respond. Aside from maintaining silence, these include vague 'no,' ambiguous refusals, counter questions, apologizing, and even lying. In fact, lying was found to be used most frequently for declining requests. Of course, we do this in many North American English-speaking communities as well; however, we prefer to term this type of response an "excuse" rather than a lie.

In Japanese society, one feels freer to be honest in refusals with more intimate interlocutors. This appears to be the case as well among many US English speakers. We need to be careful, however, not to assume that this is universal. We do know that in many societies one needs to accord a great deal of respect to elders in the family, even older siblings. Thus, how to refuse in family interactions is a different matter. In social life at least, refusals are carried out differently across cultures, and thus this speech behavior has great potential for misperceptions and miscommunication.

Other misperceptions and misunderstandings due to cross-cultural pragmatics are very aptly described in a rather early paper by Joan Rubin (1983). The focus here, as in Ueda's work, was on the speech act of refusing, an act that can be very face-threatening, as we have seen earlier (see chapter on social interaction). Rubin offers many wonderful examples of how differing rules of saying "no" cross-culturally can get one into trouble. One of my favorite is the following:

> "In parts of the Arab world and many other parts of the world one mustn't accept food the first or second time it is offered; however, refusal the third time is definitive…An anecdote was recounted by an Arab speaker's first encounter with some Americans. On his first visit to an American home, he was served some delicious sandwiches. When the hostess came to offer seconds, he refused. Much to his chagrin, the hostess didn't repeat the offer. Thus the Arab sat there, confronted by some lovely sandwiches that he couldn't eat" (14).

Rubin's piece outlines in very close detail the social parameters of saying "no." These are based on differing weight given to certain sociolinguistic variables and underlying values of different societies. In addition, she discusses the value of silence in certain communities, where silence can sometimes signal refusal or merely respect for certain interlocutors in certain contexts (e.g. among the Apache silence is used frequently in courting, responses to scolding, or mourning) (Basso 1972). One needs to know what silence means to members of different speech communities in order to accurately interpret it as a response and avoid misperceptions.

Misperceptions due to CCP differences in the social domain are important in that they are apt to interfere with the establishment of a sense of solidarity between interlocutors from societies with different norms of appropriate speech behavior. Without a sense of rapport or commonality with the "other," the establishment of friendships is prevented. Without friendship, global harmony is constrained. It is perhaps true that CCP problems are more immediately interpreted as critical in the workplace and educational domains, where access to goods and services is impeded as a result of different norms for face-to-face encounters. Because of this, we tend to overlook the importance of personal relationships as a critical first tier of cross-cultural face-to-face interactional satisfaction. The goods and services in the social domain may not be as easily identified and quantified; nonetheless, the establishment of personal relationships is of paramount importance in harmony between people of different societies and speech communities.

1.2   Cross-cultural interactions in work life

Notwithstanding the immediate importance of workplace interactions in providing access to important goods and services, there is a paucity of research on cross-cultural pragmatics in the workplace. This is surprising, given (1) the current emphasis on a global market; and (2) the fact that workplaces in the US and elsewhere are increasingly diverse. One relatively recent volume (Firth 1995) focuses on negotiation in workplace encounters; however, few of the papers included therein specifically analyze cross-cultural phenomena. One that does (Marriott 1995) analyzes what she terms as "deviations" in intercultural business negotiation. The use of the term "deviations" is interesting in and of itself, in that it lends to the perception of the negative semantic load of the term. Marriott justifies its use based on the work of Neustupny (1985), who takes the primary language used in intercultural encounters as the "base" and thus considers that which varies from that norm as "deviations."

Marriott describes in microanalytic detail a business encounter between an Australian cheese maker and a Japanese representative of a corporation in Japan that has indicated possible interest in buying or co-producing the Australian product. The data is a videotape of the encounter, triangulated with post-hoc interviews with the participants in which they viewed the taped encounter and commented on their perceptions of the communication.

Examples of communication deviations causing miscommunication are offered. These include strategies employed by the Japanese interlocutor such as clarification requests and summarizing in order to check his comprehension of the ongoing interaction. These strategies, in addition to his writing down notes after clarification, indicated to the Australian interlocutor that the Japanese interlocutor had adequately comprehended the exchange. This was shown not to be the case in the post-hoc triangulation interviews. The assumption that writing notes indicated comprehension was unfounded. Moreover, a major dissatisfaction on the part of the Australian was the feeling of uncertainty he was left with as to whether the Japanese was indeed interested in pursuing the purchase. Marriott terms this frustration "dissonance" in that the Australian felt the need to have "a more explicit personal demonstration of interest" (262).

Given what we know about cross-cultural pragmatics of Japanese (cf. Ueda 1974; Boxer 1993c above), it is not surprising that the Australian felt this sort of frustration. An understanding of Japanese interactional style would give the non-Japanese interlocutor a basis for comprehending the seeming lack of commitment. Given that the speech act of refusal is very face-threatening in Japan, it might have been the Japanese interlocutor's strategy of not committing until he was sure his company was interested. Knowledge of some of these pragmatic differences would clearly have been useful in avoiding dissatisfaction and misperceptions on the part of both interlocutors in this workplace interaction.

Davis and Henze's (1998) article on applying ethnographic perspectives to CCP illustrates how this can be done with an example from the workplace domain. In the incident described, the interlocutors were all native or near-native speakers of US English from different ethnic/cultural backgrounds with differing pragmatic norms. The characters are Rosemary, who is a team director and European-American; Sandra, a Spanish-English bilingual, and Jenny, a Chinese-English bilingual. All three were working in a non-profit organization. Rosemary, in her role as director, typically took a non-imposing stance when it came to task allocation, offering the task as up for grabs rather than assigning it to a specific person. The pattern that evolved was the following: Jenny, the Chinese-American team member, would defer to Sandra, thinking that perhaps Sandra "needed the hours" (411). Sandra cheerfully agreed to take on the tasks, eventually overloading herself.

Since the three had been classmates in graduate school in applied linguistics, they were tuned into the pitfalls of miscommunication and thus engaged in a metalinguistic discussion of their communicative styles. In so doing, they became aware of some linguistic/cultural differences that led them to certain routine behaviors. First, Jenny noted that in her culture excuses were typically made before taking on a task just in case she would be unable to successfully complete it. Sandra, on the other hand, took on a linguistic style of making light of each task as a "piece of cake" (Davis and Henze 1998: 412) and thus took on more and more. Her style was to resort to excuses/explanations only when the task was overwhelmingly difficult to complete. These two styles clearly clashed, causing Sandra to take on too much and Jenny to pass on too much to the others.

The fact that the three interlocutors in this vignette were versed in the ethnography of communication allowed them to discuss the incident from a problem-solving perspective. What they found out was that culturally-influenced communication styles led to both pragmalinguistic and sociopragmatic failure. That is to say, while Jenny considered taking on a task as a promise, Sandra's view was one of expressing good intentions in taking on the same task. These two perspectives stem from culturally conditioned value systems: From Sandra's point of view, the interpersonal is of paramount importance, even more than the task; from Jenny's perspective, however, the commitment to the task overrode "momentary discomfort in the interpersonal relationship" (Davis and Henze 1998: 415).

Davis and Henze's article does a fine job of explicating what I view as the difference between *interlanguage* pragmatics and *cross-cultural* pragmatics. While an IP perspective views the NNS as proceeding along an interlanguage continuum toward some target pragmatic norm, CCP views pragmatic differences as an area for interlocutors to critically examine:

> In terms of applications, some might favor teaching Sandra and Jenny a way to communicate agreement to a task according to middle class white American norms. This approach is based on assimilationist ideology, which sees mainstream norms as the 'target culture.' Ethnographers would lean more toward making all parties aware of the miscommunication and seeking a shared understanding of why it happened. (1998: 416).

From this same perspective derives a study in cross-cultural impression management that sets an example for two-way understanding. Bilbow (1997) examined the multicultural workplace that is present-day Hong Kong. His study specifically investigated a large airline with work teams comprised of both ethnic Chinese and those he terms "expatriates," English speakers from Australia, the US and England, for example. Employing interactional sociolinguistic methodology, Bilbow studied cross-cultural styles of interaction through the use of directives and suggestions as speech acts leading to impressions of authoritativeness. His goal was to devise a discourse model that would enable participants to recognize each other's style differences and overcome incorrect impressions based on cultural differences. Thus, the study was designed to address existing problems with the two groups' stereotypes of each other (e.g. the Chinese viewed the expatriates as aggressive and rude while expatriates often viewed the Chinese as 'reserved,' 'evasive' or 'reticent' (462).

Bilbow's findings suggest that directives and suggestions were realized differently for the two groups, resulting in misconceptions of authoritativeness or weakness in this regard. Not only were there vast differences in functional-grammatical features (e.g. grounding and elaborating), but intonation differences were seen as problematic to interpretations of each other's speech acts, since "the range of intonational variation in Chinese verbal contributions is less marked than in Western verbal contributions" (1997: 474). The resulting effect was that Westerners interpreted the Chinese directives and suggestions as lacking in emotional expression. Such discourse differences, including circumlocution used by Chinese but not by Westerners, led both groups to misinterpret each other.

The training component that derived from the analysis focused on a presentation of the findings of the study with subsequent discussion in which both groups could bring forth issues of concern. Thus, the study's application to this workplace was direct and immediate: to aid each group in understanding how differential use of speech acts creates certain impressions that may be unwarranted and that have the potential of stereotyping.

Bilbow's research is a good example of applied cross-cultural pragmatics. In a multicultural workplace such as Hong Kong, where English is the medium used but not the L1 of many workers, we need to examine what it means to have felicitous face-to-face interaction. Without raising the consciousness of cultural differences in speech behavior in such a context, the dangers of miscommunication are salient indeed. This line of research can thus be viewed in much the way that Davis and Henze (above) advocate; that is, cross-cultural pragmatics needs to be a two-way understanding. Bilbow eloquently states:

> This approach, I believe, places an appropriate emphasis on the empowerment of those groups that have traditionally been seen as deviating from the 'norm' in discourse, and the development of enabling skills on the part of all parties present in intercultural encounters (1997: 466).

The issue of interlanguage pragmatics is not relevant here, as Cantonese is the national language, while English is the official language. It is therefore a situation in which cross-cultural pragmatics is key, calling for the necessity of two-way understanding.

Here we must return once again to the crucial issue of power: Why is it that the burden of understanding falls on the Chinese here, when Hong Kong is a Chinese-speaking city? It seems clear from studies such as Bilbow's that power resides with the Westerners here as well as on their own turf. Perhaps this is a remaining vestige of colonialism. Perhaps this is related to the inherent power of the native English-speaker as "owner" of the world's current lingua franca. The study of cross-cultural pragmatics in the workplace has great potential to rectify power injustices. By making both groups aware of the other's norms, we are able to bring issues of power and dominance to the level of consciousness. This is a critical first step in equalization. In the workplace domain this equalization has serious repercussions for access to means of livelihood.

1.3   Cross-cultural interactions in educational life

The issue of equalization is nowhere more important than in the domain of education. Because of this (and because most researchers interact in this domain daily) there has been a considerable amount of research on cross-cultural pragmatics in education. CCP research is crucial in all levels of education, particularly in early childhood and elementary education. Shirley Brice Heath's *Ways With Words* (1983) is the quintessential study of CCP's effects on young children. What sets this work apart is precisely the bi-directionality of the focus: teachers and school personnel as well as parents and students were brought to an awareness of the mismatch of interactional norms between home and school in order to empower children to succeed in school. Whereas Heath's study dealt with CCP differences due to ethnic/racial differences within a speech community, a vast body of research also exists that focuses on CCP within bilingual education, that is, dealing with groups possessing different first languages. We will not deal with this research here, but consistent with the chapter on the educational domain, will focus on higher education as a means to narrow our overview.

As in lower levels of education, higher education in the US is a setting in which individuals from all parts of the world interact, often with consequences of misperceptions due to pragmatic differences. One salient example of the importance of knowing what is appropriate language and behavior in higher education are interactions between NNS teachers with their NS students. In many cases where NNSs are in the role of teacher, it is the student who has the pragmatic power, simply because the teacher is not a native speaker. This was the subject for a research project that I carried out in collaboration with colleague my Andrea Tyler (Tyler and Boxer 1996; Boxer and Tyler 1996). Tyler's work with international teaching assistants (ITAs) over several years and my own interest in gender and language sparked a series of discussions about incidents in which ITAs said certain things to undergraduates of the opposite sex that were construed by the undergraduates as inappropriate. These discussions led us to design a project that focused specifically on what verbal and nonverbal behavior might have sexual implications and therefore what teacher behavior might be perceived as sexual harassment.

We wondered whether there was language and behavior that could be construed as sexual in US contexts but not in other societies, and we also wanted to ascertain if certain sexually-tinged language might be more tolerated in societies other than the US. Given the heightened state of awareness of sexual harassment in the US, this issue seemed and continues to seem critical for the success of international graduate students teaching on US campuses. While we realized that some men from cultures outside the US bring with them negative attitudes towards women in universities and the workplace, we also suspected that some of these negative perceptions might be the result of cross-cultural misunderstanding.

In order to systematically investigate potential differences in interpretation of appropriateness and sexual intent in various teacher-student interactions, our research took a two-pronged approach. We sought the reactions of both undergraduates and ITAs to twelve scenarios of naturally occurring (and potentially problematic) interactions. We asked ITAs and undergraduates of both sexes to comment on whether the interaction was appropriate or inappropriate. A sample scenario follows:

> You have a class that meets three times per week. The TA borrowed a book from you two weeks ago. During the last class, which met on Firday, you asked if the TA happened to have brought the book to class. When the TA said, "No," you responded with, "OK, no problem." At 9:30 p.m Saturday night, the TA dropped by your apartment to return your book. The TA asked what you were doing. When you said you were just reading, the TA said, "I'm not doing anything either."

Our research participants responded to the twelve scenarios, in each case indicating whether they thought it was appropriate or inappropriate. The first study (Tyler and Boxer 1996) had the subjects respond to the scenarios presented in written form. The second study (Boxer and Tyler 1998) used video-taped re-enactments of the scenarios. In both studies, we carried out in-depth ethnographic interviews with ITAs and students of both sexes to triangualate the data and obtain further information about perceptions on both sides.

The issue of cross-cultural perceptions of sexual intent is multi-faceted and many-layered. Identity of the ITA, in terms of race, ethnicity, and gender, appeared to play an important role. Our consultants in the first study often stated that their assessments would depend on who the ITA was and the manner in which the potentially offensive language and behavior was carried out. It was for this reason that we developed the video-prompts for the second study. Each scenario was enacted twice, once with a female ITA and once with a male ITA and a student of the opposite sex.

The interpretations derived from these studies reflect culturally specific schemata of expectations for teacher-student relationships. For instance, while most US undergraduates found it inappropriate for an ITA to stop by a student's apartment unannounced, many ITAs found this scenario quite acceptable. Some of the narrative comments indicated that this would be normal and neutral in their own cultures. The key notion here is the bi-directional nature of differences in interpretations. Clearly, miscommunication involving conflicting cultural assumptions and linguistic cues is subtle and enduring. Forewarned, ITAs can make informed decisions about how they might avoid being misinterpreted and avoid cross-cultural misunderstandings concerning sexual intent.

We see how role expectations determine the context of just where the burden of pragmatic competence falls. Despite the fact that ITAs are teachers, it is incumbent upon them as NNSs to understand the sociolinguistic norms of the society in which they are teaching and work within them. Thus, the tables are somewhat turned around with ITAs. While as instructors these students wield power over undergraduates, having the responsibility of dispensing grades, as newcomers they are placed in less powerful positions than those which ordinarily prevails among professors. Undergraduates who pay hefty tuition fees complain to their parents about their inability to understand their teachers from other countries. Far worse are complaints about what are construed as violations of pragmatic norms.

The issue of power here is turned on its head. While it is true that teachers are typically the more powerful group vis à vis their students, holding in their power rewards and punishments, where the teacher is an international teaching assistant the power is diminished. First, it is diminished by the fact of not being a native speaker of the language of instruction; second, it is diminished by parental pressure on the institution for teachers who are both "comprehensible" as well as appropriate. Thus, while cross-cultural understanding ought to be a two-way issue, we clearly see here that this is not the case. Invariably, the NNS, despite playing a role that is traditionally more powerful in the institution of higher education, is cast in a less powerful position, and thus needs to more seriously understand the rules and norms of the NS students.

Academic advising sessions in higher education is the theme of a body of work by several scholars in sociolinguistics, stemming from the early work of Erickson and Schultz (1982). In that in-depth study, the authors documented in microethnographic detail the consequences of pragmatic mismatches between students and academic advisors in advising sessions. Their findings indicated that miscommunication due to linguistic, paralinguistic and extralinguistic differences between students and the advisors who play the role of gatekeepers can have life-altering consequences for the students. In other words, students who came from different ethnic and racial speech communities with interactional rules that differed from those of their advisors ran the risk of not gaining the help that they required in order to succeed in their education.

Since the publication of Erickson and Schultz' groundbreaking work on gatekeeping encounters in higher education, others have followed suit in studying various similar gatekeeping contexts. An excellent example is the work of Kathleen Bardovi-Harlig and Beverly Hartford carried out over a number of years and published by and large in the early nineties. These researchers studied the interactions of graduate students with their academic advisors, comparing the pragmatic competence of NS students with NNS students. This sort of comparison sheds light on the communicative competence needed on the part of foreign students to successfully participate in such gatekeeping encounters. I have chosen one example of this larger project (Hartford and Bardovi-Harlig 1992) to elucidate how such research is exemplary of applied sociolinguistics. The research also aptly illustrates the fuzzy line that I have drawn between what falls into the category of cross-cultural pragmatics as opposed to interlanguage pragmatics.

In this particular part of the project, the authors examined closing segments of the academic advising session. Following Schegloff and Sacks (1973) they studied appropriate timing of closings as well as the topics that qualify as permissible postsession discussion. They demonstrate just how closings in this speech event differ from those of ordinary social conversation. While in normal conversation there is preponderant evidence of pre-closing sequences, these are either absent entirely in advising event or accomplished in quite a different manner. For example, previously discussed matters are often reinvoked in the closing section of ordinary social conversation; however, they may not be reinvoked in advising interviews.

> In order to participate in the felicitous closing of an advising session, a speaker must know four things: how to close conversations in general, what work must be accomplished in the advising session proper, what constitutes appropriate timing, and what topics qualify as permissable topics.
> (Hartford and Bardovi-Harlig 1992: 98).

Two variables determine whether or not postsession talk is permitted: (1) topic; and (2) timing. Not surprisingly, NNSs had more trouble with both. Indeed, re-openings were restricted to the NNS in the data. Moreover, many NNSs were unsure of whether the interview was closed and had to specifically ask if it was the end of the session. These students had difficulty with timing their closings as well as knowing the appropriateness of topics in the pre-closing moves.

The only topics allowed in pre-closings are those that ask for information about some aspect of the institution (e.g. directions to some place on campus); and those that introduce or reinforce aspects of co-membership of the partici-pants (e.g. talk about common membership as linguists, in this case). As for timing, closings are much shorter than in social conversation, warranting only one possible topic that can be introduced.

In summary, closings in this speech event differ from those of ordinary social conversation in the disallowing of postsession conversations and reinvocations. The fact that the sessions are by and large monotopical precludes reinvocations of an earlier subtopic. Moreover, the sessions have time limitations (approxi-mately 15 to 20 minutes) that differ from conversations. Contrasting NSs with NNSs participation in these advising interviews gives insight into the commu-nicative competence necessary for felicitous advising interviews. Sometimes only by noticing violations can norms and rules be recognized.

Advising sessions in the context of higher education are clear gatekeeping encounters. The advisors, as representative of the department and institution, have the power to give or deny access to the student. Obviously, then, this case of cross-cultural pragmatics is not a matter of two-way understanding. It is a clear-cut case of the burden of pragmatic competence falling on the less powerful interlocutor, the student. In the educational domain, the conse-quences of not knowing the appropriate norms for verbal interaction are serious indeed. Let us turn now to another example of research on gatekeeping encounters in a university setting that have consequences for foreign students' developing sense of belonging.

2.   **An in-depth analysis of cross-cultural speech behavior**
       From outsiders to insiders:
       Cross-cultural gatekeeping encounters in higher education

2.1   Introduction

Higher education is now the #1 export product of the U. S. An increasing number of international students either enroll in intensive English language programs or register as full-time undergraduate and graduate students at US universities. While some of these students master the norms of face-to-face interaction in US English, making friends with the 'natives' and taking an active part in campus and community life, others remain strangers in many ways. What are the reasons and why should it concern us? The same people who live and learn together on US campuses may well be tomorrow's world economic and political leaders. For international students, their experience at US universities will undoubtedly impact any future contact with Americans, be it of a personal, business, or political nature. The stakes are high. For many, gaining entry into campus life is directly connected to their ability to gain acceptance into their new community, with direct access to the goods and services therein provided. This in turn has a direct bearing on their success in the US and on their future lives and careers when they return to their own societies. It is therefore important that we identify and remove barriers that keep foreign students from becoming involved in campus and community.

The initial contact between students arriving from their respective native countries and members of the US University community typically occurs in administrative offices. Students return to these offices whenever they need help regarding either academic or personal affairs. The purpose of this study is to investigate the key role that staff members of a large university play in helping students gain entry into campus life. We focus on gatekeeping encounters between staff members and students from varying cultural backgrounds. In so doing, we explore the dangers of negative cultural stereotyping that prevent students from gaining access to important services.

2.2   Background

Every undergraduate or graduate student who attends a university enters into a 'utilitarian, contractual relationship' with the institution. (Scollon and Scollon 1995: 135). Building on Toennies (1971), Scollon and Scollon describe the interdependency of two major types of discourse systems and the two different ways in which society can be organized. One becomes a member of a *Gemeinschaft* through birth and processes of socialization or enculturation. *Gesellschaft*, on the other hand, indicates utilitarian relationships that are contractual, rational, and instrumental, rather than based on a common history and cultural background. The discourse system of *Gesellschaft* is 'goal-directed' and 'informational', rather than 'relational' as in the *Gemeinschaft* (Scollon and Scollon 1995: 138). Clearly, no modern society is either *Gesellschaft* or *Gemeinschaft*-oriented in its entirety, but rather a mixture of both. In this study, we borrow and expand upon these notions from Toennies (1971) and Scollon and Scollon (1995). The term *Gesellschaft* will be used when the emphasis is on the institutional aspect of university life and its rules and regulations. In contrast, *Gemeinschaft* describes that aspect of the university community that stresses interpersonal relationships, solidarity, and "non-institutional forms of learning" (Scollon and Scollon 1995: 136).

We demonstrate the interdependency of *Gesellschaft* and *Gemeinschaft* on the macro-level and corresponding use of language between native and newcomer on the micro-level. Erickson and Shultz' finding that the "revelation of comembership" between student and counselor provides a "microsocial context for empathy and rapport" (1982: 41), can be extended to encounters between foreign students and staff in administrative offices. As we will see below, these personnel also play the role of de facto gatekeepers. Erickson and Shultz found that those who tend the gate in academic settings hold a dual role: Invested with institutional authority, they are obliged to act in the interest of the institution while meeting the individual student's needs (1982). Furthermore, gatekeeping processes and outcomes are heavily influenced by the "cultural communication style and social background" of the interlocutors (193). Their analysis suggests that the "game is rigged", that its outcomes are in favor of those students whose cultural communication style and social background resembles that of the gatekeeper (193). Thus, staff members who consciously work to establish a common ground are more likely to help foreign students make the transition from the *informational* to the *relational*, from "F-1 Visa type" to members of the *Gemeinschaft*.

Erickson and Shultz draw a distinction between "universalistic" and "particularistic" attributes of social identity (1982: 16). Examples of "officially relevant" or universalistic attributes are grades, scores on achievement tests, and previous course work. "Unofficially relevant," or particularistic attributes, on the other hand, are sex, race, ethnicity, social status, and language (native language, variety, dialect). In the present study we are interested in how representatives of the *Gesellschaft* and newcomers/strangers who have entered into a contractual, utilitarian relationship with the *Gesellschaft*, either hinder or help the newcomer/stranger to enter the inner circle. These interactions have the potential to transform the perception (and self-perception) of outsiders as out-group members. In other words, such interactions can serve to re-create and re-shape individual social identity as well as relational identity (Boxer and Cortés-Conde 1997).

As was mentioned in Chapter 3, Relational Identity is the bonding between individuals in particular interactions. It differs from individual identity and social identity in that it is relevant only for particular interactions with particular interlocutors. "The participants not only display identity but create new ones based on their past, present, and future relationship" (Boxer and Cortés-Conde, 1997: 282). Erickson and Shultz' notion of "performed social identity" explores the structure of moment-to-moment collaborative re-definition of individual identity within the frame of a specific localized face-to-face encounter. Boxer and Cortes-Conde's notion of 'relational identity' builds on this structural view to capture the functional consequences of this moment-to-moment building of rapport and relationship between interlocutors. These notions of identity encompass universalistic as well as particularistic attributes of both student and counselor or, in our case, staff member and student. Clearly, it is not only foreign students who encounter gatekeeping in interactions with university staff. All students are subject to such power relationships. However, the foreign student, with individual and social attributes more alien to the gatekeeper, is particularly vulnerable and has greater difficulty with passing through the gate.

As new official information is added to the student's file, staff member and student (consciously and unconsciously) register how language and non-verbal behavior are used during the encounter. Depending on the level and quality of the exchange, unofficial and nonacademic attributes of the interlocutors begin to emerge, building a basis for the discovery of commonalities and comembership and leading to the possibility of belonging on the part of the newcomer.

2.3   Method

This study takes an ethnography of speaking (Hymes 1962) approach to the collection and analysis of data, allowing for an in-depth investigation of the process of identity construction within the frame of the gatekeeping encounter.

We analyzed spontaneous transactional exchanges between staff members of international programs offices and foreign students. These exchanges were recorded as field notes and were validated through in-depth ethnographic interviews with selected participants in the study. This approach to the collection and analysis of data provides the theoretical framework for exploring two levels of sociolinguistic inquiry: (1) the macro-level phenomena of *Gesellschaft* and *Gemeinschaft*; and (2) the micro-level of social meaning, that is how native and newcomer re-define self and other during the encounter. Our analysis is grounded in theories of discourse analysis (e.g. Goffman 1967; Gumperz 1982) that take into account the problematic nature of individuals from different societies lacking shared schema for the production and interpretation of messages. We analyze exchanges between staff and student with the goal of explicating how native and newcomer re-define their perception of each other during the gatekeeping encounter. Naturally occurring talk was collected from two distinct contexts: (1) in the waiting rooms of administrators and counselors at an international programs office; and (2) in orientation meetings of an intensive English language program during a Check-In event, an Insurance Workshop, and an Activities Overview. Of course, the two contexts are different speech events with different rules for interaction. Follow-up ethnographic interviews with several staff members and students observed provided relevant information about participant attributes, thus serving as triangulation of the data.

2.4   Gatekeeping encounters in the International Programs office

In the first setting, the International Programs office waiting area, we recorded nineteen lengthy verbal sequences of speech between staff members and students. International students entered, stated their requests at the front desk, signed in, and took a seat to wait or fill out forms. While waiting, some leafed through an assortment of magazines and newspapers lying on the small table in front of the sofa. Racks were filled with forms for F-1 visas, F-1 reinstatement forms, B-1 and B-2 extension forms, J-2 visa work permit instructions, I-20 extensions, and forms for requesting forms, to name but a few. Our aim was to discover what staff members actually say and do to help international students gain entry into the *Gemeinschaft*. We analyzed the data by isolating elements of (1) official, utilitarian language or bureaucratic jargon; and (2) relational talk.

The majority of exchanges analyzed in this setting were between two female receptionists and a number of international students. These were examined for contextualization cues such as opening and closing signals, sequencing strategies, register, and backchannelling, including eye contact, smiles, and body alignment. Typically, the exchanges were brief with turns short and distributed unevenly. After the opening sequences, the staff members held the floor in disproportionate quantity relative to the students. This is not surprising, given the nature of the particular type of service encounter and what we know about NS/NNS conversation (Boxer 1993c).

One of the receptionists (R1, speaker of British English, middle aged, white) used openings that depended upon her first impression of the student. R1 had traveled extensively until a year ago when she began working in the international office. She indicated during one of our ethnographic interviews that she believes individuals' behavior is largely predictable according to their nationalities (e.g. Asians are shy, Western Europeans and Islanders bold and self-assured.). If the student spoke first, R1 was sensitive to the way that student formulated the opener. Along with 'how goes it', 'hi love,' and 'hello love,' R1 most often used 'can I help you, love', 'can I help you' and 'what can I do for you'.[1] The openings of the other receptionist (R2, young African-American woman) were the same, but without the terms of endearment. In one isolated instance, R2 addressed an Asian male with 'Can I help you, *Sir*'. Closings, like openings, reflect how staff perceive their role vis-à-vis the students. They clearly see themselves in a supportive role rather than as gatekeepers. Some examples of closings recorded are the following: 'Take care now', 'see you tomorrow', 'here you go love, see you tomorrow', 'bye, love', and 'bye, bye sweetheart' (The latter used by counselor C1; female, middle aged, of northern European descent).

The use of forms of address in this environment, particularly terms of endearment, are relevant to the analysis of *Gemeinschaft*. Who uses them, is there a pattern to their use, and how are they interpreted by the addressee? In this context, R1 and C1 used 'love' and/or 'sweetheart' with male and female students and with all women regardless of age, except for women who held a higher rank. Also, younger men who worked in the office, as well as delivery and service people, received terms of endearment. We must note that R1 speaks British English and thus uses the term 'love' quite naturally 'out of habit.' As a rule, in the US English terms of endearment between strangers may not be used reciprocally, except in certain service encounters (Wolfson and Manes 1980). Typically, lack of reciprocity indicates that the speaker and the addressee are not status equals. While some of the staff members (indicated above) used terms of endearment with students, students did not use these reciprocally with staff. This indicates the inherent status superiority of the staff members in this context. Students either used no name or first name address with all staff, with the exception of C1, who is functional head of the office. Indeed, she received title and last name from everyone.

Wolfson and Manes found that in service encounters the use of terms of endearment is "generally triggered by something in the interaction which shows the customer to be somewhat less than totally competent" (1980: 89). An examination of all instances of terms of endearment in our data indicates an overabundance of such terms when the addressee was perceived as shy, frightened, or confused. Asians, male and female, received the most terms of endearment.[2] These findings were confirmed by R1 during the ethnographic interview. She indicated that she and C1 could use terms of endearment without offending anyone, because they were older and because they 'meant' them. Analysis of the data leads us to believe that the use of terms of endearment may, in this case, serve not to build rapport but to emphasize power relationships. We assert that the use of terms of endearment here is tied to the existence of cultural stereotypes. Interviews with the staff indicate that they hold certain beliefs about students from different societies (e.g. Asians are shy). Staff members respond to students' needs based on certain beliefs about their group membership. While these beliefs seem harmless and even helpful on the surface, the resultant behavior is congruent with stereotypes. Such stereotypes may "predispose people to selectively perceive whatever reinforces the stereotypes and ignore whatever does not .... This completes the negative cycle ... which is difficult to arrest and in which even people who feel goodwill towards other groups find themselves admitting, reluctantly, that the negative stereotypes are apparently confirmed within their experience" (Chick 1985: 316–317).

All students appropriately interpreted openings with rising intonation and with or without terms of endearment as an invitation to voice their requests. They either moved closer to the desk or addressed the staff member from the center of the room. Those who moved closer spoke in low hushed tones; the others spoke up loudly and clearly. With few exceptions, everyone who wanted to see one of the three counselors adhered to the same protocol. Students used routine utterances like 'I am here for ...' (name of counselor); 'I need to see ...;' ' can I possibly sign up with ...;' 'I need an appointment with ...;' 'I have an appointment with ...;' Responses of R1 and R2 signaled the need for order and the high value placed on time: 'Sign in for her, please'. 'O. K., love. Sign in on this sheet'. 'Everyone has to sign in, you know'. 'Sign in. You can't do anything unless you sign in'.

The protocol was challenged in two out of the nineteen observed encounters. A female student from the Netherlands rushed in and requested to see C1:

S: Do you know if Ms. C. is here?
R1:   Yes, she is here, but someone is with her.
S: Do I need an appointment with her? I sent her an e-mail.
R1:   If you want to wait.
S: O. K., I'll wait.

S's English was fluent and virtually accent-free. Moreover, it was pragmatically competent. She stated her request in a much more matter-of-fact manner than most other non-native speakers in this setting. Indeed, the receptionist understood the illocutionary force of the apparent question for the request that it was. Zero terms of endearment were used in this exchange. Relational identity display/development, albeit momentary, was evident. S still had to wait; however, she achieved her objective with little resistance from the staff member.

As S stood waiting, she offered us information about her studies, native country, and future plans to settle in the US. She was at the office that day to get help with work permits and insurance and indicated a prior warm relationship with C1. In C1's office, the two exchanged pleasantries as forms were passed back and forth. C1 called the student by her first name or 'love', while she received title and last name (recall that C1, unlike R1, is not British). The following is a segment of that exchange.

S: ... this it?
C1:   Yes, O. K. love. You are staying for how long? Six months? O. K. six times 41 is 246 O. K. Remember ... do you see? There, you are in business, O. K.?
S: What does it mean 'beneficiary'?
C1:   Life insurance built in. If you die your relatives get 10,000 dollars.
S: I don't intend to.
C1:   That's it, love. That's it. Takes so much time. I know, love.
S: ... all that trouble ...

The encounter was brief, and business at hand was taken care of efficiently. From an earlier conversation with C1, we knew that she believed Europeans to be straightforward, as opposed to Americans who 'danced around the subject'. As two Europeans, the speakers were well-aligned. From the way the student, S, and C1 interacted, we concluded that they had established prior comembership. Although C1 used 'love' repeatedly, it was neither shyness nor lack of confidence on the part of the recipient that prompted this term of endearment. Indeed, in the ethnographic interview with this student, she indicated that she did not interpret it as belittling or condescending. The use of terms of endearment can have double meaning: It can serve to increase Relational Identity with interlocutors having a prior relationship; or it can serve to emphasize a power differential between interlocutors of unequal status in a specific context. The case with S and C1 is an example of the former.

The second student who challenged the protocol was a black female from the Caribbean. She entered quickly and stopped several steps from the receptionist's desk, requesting to see the counselor immediately:

S: I need to see Ms. C.

R1:   You know, she is going to lunch now. It *is* lunch time. How about an appointment?

S: No. No, that won't do. (She shook her head emphatically and looked like she was heading straight for the counselor's office.) Can I see her for a second before she goes to lunch?

R1:   Well, all right. Sign in. Can't do anything unless you sign in. All right.

Much like in the previous encounter, a confident demeanor received zero terms of endearment. The student's distinguishing personal characteristics together with a previously acquired sense of belonging emerged during this encounter. As a result of her assertiveness, the young woman did not have to wait until after lunch to see the counselor, but she still had to sign in. This encounter clearly reflects the underlying tension between the universalistic/institutional aspect of the system on the one hand, and the particularistic/non-institutional aspect of interpersonal relationships on the other.

The next report of an exchange between an Asian male and one of the counselors (C2, middle aged, White, North American) is an example of complete misalignment between two speakers. C2 walked up to the Asian male who had been standing at the door for about fifteen minutes (the same student who had received *Sir* from R1 earlier). She handed him the form that she thought he had requested:

C2:   So, you see ... (She points to the bottom of the page.)

S: Oh, actually ... I already have this. I need ...

C2:   (loudly, as she turns and walks away) You have to tell me specifically what you want. Time is of the essence around here.

The student's responses were incomprehensible. Stuttering and stammering, he was visibly shaken by the encounter. While C2 walked back to her cubicle loudly complaining about the waste of time caused by people who fail to provide the correct information in the first place, the student was leaning against the doorjamb with eyes downcast. Within a few minutes, C2 returned, now smiling. While the student apologized profusely, C2 led him out the door, speaking now in a reassuring, accepting tone, possibly trying to make him understand why she had reacted so strongly.

The account of face-threatening acts (FTAs) offered by Brown and Levinson (1987) is helpful in analyzing the above interaction. Building on Goffman's work (1967), they argue that by attending to one's own face needs, one might threaten the other's. Politeness strategies are a means for balancing these conflicting needs. Because C2's face had been threatened, her immediate, face-saving attempt was to retaliate. By publicly expressing her frustration about the perceived face threat, she in turn performed an FTA to the student. Once she returned with the correct form and the student apologized, C2 became concerned with saving face. In this encounter, the weightiness or seriousness of the threat was determined by the degree of social distance between C2 and the student, the power C2 held over him, and by the value that Western cultures place on time.

The interview with C2, who no doubt holds a very difficult and trying position, provided valuable background information for the analysis of the above encounter. C2 is responsible for admission and immigration issues. We talked in her office while she was doing, in her own words, 'mindless paperwork.' She indicated that in spite of never having traveled abroad, she enjoys meeting the students and learning about their cultures. In her opinion, the office staff is 'not all business.' They also try to take a personal interest in helping foreign students make the adjustment to life in the U. S. C2's experience with 'internationals' has taught her that students who have passed the TOEFL understand 'more than they let on.' 'If they don't understand, it would be their own fault, because they do not mix enough with Americans. It's stressful if they get in trouble with immigration, but, you know, ignorance of the law ....' C2 may have misperceived the students' abilities and judged too harshly. She assigned a heavy burden of understanding to the students, who may not really have achieved full communicative competence. ESL professionals widely agree that a score of 550 or 600 on TOEFL does not assure full sociolinguistic and pragmatic competence. It certainly does not guarantee knowledge of bureaucratic workings and immigration law.

Just how difficult it can be to deal with bureaucratic workings and the language of forms is illustrated by the experience of a student from India, whose health insurance proved to be insufficient. His frustration is obvious in the following exchange:

R2: How can I help you?
S: Health insurance. I've already got health insurance.
R2: But it might not cover all the things we require, O. K.?
S: That's gonna take forever.
R2: Buy this insurance; this is O. K. with us.
S: Is there another way to do it?
R2: Fill out this form.
S: How much?
R2: 176 Dollars. Fill out this form, please.

After the student had filled out the form, he went back to the desk and requested a receipt for payment:

S: Can I get a receipt?
R2: You have to fill out a request for a receipt. (She laughs, trying to make light). There are forms for everything.

The student was not laughing. He returned the next day because he had failed to include his wife in the insurance plan. This time, he talked to R1:

R1: Check it to make sure everything is correct.
S: No ... (S's voice trails off, R1 waits)
R1: It's not?
S: ... for my wife ... I purchase additional ... (S's voice trails off, but R1 waits)
R1: Oh! If you have a seat, I'll do it for you again.

R1 did not question the student, and she allowed him time to finish his turn, but he never did. When she was finished typing the information on the form, R1 came out from behind the desk and walked to the student, who was sitting in the waiting area reading a magazine:

R1: Check this, please, before I put the signature on it. All right?
S: humm ...
R1: (Again she waits) All right. (A friendly, gentle, but firm voice was maintained.)
S. Zero response. (R1 signs form and student leaves.)

R1 was tuned in to the frustration that this older, married Indian student experienced. She did not perceive him as shy and helpless, and she did not address him with an endearment term, probably because of his age and marital status. In this exchange, she was doing a lot of face work to keep a semblance of politeness, since it seemed apparent that this student had reached the end of his rope.

During the ethnographic interview, R1 freely discussed her exchange with the student from India. It became obvious that both her verbal and nonverbal behavior was based on her sense of what was socially appropriate and her passion 'to take care of people.' In her own words: 'I like taking care of people. I feel for them. I don't mind doing the work.' Pamela Fishman's (1983) findings on the work women do in conversation is relevant to the present discussion. All staff members in our data are women. Fishman's research on women's work as listeners has shown that women do far more work to generate a flow of messages than the men they talk to. She suggests an 'unequal distribution of work in conversation' based on her observations of differential use of conversational strategies (1983: 98). The analysis of the data for this study reveals instances of women doing conversational 'shitwork,' actively engaging in strategies to encourage relational talk. They unlocked the gate, but did not open it. Quite possibly, their perceived roles as representatives of the institution interfered with their attempts to meet the needs of the foreign students more fully.

The work that these women did was not always sufficient to result in relational talk and gate opening, particularly when the student did not recognize and seize upon the opportunity. Indeed, it must be a two-way street. The data confirms that while staff women attempted small talk, there was little uptake by their interlocutors, indicating a lack of knowledge on the part of the NNS of how to successfully participate in relational talk. In one instance, R1 asked a female student 'everything O. K., love?' The student merely answered with a back channel and left. R1's attempt to start a conversation with another student about his native country only drew a smile. Lack of shared contextualization cues can cause missed opportunities for Relational Identity Development. Stereotypes are likely to be reinforced in such instances. Gates close that might otherwise be opened. *Gemeinschaft* is stifled; *Gesellschaft* persists.

2.5   Gatekeeping encounters in an English language program

The second setting for our data collection was an intensive English language program. Here, students from the world over come to spend a semester or two (or in rare cases more) to perfect their language skills. Most of them plan to attend a US university as graduate or undergraduate students. Some plan to return to their countries with the hope that knowledge of the English language will help further their careers. We collected and analyzed data from three different orientation sessions for new students and conducted ethnographic interviews with the two staff members who were in charge of the sessions.

A Check-In event and an Insurance Workshop were very similar in that they dealt with immigration and admission requirements. In both, the foreign students sat in classrooms and listened to instructions by the staff member on how to fill out check-in and health insurance forms. Clearly these are speech events that differ from the encounters in the International Programs Office discussed above. Here the rules were such that students were receiving information as a group, and they had to follow instructions. They participated as interlocutors when they had difficulty understanding and requested clarification.

Both workshops were led by a senior member of the English language program with seventeen years of on-the-job training. We will refer to this staff member as E1 (female, White, North American). At the beginning of the Check-In, E1 introduced herself as the person who had sent out the I-20's (the I-20 is an immigration permission document). The newcomers learned to write their dates of birth and names in the proper order. They found out about 'waivers', what it means to 'sue' someone, and that they had two weeks to be immunized. Another staff member went around the room and collected passports from the students in order to create a file on each individual. Later, during the insurance workshop, terms like 'mandatory', 'expire', and 'beneficiary' were discussed. When E1 had asked the group at the beginning 'What type are you? F-1's? Most of you? B-2's? J-2's? F-2's?' most of the new students did not know. But once the Check-In was completed, all were identified as F-1 Visas. The utilitarian, contractual relationship was thus affirmed and ratified.

As in the previous encounters in the International Programs Office waiting room setting, the importance of being on time was brought to everyone's attention when a student from South America arrived towards the end of the Check-In session. After a moment's hesitation, E1 did invite him in and used the occasion to lecture the entire assembly on the value of time in the US:

> E1: I was hoping I wouldn't have to say this. In this country we do everything by the book. If we say something starts at 9, we start at 9. In some cultures it's not important. In this culture time matters a lot. If you have an 8:30 class, you have to be there or you will be penalized. Does everybody know what penalized means? You will be marked by your teacher. Points will be taken away.

During the ethnographic interview, E1 expressed her concern about 'coming on too strong' and embarrassing students. As a result of her personality and upbringing, she has difficulty dealing with people 'who don't go by the rules.' Although she does not intend to embarrass students who are late and wishes there were a 'better way' for handling these situations, she is nevertheless convinced that they must learn. E1 is also very much aware of the way she uses language. She said that she tries to simplify abstract language about governmental regulations and relate it to examples of everyday practical living. It is imperative that students understand immigration issues. E1 believed that her experience of raising six children without a husband, in particular taking care of a disabled child, has taught her to be nurturing and patient and look at the student 'as a whole person.'

Through the years, E1 has formed some opinions about how people from various cultures behave when they are confronted with the rules and regulations in the US. For example, she perceives Saudi men as lacking respect for women; Asians, on the other hand, are very respectful, but 'they don't trust what you say.' In her experience, it is not the language that is the barrier, but rather the lack of trust that will cause frustration and miscommunication. Based on "repeated intercultural communication involving different persons, but having similar results" (Chick 1985: 302), E1 has developed negative stereotypes despite her nurturing tendencies. In her effort to understand where the other person is coming from (literally, linguistically, and figuratively speaking), she has been drawn into a cycle in which negative stereotypes will continually be reaffirmed, reducing the chances for the type of person-to-person rapport, or Relational Identity, that encourages comembership and *Gemeinschaft*.

While it is indeed a difficult task for staff members dealing with immigration and insurance issues to interject the particularistic, the professional staff at the English language program is well aware of the need to expose international students to American culture through non-institutional forms of learning. The second staff member observed and interviewed (E2, young, middle class, White), was in charge of the Interaction Program.[3] Besides receiving on-the-job training, she held an M. A. in Linguistics and her scholarly work has dealt with cross-cultural communication. E2 began working in the program as an interaction leader and later became a teacher and interaction leader trainer and supervisor. At the activities meeting, she introduced the interaction leaders to a group of new students and explained the schedule for the planned activities in a very clear, concise way without using 'foreigner talk'. The students felt comfortable with her and asked some questions about the particulars of certain excursions.

E2 expressed definite ideas about the purpose of interaction groups in the follow-up interview. They provide students with the link to the community. A large thrust of the interaction program is involving the students in community activities. E2 has a full program in which the newcomers are able to become volunteers for philanthropic causes. Volunteering, she believes, is the best way to become part of the give-and-take of a community.

E2 also was aware of the cultural differences among the students of the program, but she was very careful not to draw hard and fast stereotypes. Despite this carefulness, E2 indicated her perceptions that South American cultures 'support being outgoing; South Americans are very energetic, don't have any lull time in the conversation, and a lot of overlap. Many Asian cultures on the other hand, will respect that you are a little more reserved, and there is more lull in the conversation.' E2 does not think that international students need to sacrifice their own identity to interact in the American culture. What they do need is to understand how an American would perceive what they might say. She teaches them how Americans would interact, but they must use their own judgment in deciding how to respond.

E2's background and training set her apart from all other informants in this study. As a whole, she makes a conscious effort to relate to the "biographies" (Chick 1985: 302) of international students refusing to allow negative cultural stereotyping to interfere with genuine person-to-person *Gemeinschaft* building rapport.

2.6 Implications of the study

Although our findings are taken from a small sample of data, we believe nevertheless that they provide a window into gatekeeping mechanisms that international students must endure at large U. S. universities. Knowledge gleaned from ethnographic interviews with key informants and field notes of spontaneous face-to-face encounters between staff members and international students show sufficient convergence to support the validity of the interpretation of data for these specific contexts of interaction. The fact remains that while all students have gatekeeping to contend with, native speakers more readily share the contextualization cues that make it easier for them to achieve their goals in gatekeeping encounters. Without such shared cues, foreign students miss opportunities to pass through the gate. They cannot fall back on support systems that native speakers and members of the NS community already have in place. Gatekeepers who work with foreign students need to be trained to take into account the foreigner's lack of shared schema. While the findings will not necessarily be the same for every institution of higher education and for every staff/student encounter, they are likely applicable to similar populations in similar contexts.

2.7 Conclusion

This study has aimed to aid our understanding of how the dynamics of *Gesellschaft* and *Gemeinschaft* are played out in the face-to-face encounters between staff members as gatekeepers and those students who seek to gain entry. It has been brought to light that the microcontext of talk not only reflects macrocontexts of *Gesellschaft* and *Gemeinschaft*, but also re-creates and re-shapes the social realities of interlocutors. Staff of administrative offices play an important role in gatekeeping. They have the ability to pave the way from *Gesellschaft* to *Gemeinschaft* by establishing the appropriate balance between the universalistic and the particularistic. These staff members (in our case women) have the potential to counter the official, informational use of language with words that express interest in and concern for the personal well being of the newcomer. However, as we have seen here, there is often a real danger of falling back on cultural stereotypes that tend to keep students in the *Gesellschaft*. We have shown that despite their concern for the welfare of the foreign student, those trained on the job often succumb to negative stereotyping. As a result, gatekeeping encounters may perpetuate negative perceptions of the other and hinder individuals from gaining entry to campus life.

Much is at stake. At the turn of the century, the importance of formal training of staff members in the pragmatics of face-to-face interaction with foreign students cannot be underestimated, as higher education in the US is in the unique position to lay the foundation for a 'global *Gemeinschaft*'.

3. Conclusion: Face to face in cross cultural interactions

It is possible to assert that nowhere is face-to-face interaction more important than in cross cultural encounters, where interlocutors may possess vastly divergent norms and rules for talk. This is true in all domains. The ability to acquire cross-cultural face-to-face interactional competence is increasingly crucial in an era of pluralistic workplaces, educational settings and neighbor-hoods. There is reason to believe that a lack of competence to understand and interact harmoniously with interlocutors of diverse cultural backgrounds in the domains results in a decrease in social capital. This very fact has dire consequences for our society as a whole (Putnam, 2000). For societies such as ours, where our neighbors, co-workers and colleagues are likely to come from cultural backgrounds quite different from our own, we run the risk of preju-dice, stereotyping and ultimately alienation. The path to acceptance and inclu-sion is paved with realization that others' ways with language and non-verbal behavior is not necessarily inferior (deficient) but merely different. Under-standing these differences opens doors, not only for those who are in less powerful status, but for all of us. I have attempted to demonstrate this in the preceding pages, where I have advocated cross-cultural interaction as a two-way understanding. This goes for interactions among peoples of different societies around the world (e.g. immigrants, students benefiting from higher education in another country) but also interactions with citizens whose back-grounds are different either ethnically or racially.

Anthropologists have long understood that cultural traditions are passed down for many generations, even when migration has taken place and societies are in a diaspora. Vestiges of communication styles persist long after migration and settlement in new places. Because of this we cannot merely hope to "educate" the newcomer into a new set of norms. We have seen this time and time again, starting with subcultures living in the same region, to different racial groups interacting in schools and communities. The example of African-American vernacular English is a indicator of the fact that community norms will live on, despite the best efforts of official policies to eradicate them.

It is indeed a fact that the concept of a "melting pot" seems to be a figment of wishful thinking on the part of those who espouse homogenization. How-ever, homogeneity is not only difficult to achieve but, in the rare cases where it prevails is built on the loss of language, ethnicity, and identity. We see this phenomenon unfortunately illustrated in places where diverse societies have been arbitrarily forced together into nationhood (e.g. the former Yugoslavia). The goal of striving toward homogenization results in serious consequences of in-group/out-group miscommunication and prejudice. Understanding other groups' norms of interaction has the potential to lessen hatred.

We need not stray as far from home to distant nations to witness such situations. Cross-cultural understanding ought to start in our very families, neighborhoods, and communities. We may find that the people next door, our colleagues or co-workers, our teachers or fellow students, or even our in-laws have very different ways of speaking. We may then find that we will need to know something about these norms in order to benefit from neighborliness, workplace and educational satisfaction, and familial harmony. Without understanding these differences, we set ourselves apart from important opportunities for social, educational, and workplace networks. This is true in all domains of life.

Notes

1. Phrases and expressions in quotation marks indicate the interlocutors' own words as transcribed from interviews.

2. Over 50% of the entire international student population at this institution is Asian.

3. The Interaction Program is designed for learners to have face-to-face interaction on a daily basis with native speakers.

CHAPTER 8

Conclusion

As we have seen in the preceding chapters, the endeavor of sociolinguistics subsumes the analysis of the discourse and pragmatics of face-to-face interaction. Applying sociolinguistics is the effort to extract from such research a sense of how to navigate relationships, instill values into family and community members and, indeed, *develop* a sense of community. Whether this community is a family or workplace unit or a social, religious or educational group, knowing how talk functions within each domain helps us negotiate appropriate and felicitous participation. Depending on the stage of our life-span, discourse within certain domains takes primary or secondary position. The predominance of one discourse domain over another relies on the spheres of activity in which we find ourselves, whether by circumstance or choice. To take an example, for some the religious domain is an important sphere of interaction throughout one's life; for others, such interaction is less important by virtue of choosing not to participate in religious life or to participate only minimally. The same is true for all of the other domains. An adult who remains single and lives alone may experience familial interaction only at certain times of the year (e.g. holidays). One who works at home may not need not to participate in workplace interaction, or may participate only rarely. For those who have discontinued their formal education, as do most of us eventually, the domain of educational interaction loses its primacy of relevance. Regardless, the circumstances or choices may have important repercussions. Choosing not to participate in social groups, or being unable to do so due to a variety of circumstances, may lead to alienation. Here, the consequences are potentially severe. Participation in any domain of interaction can be made smoother through the knowledge gleaned from research into face-to-face discourse. It is for this reason that appyling sociolinguistics can have important beneficial effects for individuals and groups.

1.1   Domains and face-to-face interaction

1.1.1   The family domain

Family domain discourse spans our lifetimes. The roles, rights and obligations within families clearly shift as we move from childhood to adulthood. For youngsters, family talk is paramount in inculcating morals, ethics and values. Clearly, as we have seen, it is in the familial domain that children are socialized into adults who will become fully competent members of their speech communities. Familial interactions lay the foundation for building a participating citizenry. This is accomplished through family talk between parents and children, among siblings, and between and among other generations in family gatherings. Hence, the family is an important locus of modeling of appropriate behavior and language, as children learn from watching and listening to those around them as they grow.

To take one example, couples whose primary modes of interaction are through arguing, nagging or bickering, model this type of behavior for the children who are present. The language of families thus has the potential to perpetuate itself down through more than one generation. We have seen how gendered and generational roles are revealed in family talk. Discourse scenes in which fathers "know best" and in which mothers' lives are problematized, for example, model this structure for the children and may become the ideal from which these children generalize couples interaction. Family discourse in which girls and boys have differing rights to the floor insinuate important (though perhaps unfair) values. The values reflected in such talk may indeed be subtle and below the level of consciousness of the participants.

We have also seen, in the chapter on the familial domain, other ways in which gendered identities are enacted. The different manner in which mothers and fathers participate in frames, the amount of talk time allocated to women, children and men, the patterns of interruption and the silencing that is accomplished either overtly or covertly, are some examples of instantiating and modeling gendered and generational identities. The use of humor in the familial and the other domains has been studied and described, showing humor to be particularly useful in negotiating couples interactions. All of this has implications for paying attention to the importance of felicitous interactions with family members. The sad fact in many families is that we take these most important relationships for granted, and work less hard on doing the talk of solidarity within families than we do, for example, in our social interactions. We need to remember that the same principles that apply to social lubrication can also be effectively employed with family members. Indeed, familiarity ought not to breed contempt.

Dinner table conversation has been the most widely studied speech event in the familial domain. Despite the preponderance of sociolinguistic studies within this context, it is a sad fact that family dinnertime is fast becoming obsolete. In his prize-winning recent book on social isolation in America entitled *Bowling Alone*, Robert Putnam states: "In effect, Americans have increasingly chosen to grab a bite and run rather than sit a while and chat" (Putnam 2000: 102). This is nowhere more the case than in modern families and homes. The consequences of not sitting and chatting are beginning to be felt and will no doubt be widespread. Only by applying sociolinguistics can we begin to come to an understanding of the effects of our speech behavior or its absence. As families become disconnected, entire speech contexts become relics of the past. Without a context for child/parent and couples interaction, the setting for inculcating and modeling important speech behavior is lost to us. As family time becomes subsumed by other activities, family connections are loosened and our society suffers.

1.1.2   The social domain

Nowhere has face-to-face interaction been studied more than in the domain of social life. It is in this sphere of interaction that we go about the task of making friends. This is no small matter. Those who have a highly developed communicative competence in social interactions are able to achieve a sense of comfort in life that is unavailable to the more socially "inept." The chapter on social life outlined in detail some of the threads in recent research on what it means to have such competence, and in turn, what it entails to acquire it. That rules of speaking differ widely from one speech community to another, even those with geographic proximity, makes social interaction a delicate dance of negotiation. The analysis of speech acts that prevail in the social domain demonstrates how members of different communities build social networks, or, conversely, how individuals may unwittingly work to exclude themselves. The knowledge of how to become competent face-to-face interlocutors in the domain of social life is typically below the level of consciousness. By studying research in this domain, we begin to bring such knowledge to a conscious level. We thereby have the potential to benefit from the study of how people do things with words.

Analyses of how to carry out speech act sequences such as complimenting, inviting, giving advice, and commiserating, to offer a few examples, all lend important information to individuals who may want to know how to win others over. This is the real art of the *schmooze*. Oral invitations, for example, provide insight into a widespread fear of rejection felt by many across North American speech communities. This sort of information is not only fruitful for *learners* of the language; it is equally informative for *native speakers* who are unable to understand what exactly is going on when an interlocutor says, for example, "let's have lunch sometime." By studying real world interaction via real data on face-to-face social talk, we come to the realization that these invitations are not necessarily insincere. These "leads," as Wolfson et al. (1983) termed them, necessitate a small step forward in the form of some such response as "I would love to, when are you free?"

It is in the realm of social face-to-face interaction that the interlocutor variables of sex, ethnicity, social class, age, race, and so on can be microscopically analyzed, with conclusions benefiting all who participate in dialogue with others who are different. Studies of discourse in social life have revealed great problems in cross gender interactions, for example, that shed light on such phenomena as exclusion, discrimination and sexual harassment. This is merely one example of how applying sociolinguistics in this domain can greatly benefit us all.

Face-to-face social interaction is a phenomenon that is rapidly becoming obsolete. This may appear to be an extreme statement; however, consider what is happening in modern society. The art of chatting is quickly becoming lost to us, as we move from face-to-face interaction to another kind of "chatting," that is, via our computers. When we participate in such behavior (which can hardly be termed "speech") we are no longer face to face with our interlocutor; our computers are connected but our personal connection is drastically changed. We become, in essence, "faceless." We have the freedom to interact in ways that may not be appropriate, acceptable, or even done in our real life face-to-face interactions. We have the freedom to take on an assumed identity, for who will know the difference? In having these freedoms we lose something — that of the art of the good "schmooze:"

> …the trends in schmoozing (namely downward) are very similar in all segments of society — down among both women and men, down in all age categories, down in all social classes, down in all parts of the country, down in big cities and suburbs and small towns, down among both married couples and single people. In short, formal social connectedness has declined in all parts of American society (Putnam, 2000: 108).

It is true that the internet is indeed a "web," connecting us to all sorts of information that was previously either unavailable or at least much less accessible. Nonetheless, the transactional nature of its original benefit has now spilled over into the interactional sphere. What this has done is made interaction easier, but what kind of interaction is this exactly? While it is true that shut-ins need no longer be lonely, those of us who are *not* housebound may be unwittingly transforming ourselves into nameless, faceless members of chat groups. There are benefits and risks. We can begin to imagine the possible benefits of trying on new identities and thereby coming to a realization of what it means to be the "other." Perhaps by trying on a new gender or race in cyberspace, we will be able to come to some level of knowledge of what it means to speak as a member of those groups. Only future research on terminal-to-terminal interaction will tell of its potential benefits and drawbacks. From the perspective of the beginning of the 21st century, the world of social interaction is indeed changing.

1.1.3   *The educational domain*

For most of the readers of this book, the domain of educational interaction takes a primary place in our lives. It is for this reason that I chose to focus on higher education and the contexts of interaction that it engenders. These contexts, nevertheless, can be generalized to other educational settings. Group and peer interaction, for example, is found not only in higher education but in lower levels as well. The well-known features of classroom discourse are found on all levels. Displaying intellectual identity is an important phenomenon from early years on upward to higher education, where it is essential. The knowledge of how to go about negotiating the talk of the educational domain can have important repercussions, as we saw in chapter four.

The chapter on face-to-face interaction in the educational domain covered research specifically on classroom discourse but also on the discourse of other spheres of interaction. It was shown how knowing the norms of interaction in various contexts can help one negotiate through laboratory group settings, colloquia and seminars, advising sessions and other important gatekeeping encounters. It is possible to develop the knowledge of how to display one's intellectual identity through careful observation. However, a systematic reading and thinking about research in these contexts can facilitate the application of what we have gleaned from research to our everyday interactions in the educational setting.

How to interact in office hours and in other kinds of advising sessions, whether one is the student or the advisor, can be learned by a conscious study of what goes wrong. Indeed, it is frequently from miscommunication and unsuccessful interactions that discourse incompetence is clearly demonstrated and solutions are found. A careful reflection upon such instances can afford the participant in educational interactions a glimpse into what could have been done differently in order to bring an interaction to a more successful conclusion. It is not always easy to establish an affective bond, but knowing how to do so can help one gain a "foot in the door" rather than a "door in the face." Likewise, advisors and the institutions they represent benefit by knowing how to gain compliance on the part of their student clients. In all such gatekeeping encounters there is a tension between meeting the demands of the institution and the needs of the clients, who are, in the case of higher education, the students.

All persons involved in formal education at some point find themselves participating in various sorts of encounters, including less formal interactions in small groups — in laboratories, study groups, or colloquia. It is important to know how to display oneself as intellectually competent, and this is done more often than not through face-to-face interactions. We have seen how power relationships are manifested through talk in interaction, rendering lower status participants less able to display their intellectual identities. How to utilize powerful speech behaviors without presenting oneself as arrogant involves a careful dance of negotiation. Joking, teasing, challenging, asking questions and commenting, getting and holding the floor — these are all important phenomena of face-to-face discourse in higher education.

Good teaching itself involves a subtle dance of bonding with students while at the same time wielding power as a teacher/professor. Just how this is accomplished can be gleaned through applying what we learn from research in the educational domain. We have seen how congruence with students' needs and goals can make for very effective teaching. We have seen how humor and even teasing and sarcasm can have positive outcomes in classroom discourse when used effectively.

The discourse domain of education is one that everyone experiences. As an increasing number of citizens seek a higher education, it becomes ever more critical to understand how to negotiate relationships in this domain of interaction. The stakes are high.

1.1.4   *The religious domain*

Participation in religious life has the potential to fulfill needs that exceed the spiritual. A great many people also find in religious life a sense of social and intellectual satisfaction. Indeed, in modern society participation in a religious community can, in an otherwise alienating world, provide an important sense of in-group solidarity. It is precisely this fact that makes the sociolinguistic phenomena of religious interaction an important locus of study. The acquisition of what it means to have communicative competence in any given religious group depends largely on the norms of interaction of that community. These norms vary widely — from expectations of silence to the noisy giving of testimonials. Through membership in such groups and by learning and taking on the various appropriate registers, we achieve an augmented sense of social identity.

The chapter on face-to-face interaction in the religious domain described what participants of various religious sects need to know in order to be competent members. We noted that the sort of talk that takes place within the religious sphere encompasses interaction that is face-to-face, face-to-faces, and faces-to-faces. What this means is that one needs to develop communicative competence that spans one-to-one dialog, one-to-many dialog, and many-to-many dialog. The speech behaviors are various. Aside from those mentioned above (e.g. silence, testimony-giving) the registers include knowing how to do the talk of recitations, prayers, songs, evidentials, and even magical charms. Which of these behaviors predominate depends on the particular group of which one becomes a part.

The phenomenon of identity, so widely discussed at present in the social sciences generally, is nowhere more salient than in the study of religious groups and the kind of talk in which different religious groups partake. The fact that these groups frequently provide a sense of social and intellectual fulfillment is of no small consequence. This is where the line between interaction in the various domains becomes a fuzzy one. We saw in the description of the Jewish rites of passage, the Bar/Bat mitzvah, how social interaction is paramount. Through the study of speech events within the domain of religious life we see the values that are important to different groups. For that particular group, the American Jewish community, interaction in the religious service reflected the primacy placed on valuing the family and children. Recall that children were to be seen and heard, even if a solemn ceremony happened to be taking place. Moreover, from studying the greeting rituals taking place during the service, we were able to discover that social interaction — being a part of the community in a social sense — is at least as important as the religious goings-on. Thus, knowing the ritualized speech behaviors of religious groups, that which was referred to as "formatted texts," is only a part of what is needed to have communicative competence in any particular religious interaction. One also needs to know what is appropriate and acceptable with regard to social interaction. To take another example, we saw how address terms in a specific Episcopal congregation depend largely on the agreed upon norms for that group. This is true as well for any particular religious group.

As we become an increasingly mobile society, with more and more people living far from their hometowns for reasons of education, employment, and so on, religious community participation is becoming an important part of the sense of in-group belonging that is a universal human need.

1.1.5   The workplace domain

Just as social interaction is changing in modern life, so too is workplace interaction. As our work lives become a larger part of our day, with more and more people entering the full-time work force, the workplace is becoming a primary context of face-to-face discourse. Because of this, interactions with co-workers and in institutional and service encounters have a great potential impact on our lives.

The chapter on workplace interaction included a discussion of recent research within service and institutional encounters. Phenomena such as tab-building in restaurant interactions between customers and servers; how to get what you want in hairdresser and makeup counter exchanges; and how to present witness testimony in order to get across a desired point, to take a few examples, were discussed in light of what we can learn from this sort of research. Some of these types of encounters may have more serious repercussions than others. Interactions that involve life-or-death situations, such as 911 calls, clearly have potentially more serious consequences than getting the wrong haircut due to inability to communicate one's desired outcome. Clearly, the range of what we can learn from studying face-to-face discourse in service and institutional encounters spans the seemingly frivolous to the serious. Even what seems frivolous, nevertheless, may have an important impact on our everyday lives.

In the workplace itself the realm of face-to-face discourse plays a pivotal role in the happiness and well being of workers. Knowing how to participate in speech behavior that has positive consequences with co-workers can gain one job security. People are promoted who are highly regarded on a personal level. This kind of good opinion is not based on one's productivity alone. Talk in work interaction has the ability to add intangible benefits to one's 'portfolio.' To take but a few examples, we saw how the appropriate use of humor in the workplace has the potential to diffuse stressful situations and to present oneself as a valued colleague. Conversely, we saw how 'brown-nosing' accomplishes precisely the opposite. One's intelligence, fortitude, work ethic, and organizational ability will get one only so far. Without knowing the subtle features of face-to-face discourse that make one a colleague people want to have around, these other attributes will only take one so far in the domain of workplace interaction.

Some competitive workplaces are rife with speech behaviors that are typically deemed negative. The brokerage house scenario presented in the workplace chapter exemplified such talk. The bragging, boasting and bravado exemplified in that particular work setting served to boost sales while bonding the workers who were part of the 'in-group.' The problem with such talk is that it is difficult for most to sustain participation in such a workplace. Indeed, even the in-group members had short lives as brokers. Women and other outsiders needed not even attempt entrance into the inner circle.

The workplace chapter offered insights into gender differences in workplace interactions. Knowing something about these differences can help workers negotiate relationships with co-workers. One needs to come to one's own conclusions. Suffice it to say that knowing the potential consequences of different workplace interactional styles can have multiple benefits: it helps individuals fit in better; it helps to make workplace settings more harmonious; and it helps to make the world of work a more democratic one.

1.1.6   Domains in cross-cultural interaction

Face-to-face interaction is perhaps nowhere more problematic than in cross-cultural discourse. This comes as no surprise, since we all have been in some way personally involved in miscommunication stemming from differing norms of speaking. When members of two different speech communities interact face to face, there must be some effort to understand the other's communicative system and values if we are to avoid misunderstandings. Cross-cultural encounters are not always between individuals from different countries. We have seen that such interactions are potentially problematic when they take place among speakers from different ethnic, regional and racial groups as well (not to mention different sexes). It is for this reason that striving for more effective and harmonious cross-cultural face-to-face interaction is an area of crucial importance. While it is true that the world is shrinking, with communications and travel making access to other societies essentially instantaneous, the serious consequence of this situation is that we are suffering "shrinking pains."

Indeed, the need for understanding different modes of interaction has never been as important as it is today. In Chapter 7 I highlighted what I see as an essential conceptual distinction between *interlanguage* pragmatics and *cross-cultural* pragmatics. As long as the English language remains the world's lingua franca (and it is anyone's guess how long this will last), it will remain problematic to view the acquisition of native interactional norms of English as essential. The use of English as a language of wider communication makes the issue of cross-cultural communication urgent. The issue of who is the native speaker, the issue of institutionalized varieties where English is an official language (e.g. India, Nigeria), and the issue of whose norms are target-like, are obfuscated in a shrinking world.

Successful cross-cultural communication calls for a two-way understanding. This is the problem. As long as North American English, for example, has been the "target," we have been able to talk about and do research on just what the target-like norms of interaction might be. Indeed, attempts have been made to discover baseline findings of speech behavior and apply them to language learning contexts. However, this endeavor is useful only in situations in which acquirers will be interacting in *second* language situations. Situations of using English (or any other lingua franca) as a link language call for *cross- cultural* pragmatic competence more than *interlanguage* pragmatic competence.

The chapter on cross-cultural interaction focused on three domains: social life, work life and educational life. Among these, the latter two domains are those in which instrumental communication prevails. What this means is that, while the establishment of rapport is essential, it is only a first step towards other transactional communication in which goods and services are at issue. In social life, we saw some of the problems stemming from the differing use of speech acts and the different values that underlie them. The repercussions of not knowing how such norms differ are (1) the dangers of misperception; and (2) unfulfilled expectations. An ignorance of how refusals are realized, for example, can cause an interlocutor to judge the other as rude or inappropriate. More importantly, such ignorance can lead to unmet wants or needs (e.g when a polite refusal of food leads to no further offer, one is apt to go hungry!). The pitfalls of misunderstandings in cross-cultural social interactions are serious. This is precisely because the social/interactional domain lays the foundation for felicitious communication in the other more transactional domains.

Cross-cultural encounters in the workplace are varied, as we have seen. They range from culturally pluralistic workplace interactions to business transactions between individuals and groups from vastly different societies. We saw how co-workers with different ethnic backgrounds often bring to their work distinct expectations for participatory structures as members of a team. Different cultural expectations for volunteering to take on tasks as well as consummating tasks were analyzed as problematic (Davis and Henze 1998). We saw how business negotiations between English speakers and Asian interlocutors go awry due to different discourse expectations and perceptions of "the other" (Bilbow 1997; Marriott 1995). These are just a few examples of the problems that will increasingly face us as shrinking pains.

The educational domain is particularly problematic for cross-cultural pragmatics. It is in this context that gatekeeping rears its presence, serving to prevent or allow access to important goods and services to those perceived as "the other." Studies on cross-cultural miscommunication in higher education span gatekeeping encounters such as interactions in campus offices, to advising and their teachers, who dispense rewards or punishments. The potential consequences of cross-cultural miscommunication here are indeed severe, with possible legal repercussions taken against those who do not understand differing legalities of such phenomena as sexual harassment (e.g. Tyler and Boxer 1996; Boxer and Tyler 1996). As the world becomes smaller the stakes of *not* striving for mutual understanding become greater.

1.1.7   Applying sociolinguistics

Clearly, sociolinguistics is but one sub-area of applied linguistics. The part of sociolinguistics that deals with discourse phenomena falls under the rubric of micro-sociolinguistics. This "micro" aspect is directly connected to "macro" issues of language and class, ethnicity, race, gender, and most importantly, power. This is where critical discourse analysis finds its home. What critical discourse analysis tries to do is alert us to the significance of language that is manipulative, that "constructs convenient realities and persuade[s] opinion" (Widdowson 2000: 10).

The question that immediately arises is "how can we best apply findings from studies of face-to-face interaction in the domains of everyday life?" It is this critical question that has motivated the writing of this volume. Is it possible to learn from careful study of discourse in everyday life in order to solve real world problems? Critical discourse analysts firmly believe the answer is a resounding YES. Exactly how to carry out what Wodak (1989) termed "therapy" is not at all clear and has not been solved in the literature. Indeed, at least one important scholar in applied linguistics, Henry Widdowson (2000), has taken issue with what he has termed "linguistics applied". He contrasts this with applied linguistics:

...in the case of linguistics applied the assumption is that the problem can be reformulated by the direct and unilateral application of concepts and terms deriving from linguistic enquiry itself. In the case of applied linguistics, intervention is crucially a matter of mediation. Here there is the recognition that linguistic insights are not self-evident but a matter of interpretation; that ideas and findings from linguistics can only be made relevant in reference to other perceptions and perspectives that define the context of the problem. Applied linguistics is in this respect a multilateral process which, of its nature, has to relate and reconcile different representations of reality, including that of linguistics without excluding others (Widdowson 2000: 5).

I concur that the applications of what can be learned from studies on face-to-face discourse cannot be direct. First and foremost, the desired outcome of studying descriptive analyses of face-to-face interaction lies in the simple raising of awareness of how best to go about participating in talk in interaction. Issues of dominance and power are clearly important. What I have proposed, however, is broader definition, perhaps one that has not been previously considered by linguists. The work outlined in the preceding chapters deals not only with *language and power*. It deals with *power in language*. The thrust of applying sociolinguistics is in the empowerment of individual speakers in their ordinary day-to-day interactions in all spheres of life and in all stages of life — from family to workplace and everything in between. Regarding critical discourse analysis, Widdowson states: ".... Its value is precisely that it provokes appraisal" (Widdowson 2000: 5). The same is true of applying sociolinguistics.

What can be learned from applying sociolinguistics? We have seen in the preceding pages that face-to-face discourse in the domains has far-reaching implications for how speakers can become more connected into their speech communities. Speakers, of whatever language, have the ability to increase their own communicative competence in order to present themselves as they wish. Family members can learn to interact in ways that lead to increased equality and harmony. This in turn provides a healthier model for child socialization, with benefits to accrue for generations to come. Skilled social interaction increases closeness, gains friendships, and provides for many a sense of social identity that comes with group membership. Learning the talk of how to negotiate the educational domain can increase one's access to important goods and services in that context of interaction. Becoming a competent member of a religious community can greatly aid individuals in a mobile society in which family and social bonds have been loosened and severed. Knowing how to best interact with colleagues at work, in service encounters and institutional interactions, can lead to better service, increased productivity and a sense of well-being and job satisfaction. Most important, perhaps, is knowing that talk in interaction in the world as it is today will continue to involve increased cross-cultural encounters in all domains. Understanding that norms of speaking differ widely and realizing that the understanding must be two-way, will greatly enhance our chances for world peace. This is the ultimate goal of applying sociolinguistics.

Appendix

Summary of Brown and Levinson's Politeness Theory

Penelope Brown and Stephen Levinson put forth a theory of politeness in 1978 that was based on several different languages in quite different parts of the world (e.g. Tzeltal; Tamil). By studying how people interact in these speech communities, Brown and Levinson posited that there are universals in how people deal with politeness across languages. The basic concept on which this theory of politeness is based is that of "face" and "face needs" – that all people have positive face needs (involving the desire to be accepted and approved of) and negative face needs (the desire not to be imposed on). To violate either of these needs is to perform what Brown and Levinson have termed a "face-threatening act," or, as is commonly referred to in the literature in linguistics, an FTA. The theory of politeness is based on three important notions that enter into whether an FTA is performed or avoided. These are 1) P: power, or the relative status of the interlocutors to each other; 2) D: distance, or the social relationship of the interlocutors in terms of familiarity or closeness; and 3) R: the burden or weightiness of the act.

The theory posits that participants in conversational interaction take into account all three of the above notions in their decisions of how to go about speaking with each other. If one is requesting something from a hearer, for example, one typically weighs the burden on the hearer of carrying out the request, the relative power one has over the interlocutor, and their relative social distance. If interlocutors are relative strangers, a weighty request will have to be linguistically realized with hedges and softeners in order to take into account this social distance relationship. The same is true for power. One who has power over another is freer to make a request that is more difficult to carry out. An important concept deriving from Brown and Levinson is the notion of "bald-on-record." One is free, for example, to employ a bald-on-record realization of a weighty request when one has either power over the hearer or a close relationship with the hearer.

Bibliography

Apte,. 1985. *Humor and laughter.* Ithaca: Cornell University Press.

Alberts, J. K. 1990. "The use of humor in managing couples' conflict interactions." In *Intimates in Conflict: A Communication Perspective,* D.D. Cahn (ed.), 105–120. Hillsdale, NJ: Lawrence Erlbaum.

Aries, E.J. and F. Johnson. 1983. "Close friendship in adulthood: Conversational content between same-sex friends." *Sex Roles* 9(7): 1183–1196.

Attardo, S. 1994. *Linguistic theories of humor.* Berlin: Mouton de Gruyter.

Attardo, S. 2000. "Irony as relevant inappropriateness." *Journal of Pragmatics* 32: 793–826.

Auer, J.T. 1989. *The Joy of selling.* Holbrook MA: Bob Adams, Inc.

Bardovi-Harlig, K. and B. Hartford. 1993. "Learning the rules of academic talk: A longitudinal study of pragmatic development." *Studies in Second Language Acquisition.* 15. 279–304.

Bardovi-Harlig, K. and B. Hartford. 1996. "Input in an institutional setting." Studies in Second Language Acquisition 18(2): 171–188.

Barnlund, C. C. 1975. *Public and private self in Japan and the U.S.* Tokyo: Simul Press.

Basso, K. 1972. "To give up on words: Silence in Western Apache culture." In *Language and Social Context,* P.P. Giglioli (ed.), 67–86. Hammondsworth: Penguin.

Bateson, G. 1987. *Steps to an Ecology of Mind.* Northvale, N.J.: Jason Aronson.

Bateson, G. 1991. *A Sacred Unity: Further Steps to an Ecology of Mind.* New York: Harper Collins.

Bauman, R. 1974. "Speaking in the light: The role of the Quaker minister." In *Explorations in the Ethnography of Speaking,* R. Bauman and J. Sherzer (eds.), 144–160. Cambridge: Cambridge University Press.

Bell, A. 1984. "Language style as audience design." *Language in Society* 13(2): 145–204.

Beebe, L. 1995. "Polite fictions: Instrumental rudeness as pragmatic competence." In *Georgetown Roundtable on Languages and Linguistics,* J. Alatis, C. Strahle, B. Gallenberger, and M. Ronkin (eds.), 154–168. Baltimore: MD.

Beebe, L., T. Takahashi and R. Uliss-Weltz. 1985. "Pragmatic transfer in ESL refusals." In *On the Development of Communicative Competence,* R. Scarcella, E. Andersen and S. Krashen (eds.), 55–73. Rowley, MA: Newbury.

Beebe, L. and M. Cummings, 1996. "Natural speech act data versus written questionnaire data: How data collection method affects speech act performance." In *Speech Acts Across Cultures,* S. Gass and J. Neu (eds.), 65–86. Berlin: Mouton.

Beers-Fagersten, K. 2000. *A descriptive analysis of the social functions of swearing in American English.* Unpublished Ph.D. dissertation. University of Florida.

Berko-Gleason, J. 1987. "Sex differences in parent-child interaction." *In Language, Gender and Sex in Comparative Perspective,* S. Philips, S. Steele, and C. Tanz (eds.), 189–199. Cambridge: Cambridge University Press.

Berko-Gleason, J., and E. Grief. 1983. "Men's speech to young children." In *Language, Gender and Society*, B. Thorne, C. Kramerae, and N. Henley (eds.), 140–150. Rowley, MA: Newbury House.

Bilbow, G. T. 1997. "Cross-cultural impression management in the multicultural workplace: The special case of Hong Kong." *Journal of Pragmatics* 28: 461–487.

Blum-Kulka, S. 1982. "Learning to say what you mean in a second language: A study of speech act performance of learners of Hebrew as a second language." *Applied Linguistics* 3(1): 29–59.

Blum-Kulka, S. 1990. "You don't touch lettuce with your fingers: Parental politeness in family discourse." *Journal of Pragmatics* 14: 259–288.

Blum-Kulka, S., B. Danet, and R. Gherson. 1985. "The language of requesting in Israeli society." In *Language and Social Situations*, J. Forgas (ed.), 113–139. New York: Springer-Verlag.

Blum-Kulka, S, J. House-Edmondson, and G. Kasper, (eds.). 1989. *Cross-Cultural Pragmatics: Requests and Apologies*. Norwood, N.J.: Ablex.

Bourdieu, P. 1991. *Language and symbolic power*. London: Polity Press.

Boxer, D. 1993a. *Complaining and commiserating: A speech act view of solidarity in spoken American English*. New York: Peter Lang.

Boxer, D. 1993b. "Social distance and speech behavior: The case of indirect complaints." *Journal of Pragmatics* 19: 103–125.

Boxer, D. 1993c. "Complaints as positive strategies: What the learner needs to know." *TESOL Quarterly* 27: 277–299.

Boxer, D. 1996. "Ethnographic interviewing as a research tool in speech act analysis: The case of complaints." In: *Speech acts across cultures*, Susan Gass and Joyce Neu (eds.), 217–239. Berlin: Mouton

Boxer, D. and L. Pickering. 1995. "Problems in the presentation of speech acts in ELT texts." *ELT Journal* 49(1): 44–58.

Boxer, D. and F. Cortes-Conde. 1997. "From bonding to biting: Conversational joking and identity display." *Journal of Pragmatics* 27: 275–294.

Boxer, D. and A. Tyler. 1996. "A cross-linguistic view of sexual harassment." In *Gender and Belief Systems*, N. Warner, J. Ahlers, L. Bilmes, M. Oliver and S. Wertheim (eds.), 85–97. Berkeley, CA: Berkeley Women and Language Group Conference.

Boyle, R. 2000. "'You've worked with Elizabeth Taylor!': Phatic functions and implicit compliments." *Applied Linguistics* 21(1): 26–46.

Bresnahan, M.. 1992. "The effects of advisor style on overcoming client resistance in the advising interview." *Discourse Processes* 15: 229–247.

Brown, G. and G. Yule. 1983. *Teaching the Spoken Language*. Cambridge: Cambridge University Press.

Brown, P. and Levinson, S. 1987. *Politeness: Some universals in language usage. Studies in interactional sociolinguistics* (Vol. 4) Cambridge: Cambridge University Press.

Brown, R.W. and M. Ford. 1961. Address in American English." *Journal of Abnormal and Social Psychology* 62: 375–385.

Brown, R.W. and A Gilman. 1960. "The pronouns of power and solidarity." In *Style in Language*, T. Sebeok (ed.), 254–276. Cambridge, MA: MIT Press.

Butler, S. and Snizek, W. 1976. "The waitress-diner relationship." *Sociology of Work and Occupations* 3 (2): 209–222.

Cameron, D. 1996. "The language-gender interface: Challenging co-optation." In *Rethinking Language and Gender Research: Theory and Practice*, V. Bergvall, J. Bing and A. Freed (eds.), 31–53. London and New York: Longman.

Cameron, D. 1997. "Performing gender identity: Young men's talk and the construction of heterosexual masculinity." In *Language and Masculinity*, Sally Johnson and Ulrike Hanna Meinhof (eds.), 47–64. Oxford: Blackwell Publishers.

Chambers, J. K. 1995. *Sociolinguistic Theory*. Oxford: Blackwell.

Chiaro, D.. 1992. *The language of jokes: Analysing verbal play*. London: Routledge.

Chick, K. 1985. "The interactional accomplishment of discrimination in South Africa." *Language in Society* 14(3): 299–326.

Chick, K. 1989. "Intercultural communication as a source of friction in the workplace and in educational settings in South Africa." In *English Across Cultures, Cultures Across English*, Ofelia Garcia and Ricardo Otheguy (eds.), 139–160. Berlin: Mouton de Gruyter.

Chick, K. 1996. "Intercultural communication." In *Sociolinguistics and Language Teaching*, S. MacKay and N. Hornberger (eds.), 329–348. Cambridge: Cambridge University Press.

Clark, H. and J. French. 1981. "Telephone goodbyes." *Language in Society* 10(1): 1–19.

Coates, J. 1996. *Women Talk*. Oxford: Blackwell Publishers

Cohen, A.D. 1996. "Verbal reports as a source of insights into second language learning strategies." *Applied Language Learning* 7 (1/2): 5–24.

Cohen, A.D. and E. Olshtain. 1981. "Developing a measure of sociolinguistic competence: The case of apology." *Language Learning* 31(1): 113–134.

Conefrey, T.. 1997. "Gender, culture and authority in a university life sciences laboratory." *Discourse and Society* 8(3): 313–340.

Cook, L. 1995. *Magical Language*. Unpublished Ph.D. dissertation. University of Florida.

Coupland, J. 2000. *Small Talk*. Harlow, England: Pearson Education.

Coupland, J., N. Coupland and J. D. Robinson. 1992. "'How are you?': Negotiating phatic communication." *Language in Society* 21: 207–230.

D'Amico-Reisner, L. 1985. *An ethnolinguistic study of disapproval exchanges*. Unpublished Ph.D. dissertation. University of Pennsylvania.

D'Amico-Reisner, L. 1993. "That Same Old Song and Dance. " Paper presented at AILA (International Association of Applied Linguistics).

D'Amico-Reisner, L. 1999. "Avoiding direct conflict through the co-construction of narratives about absent others: Gossip as a positive speech activity in the talk of close female friends." Paper presented at American Association of Applied Linguistics, Stamford, CT. March.

Davies, A.. 1988. "Talking in silence: Ministry in Quaker meetings." In *Styles of Discourse*, Nikolas Coupland (ed.), 105–137. New York: Croom Helm.

Davies, C. 1987. "You Had To Be There: The Pragmatics of Improvisational Joking in Relation to a Sociolinguistic Theory of Conversation." Unpublished Ph.D. dissertation, University of California, Berkeley.

Davis, K. and R. Henze. 1998. "Applying ethnographic perspectives to issues in cross-cultural pragmatics." *Journal of Pragmatics* 30: 399–419.

DeCapua, A. 1989. *Complaints in German and English.* Unpublished doctoral dissertation, Columbia University.

DeCapua, A. and J. F. Dunham. 1993. "Strategies in the discourse of Advice". *Journal of Pragmatics* 20: 519–531.

De Francisco, V. L. 1991. "The sounds of silence: How men silence women in marital relations." *Discourse and Society* 2(4): 413–423.

Di Pietro, R. 1987. *Strategic Interaction: Learning Languages Through Scenarios.* Oxford: Oxford University Press.

Drew, P. 1987. "Po-faced receipts of teases." *Linguistics* 25: 219–253.

Drew, P. and J. Heritage. 1992. *Talk at work: Interaction in institutional settings.* Cambridge: Cambridge University Press.

Duranti, A. 1988. "Ethnography of speaking: Toward a linguistics of the praxis." In *Linguistics: The Cambridge Survey,* F.J. Newmeyer (ed.), 210–228. Cambridge: Cambridge University Press.

Eastman, C. and R. Stein. "Language display: Authenticating claims to social identity." *Journal of Multilingual and Multicultural Development* 14(3): 187–202.

Edelsky, C. 1981. "Who's got the floor?" *Language in Society* 10(3): 383–421.

Edelsky, C., and K. Adams. 1990. "Creating inequality: Breaking the rules in debates." *Journal of Language and Social Psychology* 9(3): 171–190.

Eisenberg, A. R. 1986. "Teasing: Verbal play in two Mexicano homes." In *Language Socialization Across Cultures,* Bambi Schieffelin and Elinor Ochs (eds.), 183–198. Cambridge: Cambridge University Press.

Eisenstein, M. and J. Bodman. 1986. "I very appreciate: Expressions of gratitude by native and nonnative speakers of English." *Applied Linguistics* 7(2): 167–185.

Eisenstein, M., J. Bodman and M. Carpenter. 1988. "Greetings in native and non-native speech." Paper presented at N.Y. State TESOL (Teachers of English to Speakers of Other Languages), January.

Ely, R., J. Berko Gleason, B. Narasimhan, and A. McCabe, 1995. "Family talk about talk: Mothers lead the way." *Discourse Processes* 19: 201–218.

Erickson, F. and J. Schultz. 1982. *The Counselor as Gatekeeper.* New York: Academic Press.

Ervin-Tripp, S. 1976. "Is Sybil there? The structure of American directives." *Language in Society* 5(1): 25–66.

Fairclough, N. 1989. *Language and Power.* London: Longman.

Fairclough, N. 1992. *Discourse and Social Change.* Cambridge: Polity Press.

Fairclough, N. 1995. *Critical Discourse Analysis: The Critical Study of Language.* London and New York: Longman.

Ferguson, C. 1986. "The study of religious discourse." In *Languages and Linguistics: The Interdependence of Theory, Data, and Application.* Georgetown Round Table on Languages and Linguistics, 1985, James Alatis and Deborah Tannen (eds.), Washington, D. C.: Georgetown University Press.

Firth, A. 1995. *The Discourse of Negotiation.* Oxford: Pergamon.

Fishman, J. 1972. "Domains and the relationship between micro and macrosociolinguistics." In *Directions in Socioinguistics,* J. Gumperz and D. Hymes, (eds), 435–453. Oxford: Blackwell.

Fishman, P. 1983. "Interaction: The work women do." *In Language, Gender and Society*, B. Thorne, C. Kramarae, and N. Henley, (eds), 89–101. Cambridge: Newbury.

Foster, M. 1989. " 'It's cookin' now:' A performance analysis of the speech events of a Black teacher in an urban community college." *Language in Society* 18: 1–29.

Fraser, B. 1981. "On apologizing." In *Conversational Routine*, F. Coulmas (ed.). The Hague: Mouton.

Fraser, B, E. Rintell and K. Walters. 1980. "An approach to conducting research on the acquisition of pragmatic competence in a second language." In *Discourse Analysis in Second Language Acquisition*, D. Larsen-Freeman (ed.), 75–91. Rowley, MA: Newbury.

Freed, A. 1994. "The form and function of questions in informal dyadic conversation." *Journal of Pragmatics* 2(6): 621–643.

Freed, A. and A. Greenwood. 1996. "Women, men and type of talk: What makes the difference?" *Language in Society* 25(1): 1–26.

Gee, J. P. 1990. *Social Linguistics and Literacies: Ideology in Discourses*. London: Falmer.

Gee, J. P. 1999. *An Introduction to Discourse Analysis: Theory and Method*. London: Routledge.

Gibbs, R. 2000. "Irony in talk among friends." *Metaphor and Symbol* 15, (1/2): 5–27.

Giora, R. 1995. "On irony and negation." *Discourse Processes* 19: 239–264.

Girard, J. and R. Casanove. 1992. *How to sell yourself*. NY: Warner Books.

Goffman, E. 1967. *Interaction Ritual: Essays on Face to Face Behavior*. Garden City, N.Y: Doubleday.

Goffman, E. 1971. *Relations in Public*. New York: Harper Colophon.

Goffman, E. 1974. *Frame Analysis*. NY: Harper & Rowe.

Goffman, E. 1983. *Forms of Talk*. Philadelphia: University of Pennsylvania Press.

Goldschimidt, M. 1993. *For the favor of Asking*. Unpublished doctoral dissertation. University of Pennsylvania.

Goldsmith, D. J. 1999. "Content-based resources for giving face sensitive advice in troubles talk episodes." *Research on Language and Social Interaction* 32(4): 303–336.

Goodwin, M. H. 1993. "Tactical uses of stories: Participation frameworks within boys' and girls' disputes." In *Gender and conversational interaction*, Deborah Tannen (ed.), 110–143. New York: Oxford University Press.

Grief, E., and J. Berko-Gleason. 1990. "Hi, thanks and goodbye: More routine information." *Language in Society* 9(2): 156–166.

Greenfield, L. 1968. Spanish and English usage self-ratings in various situational contexts. In J. Fishman (ed.), *The Measurement and Description of Language Dominance in Bilinguals*, Seventh Progress Report. New York: Yeshiva University.

Greenwood, A. and A. Freed. 1992. "Women talking to women: The function of questions in conversation." In *Locating Power*, K. Hall, M. Buchholtz and B. Moonwoman (eds.), 197–206. Berkeley, CA: Berkeley Women and Language Group.

Gumperz, J. 1982. *Language and Social Identity*. Cambridge: Cambridge University Press.

Gumperz, J. 1982. *Discourse strategies*. Cambridge: Cambridge University Press.

Hall, B.and Valde, K. 1995. "Brown-nosing as a cultural category in American organizational life." *Research on Language and Social Interaction* 28 (4): 391–419.

Hall, J.K. 1993. "Oye, oye lo ques ustedes no saben: Creativity, social power and politics in the oral practice of chismeando." *Journal of Linguistic Anthropology* 3(1): 75–98.

Hamilton, C. T. 1997. "Repetition and reformulation in hairdressing encounters." Unpublished manuscript, University of Florida.

Hamilton, H. 1995. "The aging of a poet: Intertextuality and the co-construction of identities the open family letter exchange." Paper presented at the Georgetown Linguistics Society, Washington, D.C., February 18.

Hartford, B. and K. Bardovi-Harlig. 1992. "Closing the conversation: Evidence from the academic advising session." *Discourse Processes*, 15: 93–116.

Hayashi, R. 1988. "Simultaneous talk from the perspective of floor management of English and Japanese speakers." *World Englishes* 7(3): 269–288.

He, A. W.. 1998. *Reconstructing Institutions: Language Use in Academic Encounters*. Greenwich, Connecticut: Ablex.

Heath, S. B. 1983. *Ways With Words: Language, Life and Work in Communities and Classrooms*. Cambridge: Cambridge University Press.

Herbert, R. 1986. "Say 'thank you' — or something." *American Speech* 61(1): 76–88.

Herbert, R. 1990. "Sex-based differences in compliment behavior." *Language in Society* 19(2): 201–224.

Hewitt, R. 1997. "Taxing and Box out." In *Language and Masculinity*, Johnson, Sally and Ulrike Hanna Meinhof (eds.), 27–46. Oxford: Blackwell Publishers.

Hill, J. 1993. "Is it really 'no problemo'? Junk Spanish and Anglo racism." SALSA I (Symposium About Language and Society — Austin). *Texas Linguistic Forum* 33, 1–12. Austin, TX: University of Texas.

Holmes, J. 1988. "Compliments and compliment responses in New Zealand English." *Anthropological Linguistics* 28(4): 485–508.

Holmes, J. 1989. "Sex differences and apologies: One aspect of communicative competence." *Applied Linguistics* 10(2): 194–213.

Holmes, J. 1990. Apologies in New Zealand English." *Language in Society* 19(2): 155–199.

Holmes, J. 1995. *Women, men and politeness*. London: Longman.

Hornberger, N. 1985. *Bilingual Education and Quechua Language Maintenance in Highland Puno, Peru*. Unpublished Ph.D. Dissertation, University of Wisconsin.

Hornberger, N. 1988. *Bilingual Education and Language Maintenance: S Southern Peruvian Quechua Case*. Berlin: Mouton de Gruyter.

Hymes, D. 1962. "The ethnography of speaking." In *Anthropology and Human Behavior*, T. Gladwin and W.C. Sturdevant (eds.), 15–53. The Hague: Mouton.

Jacobs-Huey, L. 1996. "Negotiating social identity in an African-American Beauty Salon." In *Gender and Belief Systems*, N. Warner, J. Ahlers, L. Bilmes, M. Oliver and S. Wertheim (eds.), 85–97. Proceedings of the 1996 Berkeley Women and Language Group Conference. Berkeley, CA: University of California.

Jesperson, O. 1922. *Language: Its Nature, Development and Origin*. London: Allyn and Unwin.

Johnstone, B. 1993. "Community and contest: Midwestern men and women creating their worlds in conversational storytelling." In *Gender and conversational interaction*, D. Tannen, (ed.), 62–80. New York: Oxford University Press.

Johnstone, B. K. Ferrara and J. M. Bean. 1992. "Gender, politeness and discourse management in same-sex and cross-sex opinion poll interviews." *Journal of Pragmatics* 18:

405–430.

Jorgensen, J. 1996. "The functions of sarcastic irony in speech." *Journal of Pragmatics* 26 (5): 613–634.

Kasper, G, and Dahl. M. 1991. "Research methods in interlanguage pragmatics." *Studies in Second Language Acquisition* 13(2): 215–247.

Kasper, G. and K. Rose. 1999. "Pragmatics and SLA". *Annual Review of Applied Linguistics* 19: 81–104.

Katriel, T. 1986. *Talking Straight: Dugri speech in Israeli Sabra Culture.* Cambridge: Cambridge University Press.

Kendall, Shari. 2000. "The balancing act at home: Framing gendered identities at dinnertime." Paper presented at American Association of Applied Linguistics, Vancouver. March 9.

Kiesling, S. F. 1997. "Power and the language of men." In *Language and Masculinity,* S. Johnson, U. Meinhof, (eds.), 65–85. Oxford: Blackwell Publishers.

Kim, D. 2001. *Apologies in Korean and English.* Unpublished Ph.D. dissertation. University of Florida.

Knapp, M., R. Hopper and R. Bell. 1984. "Compliments: A descriptive taxonomy." *Journal of Communication* 34(4): 12–31.

Kotthoff, H. 1986. "Scherzen und lachen in Gesprachen von Frauen und Maennern." *Der Deutschunterricht: Beitrage zu Seiner Praxis und Wissenschaftlichen Grundlegung.* 38(3): 16–28.

Kotthoff, H. 1996. "Impoliteness and conversational joking: On relational politics." *Folia Linguistica* 30(3–4): 299–324.

Kruez, R. 1996. "The use of verbal irony: cues and constraints." In *Metaphor: Implications and Applications,* J. Mio and A. Katz, (eds.), 23–38. Mahwah, N. J.: Lawrence Erlbaum.

Le Page, R. B. and A. Tabouret-Keller. 1985. *Acts of Identity.* Cambridge: Cambridge University Press.

Labov, W. 1966. *The Social Stratification of English in New York City.* Washington, D.C.: Center for Applied Linguistics

Labov, W. 1972. *Sociolinguistic Patterns.* Philadelphia: University of Pennsylvania Press.

Lakoff, R. 1973. "Language and woman's place." *Language in Society* 2(1): 45–80.

Lamoureux, E. L. 1988/89. "Rhetoric and conversation in service encounters." *Research on Language and Social Interaction* 22: 93–114.

Lebra, T. 1984. *Japanese women: Constraint and fulfillment.* Honolulu: University of Hawaii Press.

Lewis, M. 1989. *Liar's Poker.* New York: Norton and Co.

Long, D.and A. Graesser. 1988. "Wit and humor in discourse processing." *Discourse Processes* 11: 35–60.

Luria, M.S. and R. Hoffman (eds.). 1974. *Middle English Lyrics.* N. Y: W.W. Norton & Co.

Malinowski, B. 1923. "The problem of meaning in primitive languages." In *The Meaning of Meaning,* C. le Ogden and I.A. Richards (eds.), 146–52. London: Routledge and Kegan Paul.

Malone, M. 1995. "How to do things with friends: Altercasting and recipient design." *Research on Language and Social Interaction* 28(2): 147–170.

Maltz, D. N. 1985. "Joyful noise and reverent silence: The significance of noise in pentecostal worship." In *Perspectives on Silence*, D. Tannen and M. Saville-Troike (eds.), 113–137. Norwood, N.J.: Ablex.

Maltz, D.N. and R. Borker. 1983. "A cultural approach to male/female miscommunication." In *Language and Social Identity*, J. Gumperz, (ed.), 195–217. New York: Cambridge University Press.

Manes, J. and N. Wolfson. 1981. "The compliment formula." In *Conversational Routine*, F. Coulmas (ed.), 115–132. The Hague: Mouton.

Marriott, H. 1995. "'Deviations' in an intercultural business negotiation." In *The Discourse of Negotiation: Studies of Language in the Workplace*, Alan Firth, (ed.), 247–268. Oxford: Pergamon.

Martyna, W.. 1983. "Beyond the he/man approach: The case for non-sexist language." In *Language, Gender and Society*, B. Thorne, C. Kramarae and N. Henley (eds.), 25–37. Cambridge: Newbury House.

Maynard, D. 1998. "Praising versus blaming the messenger: Moral issues in deliveries of good and bad news." *Research on Language and Social Interaction*, 31(3/4): 359–395.

Maynard, S. 1986. "On backchannel behavior in Japanese and English casual conversation." *Linguistics* 24: 1079–1108.

McElhinny, B. 1995. "Challenging hegemonic masculinities." In *Gender Articulated: Language and the Socially Constructed Self*, Kira Hall and Mary Bucholtz, (eds.), 218–243. New York: Routledge.

Meier, A. J. 1998. "Apologies: What do we know?" *International Journal of Applied Linguistics* 8: 215–231.

Merritt, Marilyn. 1977. "The playback: An instance of variation in discourse." In *Studies in Language Variation: Semantics, Syntax, Phonology, Pragmatics, Social Situations, Ethnographic Approaches*, Ralph Fasold and Roger Shuy, (eds), 198–208. Washington, D.C.: Georgetown University Press.

Merritt, M. 1984. "On the use of OK in service encounters." In *Language in Use: Readings in Sociolinguistics*, John Baugh and Joel Sherzer, (eds), 139–148. Englewood Cliffs, N.J.: Prenctice Hall.

Mey, J. 1993. *Pragmatics: An Introduction*. Oxford: Blackwell Publishers.

Miller, L., L.Cooke, J. Tsang, and F. Morgan. 1992. "Should I brag? Nature and impact of positive and boastful disclosures for women and men." *Human Communication Research* 18 (3): 364–399.

Miller, P. 1986. "Teasing as language socialization and verbal play in a white working class community." In *Language Socialization Across Cultures*, B. Schieffelin and E. Ochs (eds.), 199–212. Cambridge: Cambridge University Press.

Milroy, L. 1980. *Language and Social Networks*. Oxford: Blackwell.

Moyna, M. I. 1994. "'Nosotros los Americanos': Humourous code-switching and borrowing as a means to defuse culture shock." Unpublished ms., University of Florida.

Myers-Roy, A. 1981. "The function of irony in discourse." *Text* 1(4): 407–423.

Nelms, J. 2001. *A descriptive analysis of the functions and uses of sarcasm in higher education classroom discourse*. Unpublished Ph.D. dissertation. University of Florida.

Nelms, J., S. Attardo, and D. Boxer. 2000. "The least disruption principle: Sarcasm revisited." Paper given at the Fourteenth Annual International Conference on Pragmatics and Language Learning. Urbana, IL.

Neustupny, J.V. 1985. "Language norms in Australian-Japanese contact situations." In *Cross-Cultural Encounters: Communication and Miscommunication*, J.B. Pride (ed.), 44–64. Melbourne: River Seine.

Norrick, N.1994. *Conversational Joking: Humor in Everday Talk*. Bloomington, IN· Indiana University Press.

Ochs, E.and C. Taylor. 1992. "Family narrative as political activity." *Discourse and Society* 3(3): 301–340.

Ochs, E. and C. Taylor. 1995. "The 'father knows best' dynamic in dinnertime narratives." In *Gender articulated: Language and the socially constructed self*, Kira Hall and Mary Bucholtz, (eds), 97–120. New York: Routledge.

Ochs, E., R.Smith and C. Taylor. 1996. "Detective stories at dinnertime: Problem-solving through co-narration." In *The matrix of language*, Donald Brenneis and Ronald K.D. MacCauley, (eds.): 39–55. Boulder: Westview Press.

Olshtain, E., and A. D. Cohen. 1983. "Apology: A speech act set." In *Sociolinguistics and Language Acquisition*, Nessa Wolfson, (ed.), 18–35. Rowley, MA: Newbury.

Olshtain, E. and A. D. Cohen. 1987. "The learning of complex speech act behavior." Paper presented at the Colloquium on sociolinguistics and TESOL, TESOL Miami, Florida. March.

Olshtain, E. and L. Weinbach, 1993. "Interlanguage features of the speech act of complaining." In *Interlanguage Pragmatics*, Shoshana Blum-Kulka and Gabriele Kasper, (eds.), 108–122. Oxford University Press.

Owen, M. 1980. *Apologies and Remedial Interchanges*. The Hague: Mouton.

Oxford English Dictionary. 1971. Second edition. Oxford: Clarendon.

Phillips, S. U. 1973. "Teasing, punning and putting people on." Paper presented at the conference of the American Anthropological Association, New Orleans, November.

Pike, K. 1960. *Language in Relation to a Unified Theory of the Structure of Human Behavior*. Glendale, CA: Summer Institute of Linguistics.

Pomerantz, A. 1978. "Compliment responses: Notes on the cooperation of multiple constraints." In *Studies in the Organization of Conversational Interaction*, J. Schenkein (ed.), 79–112. New York: Academic Press.

Putnam, R. D. 2000. *Bowling Alone*. New York: Simon and Schuster.

Prieto, V. 2001. "The language of religion in three Spanish-speaking Protestant communities in the US." Unpublished M.A. thesis, University of Florida.

Random House Dictionary of the English Language. 1987. Second edition, unabridged. New York: Random House.

Rabin, C. 1976. "Liturgy and language in Judaism." In *Language in Religious Practice*, William Samarin, (ed.), 131–156. Rowley, MA: Newbury House.

Rabinowitz, J. 1993. *An ethnolinguistic study of the Offer as a speech event*. Unpublished Ph.D. dissertation. University of Pennsylvania.

Rodriguez, N. and A. Ryave. 1995. "The competitive management of face: A case study of mentally retarded adult male interaction." *Semiotica,* 103(1–2): 97–117.

Rosser, S. V. 1997. *Re-engineering Female-Friendly Science.* N.Y.: Teachers College Press of Columbia University.

Rosser, S. V. 2000. *Women, Science and Society: The Crucial Union.* N.Y.: Teachers' College Press of Columbia University.

Rubin, J. 1983. "How to tell when someone is saying 'no' revisited." In *Sociolinguistics and Language Acquisition,* N. Wolfson and E. Judd (eds.), 10–17. Rowley, MA: Newbury.

Rudolph, D. E. "Constructing an apprenticeship with discourse strategies: Professor-graduate student interactions." *Language in Society* 23: 199–230.

Salmonsohn, K. 1996. *How to succeed in business without a penis: Secrets and strategies for the working woman.* NY: Random House.

Samarin, W. 1976. "The language of religion." In *Language in Religious Practice.* William Samarin (ed), 3–13. Rowley: Newbury House.

Sattell, J. 1983. "Men, inexpressiveness, and power." In *Language, Gender and Society,* B. Thorne, C. Kramarae and N. Henley (eds.), 119–124. Cambridge: Newbury House.

Schegloff, E. and H. Sacks. 1973. "Opening up closings." *Semiotica* 7(3/4): 289–327.

Schieffelin, B. 1986. "Teasing and shaming in Kaluli children's interactions." In *Language Socialization Across Cultures,* B. Schieffelin and E. Ochs (eds.), 165–181. Cambridge: Cambridge University Press.

Schiffrin, D. 1988. "Sociolinguistic approaches to discourse: Topic and reference in narrative." In *Linguistic Contact and Variation,* K. Ferrara et.al. (eds.), 1–28. Austin: University of Texas Press.

Schiffrin, D. 1994. *Approaches to Discourse.* Cambridge, MA: Blackwell Publishers.

Schiffrin, D. 1996. "Narrative as self-portrait: Sociolinguistic constructions of identity." *Language in Society* 25: 167–203.

Schneider, D.M. 1968. *American Kinship: A Cultural Account.* Englewood Cliffs, NJ: Prentice-Hall.

Scollon, S. W. and R. Scollon. 1995. *Intercultural communication. A discourse approach.* Oxford: Blackwell Publishers.

Scott, Karla D. 2000. "Crossing cultural borders: 'girl' and 'look' as markers of identity in Black women's language use." *Discourse and Society,* 11(2): 237–248.

Selnow, G. 1985. "Sex differences in uses and perceptions of profanity." *Sex Roles,* 12(3/4): 303–312.

Sequeira, D. 1993. "Personal address as negotiated meaning in an American church community." *Research on Language and Social Interaction* 26 (3): 259–285.

Sherzer, J . 1983. *Cuna ways of speaking.* Austin, Texas: University of Texas Press.

Siconolfi, M. and J.Auerbach. 1996, September 19. "Trading obscenities: Brokers are told to curb gutter talk." *The Wall Street Journal*: 1, 14.

Sniad, T. 1998. "Games with face: Status vs. solidarity in cosmetic service encounters." Unpublished M.A. thesis, University of Florida.

Spencer-Oatey, H.1995. "Reconsidering power and distance." *Journal of Pragmatics,* 26(1): 1–24.

Spradley, J.1979. *The ethnographic interview.* New York: Holt, Reinhart and Winston.

Statham, A. 1987. "The gender model revisited: Differences in the management styles of men and women." *Sex Roles* 16 (7/8), 409–429.

Straehle, C. 1993. " 'Samuel? Yes, dear?' Teasing and conversational rapport." In *Framing in Discourse*, D. Tannen (ed.), 210–221. Oxford: Oxford University Press.

Szuchewycz, B. 1994. "Evidentiality in ritual discourse: The social construction of religious meaning." *Language in Society* 23(3): 389–410.

Tannen, D. 1989. *Talking Voices: Repetition, Dialogue, and Imagery in Conversational Discourse*. Cambridge: Cambridge University Press.

Tannen, D. 1990. *You just don't understand: Women and men in conversation*. New York: William Morrow.

Tannen, D. 1993. *Framing in Discourse*. Oxford: Oxford University Press.

Tannen, D. 1994. *Talking from nine to five*. NY: William Morrow and Company.

Tannen, D. 1995. "The power of talk: Who gets heard and why." *Harvard Business Review*, (Sept.-Oct.): 242–259.

Taylor, C. 1995. " 'You think it was a fight?': Co-constructing (the struggle for) meaning, face, and family in everyday narrative activity." *Research on Language and Social Interaction* 28(3): 283–317.

Thomas, J. 1983. "Cross-cultural pragmatic failure." *Applied Linguistics* 4(2): 91–109.

Thorne, B. and N. Henley, (eds.) 1975. *Language and sex: Difference and dominance*. Rowley, MA: Newbury House.

Thorne, B. C. Kramarae and N. Henley (eds.). 1983. *Language, Gender and Society*. Cambridge: Newbury House.

Toennies, F. 1971. *Ferdinand Toennies on Sociology: Pure, applied and empirical: selected writings*. Chicago: University of Chicago Press.

Tracy, K. 1997. "Interactional trouble in emergency service requests: A problem of frames." *Research on Language and Social Interaction* 30(4), 315–343.

Tracy, K. and J. Carjuzaa. 1993. "Identity enactment in intellectual discussion." *Journal of Language and Social Psychology* 12(3): 171–194.

Tracy, K. and N. Muller. 1994. "Talking about ideas: Academics' beliefs about appropriate communicative practices." *Research on Language and Social Interaction* 27(4): 319–349.

Tracy, K. and J. Naughton. 1994. "The identity work of questioning in intellectual discussion." *Communication Monographs* 61: 281–302.

Troemel-Ploetz, S. 1991. "Selling the Apolitical." *Discourse and Society* 2(4): 489–502

Troemel-Ploetz, S. 1994. " 'Let me put it this way, John': Conversational strategies of women in leadership positions." *Journal of Pragmatics* 22: 199–209.

Twitchen, J., J.Gumperz, T.C. Jupp and C. Roberts. 1979. *Cross Talk*. London: British Broadcasting Corporation.

Tyler, A. and D. Boxer. 1996. "Sexual harassment? Cross-cultural/cross-linguistic perspectives." *Discourse and Society* 7(1):107–133.

Ueda, K. 1974. "Sixteen ways to avoid saying 'no' in Japan." In *Intercultural Encounters with Japan*, J. Condon and M. Saito (eds.). Tokyo: Simul Press.

Van Dijk, T. 1983. "Cognitive and conversational strategies in the expression of ethnic prejudice. *Text* 3(4): 375–404.

Van Dijk, T. 1988. "Social cognition, social power and social discourse." *Text* 9(1/2): 129–157.

Van Dijk, T. 1989. "Critical news analysis." *Critical Studies* 1(1): 103–126.

Van Dijk, T. 1993. "Principles of critical discourse analysis." *Discourse and Society* 4(2): 249–283.

Van Dijk, T. 1996. "Discourse, power and access." *In Texts and Practices: Readings in Critical Discourse Analysis,* Carmen Rosa Caldas-Coultard and Malcolm Coultard (eds.), 84–104. London: Routledge.

Van Dijk, T. 1998. "Discourse analysis unlimited." *Discourse and Society* 9(2): 147–148.

Ventola, E. 1987. *The structure of social interaction.* London: Frances Pinter

Vinton, K. 1989. "Humor in the workplace: It is more than telling jokes." *Small Group Behavior* 20 (2), 151–166.

Wardaugh, R. 1986. *An introduction to sociolinguistics.* Oxford: Basil Blackwell

Webster, J. 1988. "The language of religion: A sociolinguistic perspective." In Registers of Written English, M. Ghaddesy (ed.), 85–107. London: Pluter.

Weinstein, E. and P. Deutschberger. 1963. Some dimensions of altercasting. *Sociometry* 26: 454–466.

West, C. 1984. "When the doctor is a lady: Power, status and gender in physician-patient encounters." *Symbolic Interaction,* 7: 87–195.

West, C. 1990. "Not just 'doctor's' orders: Directive-response sequences in patients' visits to women and men physicians." *Discourse and Society* 1(1): 85–112.

West, C. 1995. "Women's competence in conversation." *Discourse and Society* 6(1): 107–131.

West, C.and A. Garcia. 1988. "Conversational shift work: a study of topical transitions between women and men." *Social Problems* 35(5): 551–575.

Wetzel, P. 1988). "Are powerless communication strategies the Japanese norm?" *Language in Society* 17(4): 555–564.

White, S. 1989. "Backchannels across cultures: A study of Americans and Japanese." *Language in Society* 18(1): 59–76.

Wiley, N. (1994). *The Semiotic Self.* Chicago: University of Chicago Press.

Widdowson, H. 2000. "On the limitations of linguistics applied." *Applied Linguistics* 21(1): 3–25.

Wodak, R. 1989. *Language, Power and Ideology: Studies in Political Discourse.* Amsterdam: John Benjamins.

Wodak, R. 1996. "The genesis of racist discourse in Austria since 1989." In *Texts and Practices: Readings in Critical Discourse Analysis,* C. Caldas-Coultard and M. Coultard (eds.), 107–128. London: Routledge.

Wodak, R. 1999. "Critical discourse analysis at the end of the 20th century." *Research on Language and Social Interaction* 32(1–2): 185–193.

Wolcott, H.F. 1987. "On ethnographic intent." In *Interpretive Ethnography of Education at Home and Abroad.,* Spindler, G. and L. Spindler (eds.), 37–57. Hillsdale, N.J.: Lawrence Erlbaum.

Wolfson, N. 1976. "Speech Events and natural speech: Some implications for sociolinguistic methodology." *Language in Society* 5(2): 189–209.

Wolfson, N. 1979. "Let's have lunch together sometime: Perceptions of insecurity." Paper presented at 13th annual TESOL convention, Boston.

Wolfson, N. 1981. "Compliments in cross-cultural perspective." *TESOL Quarterly* 15(2): 117–124.

Wolfson N.1988. "The bulge: A theory of speech behavior and social distance." In *Second language discourse A textbook of current research*, J. Fine (ed.), 21–38. Norwood, NJ: Ablex.

Wolfson, N., L. D'Amico-Reisner, and L. Huber. 1983. "How to arrange for social commitments in American English: The invitation." In *Sociolinguistics and Language Acquisition*, N. Wolfson and E. Judd (eds.), 116–128. Rowley, MA: Newbury.

Wolfson, N. and Manes, J. 1980. "Don't 'dear' me!" *In Women and Language in Literature and Society*, S. McConnell-Ginet, R. Borker, & N. Furmen (eds.), 79– 92. New York: Praeger Publishers.

Wolfson, N. , T. Marmor and S. Jones, 1989. "Problems in the comparison of speech acts across cultures." In *Cross-Cultural Pragmatics: Requests and Apologies*, S. Blum-Kulka, J. House-Edmondson, and G. Kasper, (eds.), 174–196. Norwood, N.J.: Ablex.

Yedes, J. 1996. "Playful teasing: Kiddin' on the square." *Discourse and Society* 7(3), 417–438.

Index